G20@2023

THE ROADMAP TO INDIAN PRESIDENCY

G20@2023

The Roadmap to Indian Presidency

V. SRINIVAS

Foreword by

Harsh Vardhan Shringla

INDIAN COUNCIL OF WORLD AFFAIRS

PENTAGON PRESS

First published in 2023 by

PENTAGON PRESS LLP
206, Peacock Lane, Shahpur Jat
New Delhi-110049, India
Contact: 011-64706243

Typeset in Palatino, 10.5 Point
Printed by Aegean Offset Printers, Greater Noida, U.P.

ISBN: 978-93-90095-74-2 (HB)

www.pentagonpress.in

*Dedicated to my late wife, Smt. Satyasree Pamulaparthy,
and our two beloved children, Snigdha and Pranav*

Contents

ANNEXURES: Summit Leader's Communiques: 2014-2022

आज़ादी का
अमृत महोत्सव

मुख्य जी-20 समन्वयक
G20 Chief Coordinator

सत्यमेव जयते

G20
भारत 2023 INDIA

Foreword

'G20@2023: The Roadmap to Indian Presidency'

With India taking over Presidency of the G20, there has been a lot of interest in the G20 and the role India has played in this organization.

One of our foremost experts on the G20 is none other than V. Srinivas, currently Secretary Administrative Reforms, Ministry of Personnel, Government of India. Srini, as he is known to all, has had the unique experience of working as Chief of Staff to India's Finance and Foreign Ministers. This gave him the opportunity to gain a unique and privileged insight into the working of this influential global body. He has followed this up with very detailed and painstaking research based on which he has compiled his book.

The book traces the origins of the G20, its workings and track- record, India's role and contributions. What interested me was his account of the initiatives taken by Prime Minister Shri Narendra Modi in the last nine summits of the G20. This assumes special significance as India assumes Presidency of the G20. Srini's recommendations for India's Presidency also need to be read with care and attention by all those associated with the process.

On 8 August, 2022, the Indian Council for World Affairs (ICWA) hosted a talk by Srini entitled 'G20@2023: A Roadmap to India's Presidency'. This is what Srini had to say on the occasion. "For a Nation deeply committed to multilateralism and democracy, the G20 Presidency would be a very significant moment in India's history. India's inclusive governance model with emphasis on multilateralism promises one of the finest years of G20 leadership where multilateralism can flourish and the G20 can make a serious contribution to making globalization fairer, sustainable while transforming the processes of international negotiations. Prime Minister

Tel: +91-11-24100146, 24100147 • E-mail: chiefg20coord@mea.gov.in / pschiefg20coord@mea.gov.in
भारत सरकार, जी-20 सचिवालय, सुषमा स्वराज भवन, नई दिल्ली-110021
Government of India, G20 Secretariat, Sushma Swaraj Bhawan, New Delhi-110021

Modi has attended an average 25 meetings in each of the eight G20 Summit Meetings he has attended. These included bilateral meetings, pull-aside engagements, meetings of the RIC, the JAI and BRICS groupings. Prime Minister Modi has led the G20 for adopting more effective dealings convergent with the original purpose of promoting sustainable growth and financial stability, as also address a number of global challenges such as reform of multilateral institutions, climate change, fight against technology driven terrorism".

There is little doubt that the G20 would be the most high-profile international event hosted by India. As such, it would provide an opportunity for the nation to place its priorities and narratives on the global agenda. It would also provide a unique opportunity to showcase India's progress and development, as well as its rich cultural heritage and diversity and tourism potential.

The G20's initial focus was on financial and socio-economic issues. Since it was raised to the leaders' level, the G20 has evolved to bring contemporary issues under its fold and has become more comprehensive in its approach. As a founding member of the G20, India has used the platform to raise issues of vital importance, especially those that impact the most vulnerable around the world. In his intervention, at the 'Extraordinary Virtual G20 Leaders' Summit" convened under the Saudi Arabia G20 Presidency in 2020, Prime Minister Modi spoke about 'human centric globalisation'.

As G20 President, India will set the agenda for the year, identify the themes and focus areas, conduct discussions, and deliver outcome documents. New Delhi will identify, highlight, develop and strengthen international support for priorities of vital importance in diverse social and economic sectors, ranging from energy, agriculture, trade, digital economy, health and environment to employment, tourism, anti-corruption and women's empowerment, including in focus areas that impact the most vulnerable and disadvantaged.

India has prepared meticulously to organise the G20 in over 50 cities over the next year, under the theme "Vasudhaiva Kutumbakam",— "One Earth, One Family, One Future". The G20 website, www.g20.org was launched by the Prime Minister on 08 November, 2022.

Srini has researched extensively on G20's leadership response to the current global challenges to multilateralism. His scholarly acumen in presenting India's viewpoint of "Reforming Multilateralism" is seen throughout the book. It is important to mention that the issue of 'G20' has been most deftly handled by him since he has worked closely with the issues at hand during the course of his outstanding career. He has been able to impart insights armed with the knowledge of a scholar and the practical experience of a bureaucrat.

His last book on 'India's Relations with the International Monetary Fund: 25 years in Perspective-1991-2016' created a stir among reading enthusiasts, and his recent research on 'G20@2023: The Roadmap to Indian Presidency', could not have been better timed.

Harsh Vardhan Shringla

Preface

The G20, comprising the world's major economies, with 19 member-countries and the European Union, has been at the forefront of battling financial crisis—the Global Financial Crisis of 2008-09, the Eurozone Crisis of 2010, and the COVID-19 pandemic of 2019. The entire range of crisis response measures—accommodative monetary stance, fiscal stimulus, debt and deposit guarantees, capital injection, asset purchases, and currency swaps were all derived from G20 deliberations. One can say that as the designated forum for international economic cooperation, the G20 has formulated an agenda for strong, sustainable and balanced growth, strengthened the international financial regulatory system, reformed the mandate, mission and governance of the IMF, deliberated on energy security and climate change, identified the optimum pandemic response and placed quality jobs at the heart of the recovery.

The G20 established the Financial Stability Board in its efforts for strengthening financial regulation and has been at the forefront for shifting five per cent quota shares in the IMF to dynamic emerging market economies and developing countries from over-represented countries. The G20 agenda diversified to include climate change, energy security, food security, skill development, science and technology, health care, women and gender-related issues, agriculture and labour. The G20 today represents the foremost facet of multilateralism.

The first G20 Leaders Summit was held in 2008. The size and scale of G20 has grown significantly over the past seventeen Summit meetings. The Italian Presidency in 2021 conducted 175 meetings in the run up to the Leaders' Summit. The Indian Presidency has announced over 200 meetings in the run up to the New Delhi 2023 summit. The Sherpa Track coordinates the Ministerial and Development meetings and the Finance Track coordinates the Finance Ministers and Central Bank Governors meetings.

Multilateralism in the G20 works through multilateral institutions—the International Monetary Fund, the World Bank, the World Trade Organization, the International Labour Organization, the Financial Stability Board, the Organization for Economic Cooperation and Development and the United Nations Framework for Climate Change. The Engagement Groups include Business 20, Labour 20, Think 20, Civil 20, Youth 20, Urban 20 and Women 20.

The G20 undertook significant initiatives for the reform of multilateral institutions. The IMF and Financial Stability Board ensured enhanced surveillance of the world economy, stronger financial sector regulation, and 2010 Quota and Governance Reform. The World Bank worked on Sustainable Development Policies, and raising the collective GDP by an additional two per cent. The WTO's 12th Ministerial Conference sought to reduce trade barriers. The World Health Organization set up the Financial Intermediary Fund and COVID-19 Tools Accelerator. The ILO led the initiative for Women at Work in G20 countries. The 2016 Hangzhou Summit and the 2021 Riyadh Summit represented significant milestones for Multilateralism.

Since the onset of the COVID-19 pandemic, the G20 Action Plan, ACT Accelerator and COVAX as also the debt service suspension initiative represented the major initiatives of G20 to fight the COVID-19 pandemic crisis. The G20's major global initiatives included infrastructure development initiatives of Principles of Quality Infrastructure Investment, International Taxation initiative of Base Erosion and Profit Sharing, International Financial Safety Net, Riyadh initiative for WTO Reform, and Assistance for Poor and Developing Countries especially Africa.

Prime Minister Modi's leadership in nine summit meetings from the Brisbane Summit in 2014 to the Bali Summit in 2022 was visible in ministerial communiqués, Leaders' Summit Declarations, Working Group meetings and Engagement Group meetings. His views on "this is no time for war" have found resonance in the Bali Leaders' Summit Declaration. Prime Minister Modi had also led the Buenos Aires Summit 2018 to adopt the G20 Cooperation on Economic Offenders and the Brisbane 2014 Global Protocol to Combat Money Laundering. In the Osaka Summit 2019, Prime Minister Modi's views on Coalition of Disaster Resilient Infrastructure were widely supported.

From 1 December 2022, India's greatest moment of multilateralism since Independence arrived which will culminate with the New Delhi Leaders' Summit in September 2023.

Acknowledgements

I attended the G20 Finance Ministers and Central Bank Governors meeting in New Delhi when India last chaired the G20 in New Delhi in 2002 as Private Secretary to the Finance Minister. It was a Finance Ministers and Central Bank Governors forum in those years. The plenary session lasted half a day and bilateral meetings lasted half a day.

From my years in the International Monetary Fund in 2006, I distinctly recall colleagues in G24 meetings mention that the G7 had resolved to have a more inclusive body with broader representation for addressing the world's financial challenges at Heads of Government level. Multilateralism was the only way forward to deal with global economic challenges.

My deep understanding and commitment to multilateralism emanated from my years in the MEA, DEA, IMF, ICAC, ASEM and IIAS. I followed G20 policy initiatives very closely for 20 years reading every communiqué, deliberations in every leaders summit and every ministerial meeting, engagement group and pull aside meetings.

I was encouraged by Dr. T.C.A. Raghavan, former Director–General, ICWA, to pursue a book research fellowship with ICWA to document my deep knowledge of the subject in the run up to the Indian Presidency. Thus was born the concept of this book "G20@2023: The Roadmap to Indian Presidency." I am grateful to Ambassador Smt. Vijay Thakur Singh, the Director–General, ICWA, Joint Secretary ICWA Smt. Nutan Kapoor Mahawar, and Director Research Dr. Nivedita Ray for their support and encouragement. I am grateful to Ambassador Abhay Thakur, Additional Secretary G20 Secretariat, for his constant guidànce on the subject. I wish to place on record my deep appreciation for support received from the DARPG Librarian Shri Rakesh Kumar Pal who helped with the research work and bibliography.

This is my second book research fellowship with the Indian Council of World Affairs and I have a deep admiration and respect for their structured promotion of academic work by this great institution of excellence. The subject was widely welcomed in academia. I delivered orations at ICWA, ICRIER, and JNU School for International Studies on G20 Summit meetings.

In many ways, this book "G20@2023: The Roadmap to Indian Presidency" marks the high point of my twenty years of work in various facets of multilateralism and internationalism covering diplomacy, finance and banking, trade, culture, health and multilateral institutions. I was deeply committed to timely completion of my research work and publication by December 2022 when the Indian Presidency commenced. This book is a tribute to my late wife who constantly encouraged me to pursue a path of excellence, discipline and dedication to the national cause and our beloved children who put up with my obsession to complete this book within 15 months.

The G20 Presidency would be one of the most significant milestones of Indian Democracy. A global leadership responsibility has been bestowed on India. Over the next year, the G20@2023 will be the most discussed and researched subject in India's diplomatic, economic, and academic fora receiving huge media coverage. I am glad, I could document this magic moment of India's destiny.

3 December 2022 **V. Srinivas**

G20@2023

G20: Leaders

S. No.	*Country*	*Leader*
1	India	Shri Narendra Modi, Prime Minister
2	Argentina	Mr. Alberto Fernandez, President
3	Australia	Mr. Anthony Albanese, Prime Minister
4	Brazil	Mr. Luiz Inácio Lula da Silva, President
5	Canada	Mr. Justin Trudeau, Prime Minister
6	China	Mr. Xi Jinping, President
7	France	Mr. Emmanuel Macron, President
8	Germany	Mr. Olaf Scholz, Chancellor
9	Indonesia	Mr. Joko Widodo, President
10	Italy	Ms. Giorgio Meloni, Prime Minister
11	Japan	Mr. Fumio Kishida, Prime Minister
12	Republic of Korea	Mr. Yoon Suk Yeol, President
13	Mexico	Mr. Andres Manuel Lopez Obrador, President
14	Russia	Mr. Vladimir Putin, President
15	Saudia Arabia	King Salman, Prime Minister
16	South Africa	Mr. Cyril Ramaphosa, President
17	Turkey	Mr. Recep Tayyip Erdogan, President
18	United Kingdom	Mr. Rishi Sunak, Prime Minister
19	USA	Mr. Joe Biden, President
20	European Union	Ms. Ursula von der Lyen, President

Permanent Guest Invitees

1	SPAIN	Mr. Pedro Sanchez, Prime Minister
2	African Union (AU)	Mr. Macky Sall, President of Senegal
3	Association of Southeast Asian Nations (ASEAN)	Mr. Hun Sen, Prime Minister
4	Financial Stability Board (FSB)	Mr. Randal K. Quaries, Chairperson
5	Food and Agriculture Organization (FAO)	Mr. Qu Dongyu, Director-General
6	International Labour Organization (ILO)	Mr. Guy Rider, Director-General
7	International Monetary Fund (IMF)	Ms. Kristalina Georgieva, Managing Director
8	New Partnership for Africa Development (AUDA-NEPAD)	Mr. Paul Kigame, President of Rwanda
9	Organization for Economic Cooperation and Development (OECD)	Mr. Mathias Cormann, Secretary-General
10	United Nations (UN)	Mr. Antonio Guterres, Secretary-General
11	World Bank Group (WB)	Mr. David Malpass, President
12	World Health Organization (WHO)	Mr. Tedros Adhanom, Director-General
13	World Trade Organization (WTO)	Ms. Ngonzi Okonjo-Iweala, Director-General

G20: Finance Track

S. No.	*Country*	*Finance Ministers*	*Central Bank Governors*
1	India	Smt. Nirmala Sitaraman	Shri Shaktikanta Das
2	Argentina	Mr. Santiago Cafiero	Ms. Silvina Batakis
3	Australia	Mr. Jim Chalmers	Mr. Philip Lowe
4	Brazil	Mr. Fernando Haddad	Mr. Roberto Campos Neto
5	Canada	Ms. Chrystia Freeland	Mr. Tiff Mackiem
6	China	Mr. Liu Kun	Mr. Yi Gang
7	France	Mr. Bruno Le Maire	Mr. Fracois Villeroy de Galhau
8	Germany	Mr. Christian Lindner	Mr. Joachim Nagel
9	Indonesia	Ms. Sri Mulyani Indrawati	Mr. Perry Warjiyo
10	Italy	Mr. Giancarlo Giorgetti	Mr. Ignazio Visco
11	Japan	Mr. Shunichi Suzuki	Mr. Haruhiko Karuda
12	Republic of Korea	Mr. Choo Kyung Ho	Mr. Rhee Chang-yong
13	Mexico	Rogelio Ramirez de la O	Ms. Victoria Rodriguez Ceja
14	Russia	Mr. Anton Siluanov	Ms. Elvira Nabiullina
15	Saudia Arabia	Mr. Mohammed Al-Jadaan	Mr. Fahad Almubarak
16	South Africa	Mr. Enoch Godongwana	Mr. Lesetja Kganyago
17	Turkey	Mr. Nureddin Nebati	Mr. Sahap Kavcioglu
18	United Kingdom	Mr. Jeremy Hunt	Mr. Andrew Bailey
19	USA	Ms. Janet Yellen	Mr. Jerome Powell
20	European Union	Mr. Paolo Gentiloni	Ms. Christine Lagarde

G20: Engagement Groups

S. No.	*Engagement Group*	*S. No.*	*Engagement Group*
1	Business Twenty (B20)	7	Youth Twenty (Y20)
2	Science Twenty (S20)	8	Woman Twenty (W20)
3	Labour Twenty (L20)	9	Urban Twenty (U20)
4	Parliament Twenty (P20)	10	Startup 20
5	Civil Twenty (C20)	11	Supreme Audit Institution Twenty (SAI20)
6	Think Twenty (T20)		

1

G20@2023: The Roadmap to Indian Presidency

India will be holding the G20 Presidency from 1 December 2022. For a nation deeply committed to multilateralism and democracy, the G20 Presidency is a very significant moment in India's history. Since Independence, India has engaged with multilateral institutions, and contributed to combating the challenges of contemporary global governance. India's inclusive governance model with emphasis on multilateralism promises one of the finest years of G20 leadership where multilateralism can flourish and the G20 can make a serious contribution to making globalization fairer, and sustainable while transforming the processes of international negotiations.

G20: A Brief History

The rise of the G20 represents a significant development on the global economic horizon. It is the leading forum of the world's major economies that seek to develop global policies to address today's most pressing challenges. The G20 has 19 member-countries and the European Union which represent 85 per cent of the global GDP and 75 per cent of the global trade and two-thirds of the global population. The G20 was born out of a meeting of G7 Finance Ministers and Central Bank Governors who saw the need for a more inclusive body with broader representation in addressing the world's financial challenges.

The G20 has been at the forefront of battling financial crisis—the Global Financial crisis 2008-09, the Eurozone crisis in 2010 and the COVID-19 pandemic crisis in 2020—each of which have taken a devastating toll on global growth and welfare. India's position at G20 meetings reiterate its deep commitment to multilateralism and commitment to the United Nations 2030 Agenda on Sustainable Development and Sustainable Development Goals (SDGs).

The G20, designated as the premier forum for international economic cooperation, has over the past two decades formulated an agenda for strong, sustainable and balanced growth; strengthened international financial regulatory systems; reformed the mandate, mission and governance of the International Monetary Fund; deliberated on Energy Security and Climate Change, strengthened the support for the most vulnerable countries and placed quality jobs at the heart of the recovery.

Over the past 18 years, the G20's agenda has expanded to include additional issues affecting the financial markets, trade, health care, education, anti-corruption, women's development, skill building, and youth promotion. The G20 Heads of Government and State Summit meetings have been held at Washington DC (2008), London and Pittsburgh (2009), Toronto and Seoul (2010), Cannes (2011), Mexico City (2012), Saint Petersburg (2013), Brisbane (2014), Antalya (2015), Hangzhou (2016), Hamburg (2017), Osaka (2018), Buenos Aires (2019) and Riyadh (2020). The 2021 Summit was held at Rome and Indonesia held the 2022 Presidency.

In 2016, the G20 committed itself to the Action Plan on the 2030 Agenda for Sustainable Development including the Sustainable Development Goals (SDGs) and the Addis Ababa Action Agenda on Financing for Development (AAAA). The 2030 Action Plan envisaged bold transformative steps through both collective and individual concrete actions at international and domestic levels. The G20 further sought to improve sustainable livelihoods with its endeavours in energy and climate despite the United States decision to withdraw from the Paris Agreement. The G20 assumed the responsibility for launching the Africa Partnership in recognition of its goal of fostering sustainable and inclusive economic development.

The G20 meetings have enlarged in scope and number over the years. The G20 meetings comprise the following meetings: (1) meeting of Finance Ministers and Central Bank Governors (twice a year), (2) meeting of G20 Sherpas, (3) G20 ministerial meetings on Development covering Health, Education, Digital, Labour and Employment, Women and Child Development all of which are followed by the (4) Summit meetings.

A G20 summit meeting is preceded by meetings of working groups, Sherpa meetings, Finance meetings, Engagement Group meetings and finally the Leaders' Summit meeting. There is a B20 (for business), C20 (for civil society), L20 (for labour groups and unions), S20 (for the scientific and academic community), T20 (for think tanks and research institutions), W20 (for women's groups) and Y20 (for youth leaders). There is a high level of deliberative democracy at work in the G20 meetings.

Through the years, the G20 remained committed to the principles of "strong, sustainable, balanced and inclusive growth." Since 2008, the G20 has made a major contribution to setting the global governance agenda. However, the paradigm of global governance challenges has changed in the years 2020-2022 with the corona virus pandemic, an emerging debt crisis, slowdown in global growth rates and the war in Ukraine. It's important to present the issues deliberated in the Riyadh, the Rome and Bali Summits to explain the gamut of global governance challenges in formulating a roadmap for the Indian Presidency—G20@2023.

The Riyadh Summit 2020

The G20 Riyadh Summit was held on 22 November 2020. It was the second time the G20 Leaders had met under the Saudi Presidency. An extraordinary G20 Leaders' Summit was held on March 26, 2020. The COVID-19 pandemic and its unprecedented impact in terms of lives lost, and economies affected necessitated significant multilateral efforts to find timely responses.

The G20 had to address the financing gaps in the WHO's Strategic Preparedness and Response Plan, to ensure an inclusive recovery that tackles inequalities and ensures a sustainable future. An unprecedented twenty-five G20 ministerial declarations, communiqués and statements marked multilateralism's most sustained efforts to respond to the global challenge.

The focus of the Riyadh Summit was to save lives, livelihoods and affected economies. The G20 made significant efforts to fight the challenge. The G20 Finance Ministers and Central Bank Governors met seven times in 2020, with meetings being held in February, March, April, July, September, October and November 2020. The G20 Trade and Investment Ministers met three times in March, May and September, the Health Ministers met in September and November, the Education Ministers met in June and September, the Energy, Agriculture & Water, Tourism, Environment, Labour

& Employment, Digital Economy Ministers met in April, October and November. The ministerial meetings took forward the 26 March 2020 summit recommendations to enhance global cooperation.

The G20 Economic Response envisaged a multipronged coordinated approach to fight the challenges of the pandemic.

The key features were:

(a) *The Debt Service Suspension Initiative* to be implemented by the IMF and development banks. The Financial Stability Board to monitor the financial sector vulnerabilities.
(b) *The principles of a common framework for debt beyond the Debt Sustainability Suspension Initiative* and enhancing the lending capacity of the emergency response packages by the IMF, the World Bank and Regional Development Banks.
(c) *International economic assistance was in the form of Catastrophe Containment and Relief Trust* providing immediate debt service relief for six months availed by 21 countries of sub-Saharan Africa, Debt Service Suspension Initiative availed by 46 countries in the period May-December 2020.
(d) *Rapid Financing Instrument* for 29 countries along with Emergency Response Packages by expansion of the loan resources under the Poverty Reduction and Growth Trust.

The G20 Health Ministers worked to collaborate on the COVID-19 Tools Accelerator initiative. They also strengthened the financial support for the "Access to COVID-19 Tools" and enhanced support for universal health coverage schemes.

The education ministers discussed the impact of prolonged closures of educational institutions, shared international best practices, experiences, lessons learnt to ensure learning continuity while stressing on the need to address digital divides and inequities in learning opportunities.

The G20 trade ministers sought to introduce short-term measures for trade facilitation, operation of logistics networks and transparency. They also sought to support multilateral trade systems, resilience in global supply chains and strengthen international investment.

The G20 anti-corruption ministers meeting called for Action on Corruption in fighting COVID-19, preparation of a good practices compendium for combating corruption, the Riyadh Initiative for Enhancing International Anti-Corruption Law Enforcement Cooperation and International Cooperation and Asset Recovery. They further sought to criminalize bribery.

The Saudi Presidency took up the initiative to enhance access to pandemic tools. The steps included research, development, and distribution of diagnostic tools; encourage international funding for the global pandemic and support the training of epidemiologists from all over the world.

Saudi Arabia contributed USD 500 million to the immediate funding needs to fight the COVID-19 pandemic, with the G20 member-countries pledging USD 21 billion to finance the fight against the pandemic.

The G20 also committed itself to work on affordable and equitable access to COVID-19 vaccines, therapeutic and diagnostic tools. As part of the extraordinary measures to support economies and people, the G20 injected USD 11 trillion into the global economy to support businesses and protect livelihoods. Further, the G20 committed itself to extend social safety nets to protect jobs and incomes.

The other areas of focus of the Saudi Presidency were the Riyadh initiative on the Future of the WTO, Empowerment of Women and Youth, endorsing the Circular Carbon Economy Platform, reducing land degradation and access to safely managed fresh water.

The Leaders' statement covered four broad thrust areas—Rising to the challenge together, Building a resilient and long-lasting recovery, and Ensuring an inclusive recovery that tackles inequalities and enduring a sustainable future. The Leaders' summit recognized extensive immunization as a global public good. At the Riyadh Summit, the G20 had succeeded in sending a message of hope and reassurance to people around the world by adopting the communiqué. The G20's joint and individual actions were important to overcome the global challenge.

Clearly, the roadmap ahead of the G20-Riyadh Summit was global resilience. A global alliance in development and distribution of vaccines, protecting climate and environment, governing the digital economy and technology and upholding the international institutions and governance was the call of the day. The overhauling of health systems entails developing resilient health systems which are vigilant, responsive, flexible and equitable. Vaccine finance was a major challenge that needed to be addressed. Further, there existed challenges regarding inequalities within countries as also between countries. Vaccine nationalism was being witnessed.

Improved global governance entailed bolstering the efforts of the United Nations and multilateral institutions. The IMF approved a record number of loans in a short time with low conditionality. The WHO was to be developed as the world's rapid response force on global health. Another major step envisaged was enhancing the effectiveness of the WTO. Stopping the debt pandemic represented a major challenge. The borrowing needs of several countries had skyrocketed and more transparency in debt data and debt contracts was needed. Besides, there was no success in getting private lenders to follow the DSSI. Global growth in 2020 had declined to (–)4.4 per cent and partial recovery projections stood at 5.2 per cent for 2021.

The Rome Summit 2021

On 30-31 October 2021, Italy hosted the G20 Summit at Rome. The Rome Declaration's priorities were outlined as People, Planet and Prosperity. Within these three inter-connected pillars, the Italian Presidency took the lead in

- *Evolving a swift international response to the pandemic*—providing equitable and worldwide access to diagnostics, therapeutics and vaccines—while building resilience to future related shocks.
- *The G20 looked at rapid recovery beyond the crisis towards reducing inequalities*, women's empowerment, younger generations, protecting the most vulnerable by creating new jobs, social protection and food security.
- *The third major pillar was sustained prosperity*. A prosperous future that required proper harnessing of the main drivers of growth and innovation, bridging the digital divide and making digitalization an opportunity for all, improve productivity and, in short, leave no one behind.

The G20 Rome Summit was held against the backdrop of the global economy witnessing a sharp economic recovery. G20 economies had initiated policy measures to provide direct fiscal support for vulnerable households. Brazil, Germany, Russia and the USA extended unemployment benefits, and provided targeted support to affected sectors and firms.

Several G20 economies, Italy, South Africa and Spain, did not have much fiscal space. They had to undertake structural reforms in tax structure reform, trade liberalization, and active labour market policies to support a sustainable recovery. Additional resources and public investments were made in education and health sectors and for greater access to digital infrastructure and job creation.

In the run-up to the Rome Declaration, there were 20 ministerial declarations and communiqués starting with the G20 Finance Ministers and Central Bank Governors meeting communiqué, the G20 Joint Finance and Health Ministers communiqué, G20 Tourism Ministers communiqué, the G20 Education Ministers declaration, G20 Labour and Employment Ministers declaration, G20 Environment communiqué, G20 Digital Ministers declaration and the G20 Trade Ministers communiqué. *A G20 plus Qatar "Extraordinary Leaders" meeting on Afghanistan* was held virtually to discuss the response to a looming humanitarian crisis in the country on 12 October 2021.

The Rome declaration noted that global economic activity was recovering at a solid pace with the effective rollout of vaccines and continued policy support. However, economic recovery is uneven across countries and G20 leadership is needed to provide funding for vaccines, diagnostics, therapeutics through the ACT accelerator and vaccines. The Rome declaration commits the G20 to determinedly address the adverse consequences of the pandemic by avoiding any premature withdrawal of the support measures. The global financial safety net of the G20 would help vulnerable countries significantly.

The extension of the G20 Debt Service Suspension Initiative (DSSI) at the end of 2021, the G20 Common Framework for Treatment of Debt beyond the DSSI and the USD 650 billion SDR allocation were significant measures. The DSSI benefitted 50 countries and the G20 called on private creditors and bilateral creditors to provide debt treatment on similar lines as DSSI. These initiatives helped address unsustainable debt burdens and provide long-term reserves to low income, emerging market and developing countries.

On 30 November 2021, the Italian Presidency came to an end and the gavel was passed onto Indonesia to lead the G20 economies.

The Italian government focused on People, Planet and Prosperity and worked for 12 months till the Leaders' summit convening 175 events, 20 ministerial meetings in various cities, two special meetings of G20 Leaders on Global Health and Afghanistan, six Sherpas' meetings, 62 working groups and 60 finance track meetings.

In conclusion, it can be said that the G20 Rome Summit was a success. Consensus was achieved on several issues—the global minimum tax, setting up of a global body to respond to future pandemics and a global vaccination target of 40 per cent population by end 2021. Further, the G20 enabled rallying the forces of future global ecological protection.

G20: The Reform of Multilateral Institutions

Multilateralism in the G20 works through a number of international organizations including the United Nations, IMF, World Bank Group, OECD, WTO, ILO, FSB, and BIS contributing to the process. There also exist G20 engagement groups like Business 20, Civil Society 20, Labour 20, Think 20, and Youth 20 which contribute extensively to the G20 processes. Given the complex nature of the global policy challenges, multilateral institutions remain critically important in providing safety nets, emergency liquidity, preventing crisis from spreading and for progress in orderly debt restructuring.

In 2022, there were ample signs of a slowdown in the globalization efforts. The world witnessed the tragic humanitarian crisis in Eastern Europe as a consequence of the war in Ukraine, the Western sanctions against Russia, wide-ranging lockdowns in China including in key manufacturing hubs, all of which severely impacted the global economy. Multilateral cooperation has thus far not proved successful in peaceful resolution of the war. There also remain challenges in securing worldwide access to COVID-19 tools—tests, therapies and vaccines—to contain the corona virus pandemic.

It is in this context that the G20's efforts for reforms in multilateral institutions need to be examined.

In the past, G20 has witnessed several major successes in multilateralism and there is optimism that renewed multilateralism efforts can succeed:

- In 2008, against the backdrop of the global economic crisis and the European crisis, the G20's focus was on enhanced surveillance of the world economy through the IMF and stronger financial sector regulation through the Financial Stability Board.

- In 2015, the G20 led the IMF quota and governance reform to reflect the shares of dynamic economies in line with their relative positions in the world economy. The Paris Club, the principal international forum for restructuring official bilateral debt, was expanded to include Korea, Brazil and China.
- In 2017, the Leaders of the G20 took note of the decision of the USA to withdraw from the Paris Agreement. Despite the US withdrawal, the leaders of the G20 stated that the Paris Agreement was irreversible. "Investing in Climate, Investing in Growth" was the line of the G20 as it adopted the Hamburg G20 Climate and Energy Action Plan for Growth.

For 2022, there is commitment for (a) continued process of IMF governance reform under the 16th General review of quotas by December 2023 and (b) Resilience and Sustainability Trust received financial commitments of USD 40 billion from 12 countries including China and Saudi Arabia.

The WTO's 12th ministerial conference (MC12) was held from 12 to 17 June 2022 at Geneva. The Geneva package has given a new lease of life to the WTO. Consensus reached at the MC12 WTO ministerial meeting in securing agreements on relaxing patent regulations to secure vaccine equity, ensuring food security, subsidies to the fisheries sector and establishing a moratorium relevant to e-commerce that would continue to be relevant. The current moratorium on not imposing customs duties electronic transmissions (ET's) would come up for review in 2023.

The Financial Stability Board has made considerable progress in its multi-year program on enhancing the resilience of the non-banking financial intermediation and addressing the challenges in cross-border payments. A steering group has been set up to take this work forward

The World Health Organization has formulated 10 recommendations for a stronger WHO. Amongst them are the creation of a financial intermediary fund (FIF) to support countries against epidemics and pandemics. The FIF money would be used to address critical gaps in disease surveillance, laboratory systems, health workforce, emergency communication and management and community engagement. The other areas of work include a new platform for rapid development of and equitable access to vaccines, tests, treatments and expanding local production in all regions of the world.

The International Labour Organization continued its ongoing work on Women at Work in G20 countries with focus on increasing women's participation in labour markets, improving the quality of women's earnings, improving women's labour market security and improving working conditions.

The Indonesian Presidency

The G20 Indonesian Presidency was based on the theme, "Recover Together—Recover Stronger". The Indonesian Presidency said the world was in need of more collective action and inclusive collaboration amongst the major developed countries and emerging economies.

The priority issues for the Indonesian Presidency were global health architecture, digital transformation and sustainable energy transition. The Presidency concluded with the Bali Summit scheduled on 15-16 November 2022. The Indonesian Presidency has planned through the Sherpa tracks, 11 working groups, 1 initiative group and 10 engagement group meets to discuss and provide recommendations on the G20 agenda and priorities.

The 11 working groups covered agriculture, digital economy, education, employment, tourism, development, energy transition, environment and climate sustainability, trade, investment and industry, anti-corruption, health, joint finance and health task force and the EMPOWER initiative and women empowerment. The finance track discussed six priority areas—coordination of exit strategies, scarring effects, strengthening payment systems, development of sustainable finance, improvement of the inclusive financial system and international taxation agenda.

The Indian Presidency

India will host the G20 summit in 2023 at New Delhi. The following key issues were flagged by the Indian leadership in G20 fora in 2021:

- At the G20 leaders meet in response to the United Nations High Commissioner for Refugees report and appeal for funds for Afghanistan, on 13 October 2021, Prime Minister Narendra Modi called on the international community to provide Afghanistan with *'immediate and unhindered access to humanitarian assistance'* indicating India's willingness to work with international aid agencies that are working with displaced Afghans, particularly the one million children at the risk of starvation, in this 'make or break moment for the Afghan people.

- At the G20 finance ministers meeting in Washington DC on 14 October 2021, Finance Minister Nirmala Sitaraman said that ensuring equitable access to COVID-19 vaccines for all was crucial for transitioning from crisis to recovery and the proposed global tax deal will help address the challenges posed by digitalization of the economy. India supported the 'Framework on Base Erosion and Profit Shifting (BEPS)', that requires all jurisdictions to impose a 15 per cent tax on multinational enterprises.
- At the G20 trade ministers meet in Sorrento, Italy, on 12 October 2021, Commerce and Industries Minister Piyush Goyal put forth India's position for actively resolving new trade barriers like vaccine differentiations or COVID passports, which impose mobility restrictions and the movement of personnel needed for delivering critical services. The Commerce Minister also offered e-Sanjeevani, India's telemedicine initiative, to the entire world.

Conclusion

The G20 Indian Presidency has arrived 18 years after the Leaders summit meetings commenced and would be one of the most significant milestones of Indian democracy. It is widely felt that in times when there is a crisis of multilateralism, India has the responsibility for bringing stability to a deeply divided multi-polar world and crafting broader global responses to the challenges. The theme of the Indian Presidency is *Vasudhaiva Kutumbakam*—One Earth, One Family, One Future. The agenda for the Indian Presidency will be of healing, harmony and hope.

The IMF has said that the following instruments of financing remain relevant as debt challenges are pressing and the need for action continues to exist. The DSSI and CCRT lapsed at the end of 2021, and G20 is yet to reach a consensus on their continuation.

- The DSSI and the Common Framework are important instruments for debt relief, and efforts should be made to continue to operationalize them.
- The Catastrophe Containment Relief Trust grants for debt service relief to be strengthened through a coordinated approach for fund raising. However, the Trust has scarce resources after the sanctions

of the fifth tranche and creditors are reluctant to extend the timelines.

- The Resilience and Sustainability Trust commenced operations from 1 May 1 2022 and needs to be continued as an important source of financing for middle income countries under debt stress.
- The Fund's existing instrument of PRGT would continue to be relevant in the context of heavily indebted poor countries.

The WHO has said the following instruments would need to be pursued:

- The corona virus continues to witness new waves and the ACT-Accelerator to ensure equitable distribution of health tools would continue to need world finance.
- The Financial Intermediary Fund for pandemic prevention and response hosted by the World Bank to be truly inclusive and universally accessible.

From India's perspective the focus would be on:

- IMF Quota and governance as also that of other IFI's.
- The issues of climate financing, digital assets and capital flows are likely to continue to feature in the G20 agenda.
- There also exists an extraordinarily challenging macroeconomic environment. Nearly 60 per cent of the low-income countries are facing an unbearable debt burden. It is likely that the G20 will come together to establish new rules and timelines for the common framework.
- The G20 must continue to fight the crisis of climate change and send clear signals to decarbonize the economy.
- Lastly, G20 must do everything in its power to keep inflation in check, and protect the living standards for vulnerable people.

The External Affairs Minister has said that "for the first time in the history of the G20, India will host the G20 meetings over the year, not only in Delhi but in every State and Union Territory."

Prime Minister Modi said, "The G20 is a unique opportunity to showcase to the world that India is not just confined to Delhi, but includes every State and Union Territory."

Over 200 meetings have been planned under the G20@2023 Indian Presidency. It promises to be a challenging and exciting policy endeavour.

2

G20 Turns 18 in 2023

The G20 represents the leading forum of world's major economies that seek to develop global policies to address today's most pressing challenges.

The G20 has 19 member-countries and the European Union which represent 85 per cent of global GDP and 75 per cent of global trade and two-thirds of the global population. The G20 has been at the forefront of battling financial crises—the Global financial crisis 2008-09, the Eurozone crisis in 2010 and the COVID-19 pandemic crisis in 2020—each of which have taken a devastating toll on global growth and welfare. India's positions at G20 meetings reiterate its deep commitment to multilateralism and commitment to the United Nations 2030 Agenda on Sustainable Development and Sustainable Development Goals (SDGs).

G20: Navigating the Global Recovery

In the annals of the history of financial crisis, the London G20 Summit of April 2009 will be acknowledged as a clear turning point when the world leaders showed extraordinary determination and unity. There were sharp differences but they were debated and discussed and compromises made so as to reach the final goal of ending the financial crisis. This resulted in an agreed package of measures having both domestic and international components but all of them to be implemented in coordination and synchronization where necessary. The entire range of crisis response measures—accommodative monetary policy stance, fiscal stimulus, debt and deposit guarantees, capital injection, asset purchases, currency swaps, and keeping markets open—were derived from the G20 package. G20 leaders' summits attended by the heads of state and government represent the highest fora of multilateralism.

The G20, designated as the premier forum for international economic cooperation, has over the past two decades formulated an agenda for strong, sustainable and balanced growth; strengthened international financial regulatory systems; reformed the mandate, mission and governance of the International Monetary Fund; deliberated on Energy Security and Climate Change, strengthened the support for the most vulnerable countries and placed quality jobs at the heart of the recovery. The G20 established the Financial Stability Board (FSB) to include major emerging market economies to coordinate and monitor efforts in strengthening financial regulation. It was at the forefront of the efforts for shifting five per cent quota shares in the International Monetary Fund to dynamic emerging markets and developing countries from over-represented countries. In 2020, the G20 led the global fight against the COVID-19 pandemic with a USD 10 trillion bailout package that focused on addressing the economic and health crisis.

Over the past 15 years, the G20's agenda has expanded to include additional issues affecting the financial markets, trade, health care, education, anti-corruption, women's development, skill building, and youth promotion. The Indian Presidency of G20 in 2023 offers India a significant role and voice to influence and participate in the global decision-making processes. Climate change has been one area where the pressures of being part of an elite group worked and India accepted the challenge of cutting emissions.

The G20 heads of government and state summit meetings have been held at Washington DC (2008), London and Pittsburgh (2009), Toronto and Seoul (2010), Cannes (2011), Mexico City (2012), Rome (2013), Brisbane (2014), Antalya (2015), Hangzhou (2016), Hamburg (2017), Brisbane (2018), Osaka (2019) and Riyadh (2020). The 2021 Summit was held at Rome and Indonesia held the 2022 Presidency. India will host the G20 summit in 2023 at the New Pragati Maidan. The G20 today best represents a diverse group of stakeholders and international institutions that have come together to make globalization work better for all.

G20: Shared Benefits of Globalization

In 2016, the G20 committed itself to the Action Plan on the 2030 Agenda for Sustainable Development including the Sustainable Development Goals (SDGs) and the Addis Ababa Action Agenda on Financing for Development (AAAA). The 2030 Action Plan envisaged bold transformative steps through both collective and individual concrete actions at international and domestic levels. The G20 further sought to improve sustainable livelihoods with its endeavours in energy and climate despite the US plan to withdraw from the Paris Agreement. The G20 assumed the responsibility for launching the Africa Partnership in recognition of its goal for fostering sustainable and inclusive economic development.

The G20 meetings have enlarged in scope and number over the past decade. They comprise the following meetings:

1. Meetings of Finance Ministers and Central Bank Governors (twice a year)
2. Meeting of G20 Sherpas
3. G20 Ministerial Meeting on Development
4. Summit Meeting

The G20 has further diversified to include Climate Change, Energy, Skill Development, Health, Women, Science and Technology, Agriculture and Labour Ministers meetings.

The Washington DC Summit: November 2008

In 2008, global output was contracting at a pace not seen since the 1930s. Trade was plummeting, jobs disappeared rapidly. The world was on the edge of a depression. The Summit on Financial Markets and the World Economy was held on 15th November 2008 in Washington DC amid serious challenges to the world economy and financial markets. The leaders of the Group of Twenty expressed determination to enhance cooperation and work together to restore global growth and achieve needed reforms in the world's financial systems. The root causes of the 2008 crisis were inadequate appreciation of the risks building up in financial markets by policy makers, regulators, and supervisors in advanced countries. They also felt that inconsistent and insufficiently coordinated macroeconomic policies and inadequate structural reforms led to unsustainable global macroeconomic outcomes. These developments led to severe market disruptions.

The Common Principles for Reform of Financial Markets were the most significant decision of the summit. The leaders of the G20 formulated an action plan to implement the principles of reform by the Finance Ministers and experts. The common principles for reform were (a) Strengthening transparency and accountability; (b) Enhancing sound regulation; (c) Promoting integrity in financial markets; (d) Reinforcing international cooperation; and (e) Reforming international financial institutions.

While regulation was the first and foremost responsibility of the national regulators, the G20 decided on intensified international cooperation amongst regulators and strengthening of international standards affecting international financial stability. Effectively, the leaders of the G20 pledged to bolster investor protection, prevent illegal market manipulation, and strengthen financial market transparency. They further sought to reform the Bretton Woods institutions to adequately reflect changing economic strengths to increase their legitimacy and expand the financial stability forum by including emerging market countries.

The action plan to implement the principles of reform contained Immediate Actions by 31 March 2009 and Medium-Term Actions. The immediate actions envisaged that the IMF with its focus on surveillance and the expanded FSF with its focus on standard setting should strengthen their collaboration. The adequacy of resources of the IMF and World Bank was to be reviewed and the institutions were asked to restore emerging and developing countries access to credit and resume private capital flows essential for sustainable growth.

The maximum emphasis was on enhancing sound regulation. All G20 members were to review and report on the structure and principles of their regulatory systems to ensure compatibility with global financial systems. As part of prudential oversight, the G20 agreed that financial institutions should maintain adequate capital amounts to sustain confidence. The regulators were asked to strengthen banks' risk management practices in line with international best practices.

The leaders of the G20 confronted with a massive global financial crisis, reiterated their commitment to an open global economy. They felt that increasing financial sector regulation was necessary but nothing should be done to contract capital flows and reforms should be grounded in a commitment to free market principles. Continued partnership, cooperation, and multilateralism were the clarion call given the leaders of the G20 in Washington DC in November 2008.

The London Summit April 2009

At the London Summit of April 2009, the leaders of the Group of Twenty faced the greatest challenge to the world economy in modern times. Global economic activity was falling and turning around the global growth that depended critically on concerted policy actions and concerted policy support. The crisis had deepened since November 2008, and the global crisis required a global solution. It was in this backdrop that the leaders of the Group of Twenty adopted three major declarations—the Global Plan for Recovery and Reform, the Declaration on Strengthening the Financial System and the Declaration on Delivering Resources through International Financial Institutions.

The global plan pledged to (a) restore confidence, growth and jobs; (b) repair the financial system to restore lending; (c) strengthen financial regulation to rebuild trust; (d) fund and reform international financial institutions to overcome the crisis; (e) promote global trade and invest to underpin prosperity; and (f) build an inclusive green and sustainable recovery.

To restore growth and jobs, the central banks of the G20 took exceptional action. In line with the G20 framework for restoring lending and repairing the financial sector, they cut interest rates; governments put together the largest fiscal and monetary policy stimulus and agreed to put in place credible exit strategies from expansionary policies.

For strengthening financial supervision and regulation, the Financial Stability Board (FSB) with a strengthened mandate was established to include all G20 countries, Spain, and the European Union. The FSB was to coordinate with the IMF to provide early warning systems. To strengthen the global financial institutions, the G20 was committed to implementing the package of IMF quota and voice reforms agreed to in April 2008 and called on the IMF to complete the review of quotas by January 2011. The G20, at London, reiterated the commitment made in Washington DC to refrain from raising new barriers to investment or trade or new export restrictions, a pledge extended to the end of 2010. The G20 recognized the human dimension of the crisis, and agreed to create employment opportunities and income generating measures for those who had lost their jobs. The G20 agreed to make the best possible use of investments funded by fiscal stimulus programs towards building a sustainable recovery.

The Global Plan for Recovery and Reform was accompanied by the Declaration on Delivering Resources through international financial institutions and declaration on strengthening the financial system. The resources to the IMF were trebled to US $ 750 billion, a new SDR allocation of US $ 250 billion was made and additional resources from IMF gold sales for a US $ 1.1 trillion program lending were added. The IMF introduced a new flexible credit line (FCL) as part of its reformed and more flexible lending. The scope of regulation brought careful oversight to large and complex financial institutions given their systemic importance. The FSB was mandated to coordinate with the IMF and BIS to develop macro-prudential tools for regulation. The G20 also agreed to improve accounting standards and arrange effective oversight of credit rating agencies. Tax havens were also to be subjected to international prudential and supervisory standards.

The Pittsburgh Summit: September 2009

"It Worked" was what the leaders of the Group of Twenty said on 25 September 2009. The G20 economies had implemented wide-reaching policy measures that helped stabilize the confidence, limited the threat to financial stability, and provided impetus to economic growth. Considerable fiscal stimulus remained in the pipeline through 2010 for the G20 as a whole, and there was a positive impact on growth and employment.

G20: Building Blocks to the Framework

S. No.	*Summit*	*Key Steps*	*Description*
1	Pittsburgh September 2009	Policy and macro-economic frameworks	All G20 members shared information with each other and the IMF about their policy plans and expected performance over the next 3-5 years. The IMF examined global implications
2	Toronto June 2010	Assessment of members' policies	The IMF assessed the consistency of G20 members' policies with growth objectives and simulated upside scenarios in which collective action contributes to better outcomes for all and global rebalancing
3	Seoul November 2010	Enhanced MAP with indicative guidelines	G20 leaders gauged progress toward framework goals via indicative guidelines to identify and assess imbalances. The IMF was tasked to

S. No.	Summit	Key Steps	Description
			conduct assessment of members with large imbalances.
		Policy commitments	Each G20 member identified policy actions it would take to help achieve common growth objectives
4	Cannes November 2011	Cannes Action Plan for Growth and Jobs	G20 leaders endorsed policy actions to correct imbalances over the medium term and ensure progress towards strong, sustainable and balanced growth. The G20 committed itself to take significant strides towards a more stable and resilient international monetary system. For seven countries identified as having large imbalances, sustainability reports prepared by the IMF provided analysis of the nature of imbalances, root causes and impediments to adjustment.
5	Los Cabos June 2012	Los Cabos Growth and Jobs Action Plan	G20 leaders committed themselves to adopting policy measures to strengthen demand, support global growth, and restore confidence, address short-and medium-term risks and enhance job creation.
6	Saint Petersburg September 2013	Saint Petersburg Action Plan	G20 leaders agreed on an action plan to cooperatively boost global growth, jobs and financial stability and acknowledged the need for fiscal consolidation to reflect economic conditions
7	Brisbane November 2014	Brisbane Action Plan	G20 leaders committed themselves to comprehensive growth strategies aimed at boosting their collective GDP by more than 2 per cent above the trajectory in the October 2013 IMF WEO baseline by 2018
8	Antalya November 2015	Antalya Action Plan	G20 leaders took stock of the progress towards the implementation of growth strategies and reiterated their commitment to a full and timely implementation of the growth strategies. The action plan also focused on promoting investment and greater inclusiveness.
9	Hangzhou September 2016	Hangzhou Action Plan	G20 leaders enhanced growth strategies based on a new framework for structural reforms, including nine priority areas.

S. No.	*Summit*	*Key Steps*	*Description*
10	Hamburg, 2017	Hamburg Action Plan	G20 leaders developed resilience principles to guide the update of the growth strategies.
11	Osaka, 2018	Osaka Action Plan	G20 leaders furthered efforts to foster development and address global challenges
12	Buenos Aires, 2019	Buenos Aires Action Plan	G20 leaders built consensus for fair and sustainable development

Source: http://www.g20.org

The global economy was beginning to grow again, but the recovery was sluggish and policy support required to be sustained for the expansion to be firmly established. Financial conditions continued to improve but markets remained dependent on public support. The banking systems were undercapitalized and saddled with impaired assets. The biggest risk was a premature exit from accommodative macroeconomic policies.

The G20 faced key challenge to map a course between unwinding public interventions in a time-bound manner and maintaining market confidence for sustainability of public finances. They also needed to evolve clear communication of exit strategies. Central Banks needed to unwind their extraordinary liquidity and credit support and start tightening their monetary stance.

The path from Pittsburgh in September 2009 was to Canada in June 2010 and then to Korea in November 2010.

Toronto Summit: June 2010

The G20 noted that global recovery was moving at different paces in different countries, and individual countries needed to tailor their responses to their own circumstances. The Toronto summit communiqué said that "Those countries with serious fiscal challenges need to accelerate the pace of consolidation. This should be combined with efforts to rebalance global demand to help ensure global economic growth continues on a sustainable path".

The leaders' summit developed the G20 Framework for Strong Sustainable and Balanced Growth. The G20 sought to build on its achievement of addressing the global economic crisis by ensuring a full return to growth with quality jobs, to reform and strengthen financial systems and to create a strong and balanced global growth. The IMF released its assessment of scenarios for improving growth through the Mutual Assessment Process designed to enhance the synergy of country economic programs to achieve stronger growth worldwide. The G20 mutual assessment process was the mechanism through which the growth challenge was to be addressed.

The G20 mutual assessment process showed that appropriate collective action could increase the global GDP by 2.5 per cent over the medium term, creating tens of millions of jobs and lifting tens of millions out of poverty. The G20 mutual assessment program envisaged action in three areas: first, fiscal consolidation in advanced economies with credible fiscal plans starting in 2011; second, economies with surpluses to boost internal demand by spending on infrastructure, social safety nets and allowing exchange rate flexibility; and third, structural reforms in advanced economies encompassing changes in labour markets that would lift growth and financial reforms on a sustainable basis.

The G20 leaders' summit also made progress towards a comprehensive set of new standards to enhance strength and stability of the financial sector. A healthier and safer financial sector could play a significant role in government interventions to repair the financial system. The financial sector reform rested on four pillars—a strong regulatory framework, effective supervision, resolution of financial institutions in distress and transparent international assessment and peer review. Banks were required to hold significantly more and higher quality capital, the Financial Stability Board in consultation with the IMF was to make recommendations on improved supervision, and there would be greater commitment to the IMF/World Bank financial sector assessment program.

The leaders of the G20 supported the IMF quota reforms and agreed in parallel to deliver the other governance reforms in line with the Pittsburgh summit commitments to enhance IMF legitimacy and credibility.

The Seoul Summit 2010

In November 2010, the leaders of the G20 met in Seoul, Korea, in a meeting aimed at strengthening the international policy framework to help sustain the global economic recovery.

The communiqué said "Cohesion and cooperation defined the G20 during the crisis. This allowed decisive policy action to help avert a second Great Depression. Now the challenge is to secure the recovery and to create the growth and jobs the world needs. We all recognize that much remains to be done, but the Seoul Action Plan is a step in the right direction."

The G20 leaders agreed that the mutual assessment program should be continued and country-specific commitments should be spelt out in key policy areas. A set of indicative guidelines to help identify large imbalances that require preventive corrective actions to be taken were to be formulated by the IMF and the Financial Stability Board. Based on these guidelines the progress would be towards external sustainability and global consistency of national economic policies. The Fund's modernized surveillance mandate and instruments, including new country-specific spill-over reports on the wider impact of systemic economic policies would support this effort. With the objective of strengthening global financial stability, the G20 called upon the IMF to deepen its work on capital flow volatility.

The G20 adopted the Seoul Development Consensus for Shared Growth that sets out the G20's commitment to work in partnership and complement efforts to achieve the Millennium Development Goals. The Multi-Year Action Plan on Development sought to make a tangible and significant difference in people's lives including, in particular, the development of infrastructure in developing countries.

Cannes Summit 2011

On the eve of the Cannes Summit 2011, the IMF submitted a report titled "The G20 Mutual Assessment Process: From Pittsburgh to Cannes—IMF Umbrella Report" to take stock of the progress made in delivering upon the policy commitments made in the Seoul Action Plan, an updated assessment of G20 macroeconomic frameworks and a sustainability report on the nature of large imbalances (key imbalances being public debt and fiscal deficits; private savings and private debt; external position—trade balance). The IMF said that the G20 economies had been making progress towards the policy commitments made at the Toronto and Seoul summits. At the same time, however, the global environment had become much more challenging, as growth in advanced economies had slowed sharply and financial stress had increased. The IMF recommended swift and decisive action to secure the agreed objectives. Major advanced economies needed to articulate medium-term fiscal objectives and further financial sector reforms to resolve underlying problems and weaknesses that led to the crisis. Key emerging surplus economies needed to address impediments to rebalancing and allow greater exchange rate appreciation. All of them needed to focus on reforms including in the financial sector aimed at alleviating key impediments to higher growth.

At the Cannes Summit 2011, the G20 faced another major challenge in handling the European crisis. The global strategy for growth and jobs was built around endorsing the decisions of the European leaders to restore debt sustainability to Greece, strengthen European banks, build firewalls to avoid contagion and lay the foundation for robust economic recovery in Europe. They once again focused on efforts towards a more stable and resilient international monetary system. The big decision was that the SDR basket composition should reflect the role of currencies in the global trading and financial system and the SDR basket was to be reviewed in 2015. The G20 further agreed that the resources of the IMF should be mobilized to implement the euro area's comprehensive restructuring plan including country reforms.

The Washington Summit of 2008 had agreed that all financial markets, products and participants would be regulated or subject to oversight. The Financial Stability Board started publishing the list of global systemically important financial institutions (G-SIFIs). The G-SIFIs would be subjected to strengthened supervision, a new international standard for resolution regimes as well as additional capital requirements from 2016. Similarly, the systemically important non-bank financial institutions were to be identified. The Financial Stability Board was mandated to coordinate and monitor the G20's financial regulation agenda.

The other issues that were taken up by the leaders of the G20 included addressing commodity price volatility and promoting agriculture, improving energy markets and pursuing the fight against climate change, avoiding protectionism and strengthening the multilateral trading system, addressing the challenges of development, intensifying the fight against corruption and reforming the global governance for the 21st century. The G20 pursued dialogue and cooperation amongst the major international organizations, especially the UN, WTO, the ILO, the WB and the IMF.

Los Cabos Summit 2012

The Los Cabos Summit of 2012 of the G20 was held amidst political impasse in dealing with large imbalances in the USA and Japan. The economic activity in the major emerging market economies had decelerated on the back of spill-overs from advanced economies. The outlook for growth remained weak with huge downside risks. The euro area crisis required timely and resolute policy implementation. Financial conditions remained fragile.

The leaders of the G20 agreed that they would do everything necessary to strengthen the overall health and growth of the world economy. Their focus was to rebuild the confidence in global financial markets. They felt that the reduction in global imbalances had not been sufficient, and the policy commitments for fiscal tightening in the USA, Japan and Europe remained critical to reduce risks and secure a durable and strong recovery. Against this backdrop, the G20 adopted the Los Cobos Growth and Jobs Action Plan.

The European crisis necessitated stronger supervision and direct bank recapitalization. Public finances were to be brought back to a sustainable path. The G20 agreed to move rapidly to a more market determined exchange rate system and exchange rate flexibility and avoid persistent exchange rate misalignments. The enormous focus on exchange rate misalignment was to bring greater flexibility in the renminbi. The G20 also pledged additional resources to the IMF for crisis resolution. An amount of US$ 461 billion in pledges were received and US$ 286 billion borrowing agreements were finalized. The G20 also pledged to move faster on the financial sector regulation agenda. They also agreed for faster implementation of the Basel II, 2.5 and III measures and endorsed the charter for the Regulatory Oversight Committee.

Against the backdrop of the global economic crisis and the European crisis, the G20's focus was on enhanced surveillance of the world economy through the IMF and stronger financial sector regulation through the Financial Stability Board. The surveillance framework was strengthened through the integrated surveillance decision and mutual assessment framework. The Financial Stability Board started publication of an updated list of systemically important banks, and the framework for dealing with systemically important domestic banks. The G-SIFI supervision was intensified and greater transparency of financial institutions encouraged.

Further, the G20 promoted sustainable development policies and incorporated green growth into their agenda. They resolved to phase out medium-term inefficient fossil fuel subsidies that encouraged wasteful consumption. A G20 climate finance study group was constituted to effectively mobilize resources for climate finance.

Saint Petersburg Summit 2013

The agenda for the Saint Petersburg summit of the leaders of G20 covered a diverse range of issues. The financial issues discussed were Financial regulation, International financial architecture, Financial inclusion, Financial education, Consumer protection, Tackling tax avoidance, Promoting tax transparency and Automatic exchange of information. The developmental issues deliberated included Growth through quality jobs, Promoting development for all, Sustainable energy policy, resilience in commodity market and Intensifying the fight against corruption.

The G20's coordinated action had done much to stabilize the world economy and the financial system. Yet there was much more to be done to get the world economy to work better. Global growth remained subdued, with persisting market volatility and stability risks. While the advanced economies were gathering some momentum, the emerging markets were showing a slowdown. The Saint Petersburg Action Plan stressed the importance of cooperation as countries addressed the challenges of promoting global growth, jobs and financial stability. The action plan recognized the need for fiscal consolidation to reflect economic conditions, the need to push forward on financial oversight and regulation, and the importance of comprehensive structural reforms to support growth.

The Saint Petersburg Action Plan recognized the need for a supportive monetary policy and the need to ensure an orderly exit from unconventional monetary policies, effectively managing spill-overs. The G20 made progress on tax evasion and tax avoidance and recognized that international taxation was an important area of multilateral discussions. The G20 also continued support for IMF's 2010 quota reform and the urgent need to ratify the agreement.

Brisbane Summit November 2014

The Brisbane summit meeting of the leaders of G20 accorded the highest priority to delivering better living standards and quality jobs for people across the world. Global recovery was slow and not delivering the jobs needed. There was a shortfall in demand and risks persisted in financial markets. The G20 set itself an ambitious goal to lift the G20's GDP by at least an additional 2.1 per cent which would add US$ 2 trillion to the global economy and create millions of jobs.

To promote infrastructure investment, the G20 agreed to create a global infrastructure hub with a four-year mandate. The G20's actions to deliver quality jobs were to increase investment, trade and competition. For generating quality jobs, the G20 set up an employment working group to submit its report by 2015.

The G20 had delivered on strengthening the resilience of the global economy and stability of the financial system. The Financial Stability Board proposed that systemically important banks hold additional loss-absorbing capacity to protect taxpayers if banks failed, which was accepted by the G20. The G20 made further progress in the areas of international taxation. They further reiterated that the IMF quota and governance reforms and the 15th general review of quotas agreed in 2010 remains the G20's highest priority and urged the USA to ratify them.

The G20 agreed on several developmental issues with special emphasis on climate change. They agreed to support mobilizing finance for the green climate fund. They also sought to have a coordinated approach for Ebola.

Antalya Summit November 2015

The G20's comprehensive agenda for the Antalya summit included decisive implementation of past commitments, boosting investments as a powerful driver of growth and promoting inclusiveness so that the benefits of growth are shared. The G20 remained committed to lift their collective GDP by an additional 2 percent by implementation of growth strategies that include measures to support demand and structural reforms. The Antalya Action Plan reflected the growth priorities of the G20 along with implementation schedules for key commitments. To provide a strong impetus to boost investment, country-specific investment strategies were estimated to increase the G20 investment to GDP ratio by 1 per cent.

The G20 remained committed to strengthening resilience of financial institutions and enhancing the stability of the financial system. The G20 finalized an international common standard on total loss-absorbing capacity for systemically important banks. They agreed to strengthen the oversight and regulation of the shadow banking system to ensure resilience of market-based finance. To reach a globally fair and modern international tax system, a package of measures developed under the G20/OECD base erosion and profit sharing project were adopted, in particular, the exchange of information on cross-border tax rulings. A G20 anti-corruption plan and the G20 high level principles on integrity and transparency in the private sector were also adopted to bring transparency in the private sector. To bring transparency in the public sector, the G20 principles for promoting integrity in public procurement were adopted.

The G20's developmental agenda included adoption of the G20 and low-income developing countries framework to strengthen the dialogue on development. The 2030 agenda including the sustainable developmental goals (SDGs) remained the basic framework for the G20's developmental agenda. The G20 continued its work on global partnership for financial inclusion and on the G20 principles for energy collaboration. On climate change, the G20 reaffirmed its commitment to the below 2 degrees C goal and to contribute to the UNFCCC ahead of the Paris Conference on Climate Change.

Antalya witnessed the diversification the G20 agenda to cover energy sector issues and greater commitment to multilateral collaboration for climate change initiatives.

Hangzhou Summit September 2016

The Hangzhou consensus of the leaders of the G20 was based on a vision to strengthen the G20's growth agenda; forging synergy in fiscal, monetary and structural policies; promoting global trade through greater openness and inclusive growth. The global economic recovery was progressing and new sources of growth were emerging. There were profound shifts in the configuration of the global economic landscape.

The growth strategy was to strive to reduce excessive imbalances and promote greater inclusiveness. That said, the G20 felt that excess volatility and disorderly movements in exchange rates could have adverse implications for economic and financial stability. A new path for growth was to be charted with the G20 2016 innovation action plan which sought to pursue pro-innovation policies, investments in science, technology and innovation (STI), support skills training for STI, and mobility of human resources. They also delivered the G20 new industrial revolution action plan to strengthen SME's and address workforce skill challenges. Further, the G20 digital economy development cooperation initiative was formulated to unleash the potential of digital economy. An enhanced structural reforms agenda was adopted consistent with country-specific choices.

The G20 welcomed the entry into effect of the 2010 IMF quota and governance reform and sought early completion of the 15th quota review to reflect the shares of dynamic economies in line with their relative positions in the world economy. The Paris Club, the principal international forum for restructuring official bilateral debt, was expanded to include Korea, Brazil and China. The G20 remained committed to a resilient financial system through the Financial Stability Board.

The Hangzhou communiqué laid emphasis on robust international trade and investment as also inclusive and interconnected development. The Hangzhou comprehensive accountability report on G20 development commitments reflected the progress made over the period 2014-16. The G20 Labour ministers, G20 Agriculture ministers meetings were also included in the developmental agenda.

Further, the G20 took note of Brexit, and the uncertainty it brought to the global economy. The G20 felt its members were well positioned to address the potential economic and financial consequences of Brexit. The G20 reiterated its support for climate change and supported the green climate fund.

The Hangzhou summit reaffirmed the G20's founding spirit to bring together the major economies on an equal footing to catalyse action. The G20 had expanded into several new areas in its developmental agenda.

Hamburg Summit July 2017

The Hamburg summit decided to take concrete actions on the three aims of building resilience, improving sustainability and assuming responsibility. The highest priority was accorded to strong sustainable, balanced and inclusive growth. Further, the G20 recognized that globalization and technological change had raised living standards across the globe, but its benefits had not been shared widely enough. The Hamburg summit also resolved to tackle the common challenges to the global community including terrorism, displacement, poverty, hunger and health threats, job creation, climate change, energy security and gender inequality as a basis for sustainable development and stability.

The leaders of the G20 took note of the decision of the USA to withdraw from the Paris Agreement. The USA had announced that it would cease the implementation of its nationally determined contribution and adopted an approach that lowers emissions while supporting economic growth. Despite the US withdrawal, the leaders of the G20 stated that the Paris Agreement was irreversible. "Investing in Climate, Investing in Growth" was the line of the G20 as it adopted the Hamburg G20 climate and energy action plan for growth.

Buenos Aires Summit November 2018

The G20 leaders endorsed the Buenos Aires Action Plan, to work together to improve a rule-based international order that is capable of effectively responding to a rapidly changing world. Transformative technologies were expected to bring immense economic opportunities, new and better jobs and higher standards of living. The G20 endorsed the policy options for Future of Work by promoting decent work, vocational training and skill development. The signatories to the Paris Agreement reaffirmed their commitment to its full implementation, while the USA reiterated its decision to withdraw from the Paris Agreement, but reaffirmed its commitment to economic growth, energy access and security. The G20 also reiterated that strong and effective international financial institutions with a strong, quota based, and adequately resourced IMF at its centre by concluding the 15th general review of quotas. The G20 suggested further reform of the WTO and also recommended worldwide implementation of the OECD/G20 base erosion and profit shifting package. The G20 remained committed to prevent and fight corruption and endorsed the principles on preventing corruption and ensuring integrity in state-owned enterprises and on preventing and managing conflicts of interest in the public sector.

Osaka Summit June 2019

The G20 reiterated its goal of strong, sustainable, balanced and inclusive growth as envisaged in the 2030 Agenda for Sustainable Development. The G20 Fukuoka policy priorities on aging and financial inclusion were endorsed as also the necessary reform of the WTO and the progress made by the Global forum on steel excess apacity. Global health, Global finance and Global environmental issues and challenges were discussed. The G20 remained committed to the completion of the 15th general review of quotas of the IMF by end 2019. The importance of the energy transitions 3E+S (Energy Security, Economic Efficiency, and Environment and Safety) to transform energy systems was recognized.

Conclusion

The G20 has emerged as the world's premier forum for international economic cooperation and for forging a comprehensive and integrated narrative for strong, sustainable and balanced growth. The G20 was successful in avoiding a second Great Depression in 2009 by putting together the largest taxpayer funded bailout of the global financial system. Since then, there has been a massive regulatory oversight of financial institutions and banks. The major institutional reform that has been carried out by the G20 has been the governance reforms in the IMF and the emergence of the financial stability board as the major forum for a strong regulatory framework in the financial sector.

The G20 has diversified into climate change, energy security, agriculture, sustainable development initiatives and skill development. The landmark event of the Hamburg G20 summit meeting was that it had to deal with the USA distancing itself from global governance, poor performance of the WTO with the slow death of the Doha round of trade negotiations of the WTO, and the rise of China and Germany in the G20. The Buenos Aires summit and the Osaka summit discussed the general review of quotas of the IMF, Financial stability, Global health and Environmental challenges and Energy security.

After the Osaka summit, the agenda ahead was well laid out, with the G20 strengthening global multilateral institutions, promoting sustainable development goals, the Africa partnership and climate change. Clearly, the G20 had made a major contribution to setting the global governance agenda. To conclude, it can be said that the G20 has made a serious contribution to making globalization fairer and more sustainable while transforming the processes of international negotiations. However, the years 2020 and 2021 witnessed the COVID-19 pandemic which changed the paradigm of global governance.

3

G20: The Riyadh Summit 2020

The G20 had to address the financing gaps in WHO's strategic preparedness and response Plan, make significant efforts to build a resilient and long lasting economic recovery, ensure an inclusive recovery that tackled inequalities and ensure a sustainable future.

The G20 Riyadh summit was held on 22 November 2020. It was the second time the G20 leaders had met under the Saudi Presidency. An extraordinary G20 leaders' summit was held on 26 March 2020. The COVID-19 pandemic and its unprecedented impact in terms of lives lost, economies affected necessitated significant multilateral efforts to find timely responses. An unprecedented 25 G20 ministerial declarations, Communiqués and Statements marked multilateralism's most sustained efforts to respond to the global challenge.

At the Riyadh summit, the G20 acknowledged that coordinated global action, solidarity, and multilateral cooperation were more necessary in 2020 than ever to overcome the challenge of empowering people, safeguarding the planet and shaping new frontiers. The focus was to save lives, livelihoods and affected economies that witnessed an unprecedented shock revealing vulnerabilities in the global pandemic response representing a common challenge. The pandemic could push 26 million people in sub-Saharan Africa into extreme poverty and up to 39 million people into extreme poverty if downside risks to growth materialized. People in Kenya were cooking less frequently said newspaper reports. People in Uganda cannot sustain even one day of quarantine reflecting the high number of hand-to-mouth people working in the informal sector. Africa's pandemic crisis was set to wipe out nearly 10 years of progress in development with the GDP projected to contract by 5.4 per cent with per capita GDP back to 2010 levels. Massive financing gaps of USD 44 billion existed, and the slowdown was witnessed in the larger economies of South Africa, Nigeria, and Angola. The IMF's managing director, Kristalina Georgieva, said, "It's the long ascent, a journey that will be difficult, uncertain and prone to setbacks".

The G20 made significant efforts to fight the challenge. The G20 finance ministers and central bank governors met seven times in 2020, with meetings held in February, March, April, July, September, October and November 2020. The G20 Trade and Investment ministers met three times in March, May and September, the Health ministers met in September and November, the Education ministers met in June and September, the Energy, Agriculture and Water, Tourism, Environment, Labour and Employment, Digital Economy ministers met in April, October and November. The ministerial meetings took forward the 26 March 2020 summit recommendations to enhance global cooperation in fighting the pandemic, safeguarding the global economy and addressing international trade disputes.

The G20 economic response envisaged a multipronged coordinated approach to fight the challenges of the pandemic. The key features were the debt service suspension initiative to be implemented by the IMF and development banks, the financial stability board to monitor financial sector vulnerabilities, the principles of a common framework for debt beyond the debt sustainability suspension initiative and enhancing the lending capacity of the emergency response packages by the IMF, the World Bank and regional development banks. The G20 finance ministers said international economic assistance was in the form of a catastrophe containment and relief trust providing immediate debt service relief for six months were availed by 21 countries of sub-Saharan Africa, debt service suspension initiative were availed by 46 countries in the period May-December 2020, rapid financing instrument for 29 countries along with emergency response packages by expansion of the loan resources under the poverty reduction and growth trust.

The G20 health ministers worked to collaborate on the COVID-19 tools accelerator initiative, intensified pandemic surveillance, sought an assessment report from the WHO on the pandemic preparedness, sought finances from multilateral development banks to strengthen the financial support for the "Access to COVID-19 Tools" and enhanced support for universal health coverage schemes. The education ministers discussed the impact of prolonged closures of educational institutions, sharing of international best practices and, experiences, lessons learnt to ensure learning continuity while stressing on the need to address digital divides and inequities in learning opportunities. The G20 trade ministers sought to introduce short-term measures for trade facilitation, operation of logistics networks and transparency. They also sought to support multilateral trade systems, resilience in global supply chains and strengthen international investment. The G20 anti-corruption ministers meeting called for action on corruption in fighting COVID-19, preparation of a good practices compendium for combating corruption, the Riyadh initiative for enhancing international anti-corruption law enforcement cooperation and international cooperation and asset recovery. They further sought to criminalize bribery.

The Saudi Presidency imprint was visible at the leaders' summit meeting in November 2020. The Saudi Presidency took up the initiative to enhance access to pandemic tools. The steps included research and development and distribution of diagnostic tools; encouraging international funding for the global pandemic and supporting the training of epidemiologists from all over the world. Saudi Arabia contributed USD 500 million to the immediate funding needs to fight the COVID-19 pandemic, with the G20 member-countries pledging USD 21 billion to finance the fight against the pandemic. The G20 also committed itself to work on affordable and equitable access to COVID-19 vaccines, therapeutic and diagnostic tools. As part of the extraordinary measures to support economies and the people, the G20 injected USD 11 trillion into the global economy to support businesses and protect livelihoods. Further, the G20 committed itself to extended social safety nets to protect jobs and incomes. The other areas of focus of the Saudi Presidency were the Riyadh initiative on the future of the WTO, empowerment of women and youth, endorsing the circular carbon economy platform, reducing land degradation and access to safely managed fresh water.

The leaders' statement covered four broad thrust areas—Rising to the challenge together, Building a resilient and long-lasting recovery, ensuring an inclusive recovery that tackled inequalities and enduring a sustainable future. The leaders' summit recognized extensive immunization as a global public good and reiterated the commitments made in the extraordinary summit of March 2020. Further recognizing that the global economic recovery was subject to elevated downside risks, the G20 endorsed an action plan comprising the debt service suspension initiative (DSSI) and the common framework for debt treatment beyond the DSSI.

The G20's focus on building a resilient and long-term recovery covered systemically important sectors of health, trade and investment, transport and travel, international financial architecture, infrastructure investment, financial sector issues, digital economy, international taxation and anti-corruption. The Saudi Presidency initiated discussions on the need to address gaps in health preparedness, and proposed establishing access to pandemic tools. These discussions continued in the Italian Presidency with the WHO COVID-19 resolution to determine the global health response. The G20 endorsed the actions to support world trade and investment responses to COVID-19, and the inclusive economic growth through participation of MSME's. Discussions also centred around the future of the WTO. Further, the G20 committed itself to ensure global transportation routes and supply chains remaining open, safe and secure. They said that the restrictive measures of COVID-19 should be targeted and transparent with concrete ways to facilitate movement of people.

The G20 said that the international financial architecture needs a strong global safety net adequately resourced by the International Monetary Fund. They sought to continue further progress on the 16th general review of quotas by 2023. The G20 asked the IMF to prepare an analysis of the external financing needs of the low-income countries and develop a G20 reference framework for effective country platforms. The G20 leaders said the Financial Stability Board should continue to monitor financial sector vulnerabilities and complete the evaluation of Too Big to Fail Reforms. The G20 also formulated a roadmap to enhance cross border payments, mobilize sustainable finance and strengthen financial inclusion. On digital economy, the G20 leaders took note of the policy options to support digitalization of business models during COVID-19, secure and affordable connectivity, identify examples of best practices related to security in the digital economy and formulate a roadmap towards a common framework for measuring the digital economy. The G20 leaders called for progress in tax transparency standards on automatic exchange of information, strengthening tax capacity of developing countries and firming up a G20/

OECD framework for base erosion and profit sharing (BEPS) by mid-2021. The G20's call for action on corruption and COVID-19 envisaged the Riyadh initiative for enhancing the international anti-corruption law enforcement cooperation and endorsed the G20 anti-corruption accountability report. The G20 sought to build anti-corruption strategies, promote public sector integrity and promote integrity in PPP's.

To ensure an inclusive recovery that tackled inequalities, the G20 action plan on the 2030 agenda for sustainable development was adopted. The G20 financing for supporting industrialization in Africa was envisaged with the G20 Africa partnership and compact with Africa. Further, the G20 issued guidelines on quality infrastructure for regional connectivity and financing a sustainable framework. The G20 policy guidelines on digital financial inclusion for Youth, Women and SME's were adopted along with the G20 action plan to guide the work of global partnership for financial inclusion and the G20 menu of policy options to enhance access to opportunities for all. On employment issues, the G20 recognized that the impact of the pandemic on labour markets remained a priority. The G20 supported the policy options for adopting the social protection policies to reflect the changing patterns of work and the ILO/OECD report on the impact of COVID-19 on global labour markets. On women's empowerment, the G20 sought to ensure that the pandemic did not widen gender inequalities while stepping up efforts to reduce the gap in labour force participation between men and women by 25 per cent by 2025. Further, the Saudi Presidency initiative for empowerment and progression of women's economic representation (EMPOWER) was adopted. On education, the G20 said it was important to ensure the continuity of education in times of crisis. On the tourism sector, the G20 guidelines for inclusive community development through tourism were envisaged and the G20 guidelines for action on safe and seamless travel were adopted along with the establishment of the G20 tourism working group. The G20 leaders noted the 2020 annual international migration and forced displacement trends and policies report to G20 by the OECD.

Ensuring a sustainable future represented a significant policy challenge. The G20 initiative on clean cooking fuel and energy access and G20 energy security and market stability cooperation was accepted. Further efforts were made for leading the energy transitions to realize the "3E+S" (energy security, economic efficiency, environment, and safety). The G20 endorsed the circular carbon economy platform with the 4R framework and reiterated the support for tackling pressing environmental challenges ahead of COP 21 in Glasgow and COP 15 in Kunming. On agriculture and water, the G20 Riyadh statement sought to enhance implementation of responsible investment in agriculture and food systems. The G20 dialogue on water to share the best practices and promote innovation, new technologies and integrated water management was adopted.

The Saudi Presidency also held several side events, the important of which was the discussion on the pandemic preparedness and response. The G20 recognized that the pandemic had infected 54 million people and claimed over 1 million lives worldwide. It needed a multipronged and multilateral approach. The G20 members contributed USD 21 billion to support health systems and USD 14 billion in debt service relief to developing nations. The Saudi Presidency led the launch of "Access to COVID-19 Tools—Accelerator" and the "Global Corona virus Pledging Event". It was at this event that several leaders expressed solidarity. Ngozi Okonjo-Iweala, Gavi Board chair, said

> *"The virus is winning. Only through adequate financing for a global exit strategy like Access to COVID-19 Tools Accelerator (ACT-A) can economic vitality be restored at home and a catastrophe in the poorest countries be averted. A commitment by G20 leaders to invest USD 4.6 billion to fill the ACT's immediate funding gap will save lives, lay the groundwork for mass procurement and delivery of ACT-A tools—tests, treatments and vaccines—around the world. Another commitment of USD 24 billion is needed in 2021 for COVID-19 tools globally."*

The President of France, Emmanuel Macron, said "The only effective response to the pandemic will be a coordinated, global one based on solidarity." The Chancellor of Germany, Angela Merkel, said "A global challenge, which is what the pandemic undoubtedly is, can only be overcome with a global effort." The President of South Africa, Cyril Ramaphosa, said "We are pleased that there appears to be consensus in the G20 that access to an effective COVID-19 vaccine should be universal; it should also be fair and equitable." The President of South Korea, Moon Jae-in, said "We must work together more closely in solidarity to defeat the corona virus. I hope the efforts of G20 will inspire the world."

The Saudi Presidency promoted a holistic approach to manage emissions in all sectors through the circular carbon economy (CCE) initiative, the 4R's—Reduce, Reuse, Recycle, Remove—initiatives. They set an ambitious goal of conserving the sustainability of 1 billion hectares of degraded land by 2040. Renewables, including wind and solar, will generate 50 per cent of Saudi electricity by 2030. The G20 leaders supported the Saudi Presidency initiatives. The Prime Minister of India, Narendra Modi, said "Climate change must be fought not in silos, but in an integrated and holistic way. We should do so with a spirit of cooperation and collaboration." The President of the United States of America, Donald Trump, said "We must preserve the majesty of God's creation. Together we can protect our environment." The Prime Minister of Japan, Yoshihide Suga, said "Global environmental issues are urgent challenges. Japan will take the initiative."

In his closing remarks, King Salman said the G20 had upheld the commitment to work together to rise to the challenge of the COVID-19 pandemic to safeguard lives and livelihoods. Further, the G20 had succeeded in sending a message of hope and reassurance to all people around the world by adopting the communiqué. The G20's joint and individual actions were critical in overcoming the global challenge. The future challenges included empowering people, safeguarding the planet and shaping new frontiers.

Clearly, the roadmap ahead of the G20-Riyadh Summit was global resilience. A global alliance in development and distribution of vaccines, protecting climate and environment, governing the digital economy and technology and upholding the international institutions and governance was the call of the day. The overhauling of health systems entailed developing resilient health systems which are vigilant, responsive, flexible and equitable. Vaccine finance was a major challenge that needed to be addressed. Further, there existed challenges regarding inequalities within countries as also between countries. Vaccine nationalism was being witnessed.

Improved global governance entailed bolstering the efforts of the United Nations and multilateral institutions. The IMF approved a record number of loans in a short time with low conditionality. The WHO was to be developed as the world's rapid response force on global health. Another major step envisaged was enhancing the effectiveness of the WTO. Stopping the debt pandemic represented a major challenge. The borrowing needs of several countries had skyrocketed and more transparency in debt data and debt contracts was needed. Besides, there was no success in getting the private lenders to follow the DSSI.

The International Monetary Fund called the G20 for multilateral collaboration to end the health crisis, bridge the economy through the crisis and minimize scarring, and bolster medium-term growth and build resilience. The Fund said amidst unprecedented debt levels, it was essential to make operational the common framework for debt resolution for economies with unsustainable sovereign debt. Global growth in 2020 had declined to (–)4.4 per cent and partial recovery projections stood at 5.2 per cent for 2021.

When the G20 finance ministers and central bank governors met in Riyadh in February 2020, an uncertain economic landscape appeared with the global economy far from being on solid ground. Despite the USA-China trade deal, the global growth scenario with the corona virus represented the most pressing uncertainty. The fragile economic recovery was threatened by the health emergency and spill-over from China to other countries in terms of supply chain disruptions, tourism and travel restrictions. The G20 finance ministers focused on three important issues—trade, climate and inequality. It was felt that the USA-China trade deal had left many issues unaddressed while focusing on a limited share of the tariffs and minimum increases in China's imports from the USA. It was noted that climate-related disasters had become more frequent especially in the poorest countries. The G20 called for investments in clean energy and resilient infrastructure, as also additional carbon taxes to avert future losses. Income and wealth inequalities remained persistently high across the G20 countries and there was renewed focus on raising the standards of living and creating better-paying jobs. The low interest rate regime in the world provided an opportunity to spend more in countries where public debt was manageable. Only three G20 countries were assessed as having substantial fiscal space—Australia, Germany and Korea—while others had only 'some fiscal space', or no fiscal space as in the case of Argentina and South Africa. The theme as stated by Kristalina Georgieva, the Managing Director IMF, was "Working together, we can take necessary steps to reduce uncertainty and put the global economy on a more solid footing."

By April 2020, the COVID-19 pandemic had triggered a major health emergency and severe economic crisis. The pandemic had spread rapidly across the globe with most countries facing the impact. Infections were rising sharply and millions of jobs were lost with massive containment measures being put in place. Governments imposed restrictions on travel and made efforts to provide adequate resources to health sector spending.

Disruptions were seen in transport, hospitality, entertainment and retail businesses. Economic activity had slowly stopped with the containment measures. Remittances plummeted. There were massive cross-border spill-overs with uncertainty in the progress of the pandemic and the duration of the containment measures. In the USA, close to 10 million people made claims for unemployment insurance during the first two weeks of March 2020, which was seven times more than the worst period of the global financial crisis. A deep global recession loomed with economic output projected to shrink by three per cent. There was limited fiscal space available and the fiscal packages needed to be backed by monetary and financial sector packages to address economic challenges. There remained concerns on health care capacity, adequacy of doctors, hospital beds and inventories. It was clear that the containment measures would affect the poor and vulnerable groups most unless the social safety nets were strengthened. Governments provided tax cuts, waivers and extensions in tax payment deadlines. Governments also announced a series of credit/financial policies which included government guarantees, loans to businesses/households from government entities, and easing of credit regulations.

It was clear that containment was crucial to avert the humanitarian catastrophe in the immediate future, and significant multilateral efforts were needed to contain the crisis to reach stabilization. The steps included sharing information, ensuring financing for health care, establishing flow of medical supplies and strengthening the global financial safety net. Accordingly, the IMF's emergency financing facilities were strengthened. The catastrophe containment and relief trust (CCRT) was used to provide upfront debt relief grants and free resources in the countries to deal with the pandemic. The new arrangement to borrow was doubled and the IMF provided a USD 1 trillion lending capacity through bilateral borrowing arrangements. The G20's focus was to help save lives, protect the vulnerable and put the world economy back on the path of strong, sustainable, balanced and inclusive growth.

By July 2020, it was projected that the global economic output would decline by 4.9 per cent in 2020 which represented a deeper contraction than previously envisaged. The health and economic crisis had further worsened the economic outlook. Double-digit contractions were projected in several G20 member-countries including the USA, France, Mexico, Italy and Spain. A large proportion of the labour force filed for unemployment or job protection benefits in Canada, France, Italy, the United Kingdom and the USA. Bankruptcy filings by small firms were witnessed. There remained significant uncertainty that the spread of the disease could lead to further disruptions. The fiscal policy support in G20 countries was extensive to individuals, firms and the health sector and amounted to 10.5 per cent of the GDP. The low inflation scenario resulted in further easing of monetary policy and a low interest regime which enabled further lending.

There existed fears that rising protectionism and retreat from multilateralism would result. The IMF urged policy makers of G20 countries to continue to work together to end the health crisis by ensuring production and distribution of goods and health supplies essential to fight the pandemic. Several multilateral measures were undertaken. These included larger emergency financing using the rapid credit facility and rapid financing instrument to 70 countries amounting to USD 24.7 billion, higher loan resources for low-income countries by mobilizing resources through the poverty reduction and growth trust, additional liquidity and credit lines using the flexible credit lines and provision of debt relief using the catastrophe containment and relief trust which provided immediate debt relief for six months to 28 of the poorest and most vulnerable countries. The debt service suspension initiative provided temporary suspension of debt service payments to official bilateral creditors. Thirty-nine of the 73 eligible countries had requested to join the DSSI by June 2020. However, there remained considerable uncertainties on Non-Paris Club creditors, and the perimeter of claims covered by the DSSI. The IMF called upon the G20 member-countries to clarify the uncertainties around the G20 debt service suspension initiative so that the global community could seize on every opportunity to promote a stronger, more inclusive and greener future.

The spread of the pandemic forced G20 countries to respond rapidly to the health crisis and economic fallout. The fiscal support for fighting the pandemic covered increases in health sector spending, support for households, maintaining employment linkages, support for businesses by type and by measures. G20 member-countries focused on expansion of basic social security, frontloading of unemployment benefits, direct cash payments, expansion of sick leave benefits, deferred income tax and VAT payments, corporate tax exemptions, loan guarantees, increasing the lending capacity of financial institutions, equity injection to SME's and increase in credit lines. The focus of central bank interventions was on easing monetary policy, easing stress in foreign exchange markets, longer term funding markets, securities markets and short-term funding markets.

Fiscal support exceeded USD 10 trillion since the onset of the crisis and helped G20 countries to reduce the impact of the pandemic.

The year 2020 was one during which the global community witnessed massive losses, deep scars and sharp increases in poverty. The search for vaccines while witnessing significant progress was yet to reach fruition and new outbreaks of pandemic waves continued to occur. There were significant increases in public and private debt levels. Women and youth were the worst affected. Prolonged school closures necessitated online learning for children. The short term and long term extent of damage appeared severe. By November 2020, it was clear that the pandemic had caused massive devastation resulting in loss of lives and a deep recession. Poor and middle class sections were the worst affected with many losing their jobs. The G20 countries focused on continued efforts to provide support including USD 12 trillion in fiscal actions through the crisis to ensure an economic recovery, and boost efforts to reverse the rise in poverty. The IMF recommended that the richest countries must continue to help low-income countries with concessional financing, debt relief and grants. The reforms recommended were establishing efficient bankruptcy procedures, preventing high unemployment rates and strengthening human capital. Further, the IMF recommended concerted action on climate change front to address carbon emissions and the rise in temperatures. The first big step was to end the health crisis.

The Access to COVID-19 Tools (ACT) Accelerator represented global collaboration to accelerate development, production and equitable access to COVID-19 tests, treatments and vaccines. The ACT Accelerator was launched in April 2020 and brings together all stakeholders including governments, civil society and philanthropists. It established the COVAX facility for equitable procurement and distribution of vaccines globally, which has expedited rapid affordable COVID-19 tests and effective treatments. A massive equity gap exists between the richer and poorer countries in access to COVID-19 tools but the ACT accelerator has achieved and delivered its impact in record time when it was needed the most. Until mid-April 2021, India had supplied nearly 20 million doses to COVAX and donated 11 million doses while nearly 36 million doses were sold to 26 countries. The first doses were shipped to Bhutan and Maldives. In September 2021, India had announced that it would renew its vaccine export drive "Vaccine Maitri", and would first prioritize COVAX for neighbouring countries. Currently, 80 per cent of the six billion vaccine doses administered have been in higher and upper-middle income countries. Vaccine inequity is highest in Africa with only 3.5 per cent people vaccinated. To ensure that the vaccine policy is effective, significant ramping up of production and distribution networks in low-Income countries is necessary. A strategic review of the ACT Accelerator was been proposed by the stakeholders given the ongoing pandemic and need for more equitable access to COVID-19 tools. The strategic review objectives were to update ACT-A current work and priorities, information on rising demand and financing requirements for diagnostics, oxygen and PPE, and provide an update on COVAX outlook for 2022. The report was expected by October 2021.

4

G20: The Rome Summit 2021

Under the framework of the Italian Presidency where the priorities were outlined as People, Planet and Prosperity, the G20 took the lead in evolving a swift international response to the pandemic—providing equitable and worldwide access to diagnostics, therapeutics and vaccines—while building up resilience to future-related shocks.

On 30-31 October 2021, Italy hosted the G20 Summit, at Rome and after two days of deliberations. the G20 leaders adopted the Rome Declaration. It is an outcome of a year of negotiations and events organized by the Italian Presidency. The G20 looked at rapid recovery beyond the crisis, reducing inequalities, improving women's empowerment, younger generations, and protecting the most vulnerable by creating new jobs, social protection, and food security. The third major pillar was sustained prosperity. A prosperous future that required proper harnessing of the main drivers of growth and innovation, bridging the digital divide and making digitalization an opportunity for all, improving productivity and, in short, leave no one behind.

The G20 Rome summit was held against the backdrop of the global economy witnessing a sharp economic recovery. Growth projections in the advanced economies for 2021 are projected at 5.9 and G20 economies at 6.3 per cent. The GDP growth projections for 2022 for advanced economies stand at 4.9 per cent and G20 economies at 5.0 per cent. The G20 ministerial meetings had put in place policies that aimed to carry growth forward and improve debt outlook for most constrained G20 economies. G20 economies had several policy measures to provide direct fiscal support for vulnerable households: Russia provided targeted support; Brazil, Germany and the USA extended unemployment benefits; several economies provided targeted support to affected sectors and firms, and maintained fiscal balances below the 2019 levels. Several G20 economies like Italy, South Africa, and Spain did not have much fiscal space, and needed to undertake structural reforms like tax structure reforms, trade liberalization, and active labour market policies to support a sustainable recovery. Additional resources and public investments were made in the education and health sectors and for greater access to digital infrastructure and job creation.

In the run-up to the Rome Declaration, there were 20 ministerial declarations and communiqués starting with the G20 finance ministers and central bank governors meeting communiqué of 7 April 2021 and ending with the G20 joint finance and health ministers' communiqué of 29 October 2021. The period also witnessed the G20 Tourism ministers' communiqué of 4 May 2021, the G20 education ministers' declaration of 22 June 2021, G20 Labour and employment ministers' declaration of 22 June 2021, G20 environment communiqué of 22 July 2021, G20 digital ministers' declaration of 5 August, 2021 and the G20 trade ministers' communiqué of 12 October 2021. A G20 plus Qatar "Extraordinary Leaders" meeting on Afghanistan was virtually to discuss the response to a looming humanitarian crisis in the country on 12 October 2021.

In his opening remarks, the Prime Minister of Italy, Mario Draghi, said that after two years since the start of the pandemic, the world could finally look at the future with some optimism. Successful vaccination campaigns and coordinated action from governments and central banks have allowed the global economy to rebound. Many countries have launched recovery plans to boost growth, reduce inequalities and promote sustainability. As the world starts to rebuild its economic order, startling disparities in the global distribution of vaccines continue to pose challenges. In the high-income countries more than 70 per cent of the population has received at least one dose of vaccination while in the poorest countries this percentage roughly drops to 3 per cent. These differences are morally unacceptable and undermine global recovery. The world is close to meeting the WHO's target of vaccinating 40 per cent of the global population by the end of 2021 and all efforts must be made to reach 70 per cent by mid 2022. To address the vaccine inequality, the world must continue to invest in research, eliminate trade barriers affecting COVID-19 vaccines and enhance the predictability in delivery. There is a need to strengthen global supply chains, and expand manufacturing capacity at local and regional levels.

Prime Minister Mario Draghi said that the Italian Presidency had worked to promote an equitable recovery and witnessed key milestones. These include the global health summit in Rome which saw companies and countries make generous vaccine pledges for poorer countries, the historic agreement for a fairer and more effective international taxation system, and the allocation of 650 billion special drawing rights for countries that are most in need.

The G20 Rome Leaders' Declaration

The key features of the G20 Rome leaders' declaration pertain to health, financial support to vulnerable countries, environment, energy and climate, international taxation, trade and investment and digital economy, higher education and research. The G20 underlined the crucial role of multilateralism in finding shared and effective solutions. These include the need to support countries with vulnerable populations to overcome the pandemic, the need to work on the shared vision to combat climate change, to achieve gender equality and to broadly share the benefits of digitalization.

The Rome declaration noted that global economic activity was recovering at a solid pace with the effective rollout of vaccines and continued policy support. However, the economic recovery is uneven across countries and G20 leadership is needed to provide funding for vaccines, diagnostics, and therapeutics through the ACT accelerator and vaccines. The Rome declaration commits the G20 to determinedly address the adverse consequences of the pandemic by avoiding any premature withdrawal of the support measures. The global financial safety net of the G20 would help vulnerable countries significantly.

The extension of the G20 debt service suspension initiative (DSSI) to the end of 2021, the G20 common framework for treatment of debt beyond the DSSI and the USD 650 billion SDR allocation are significant measures. The DSSI has benefitted 50 countries and the G20 called on private creditors and bilateral creditors to provide debt treatment on similar lines as DSSI. These initiatives will help address unsustainable debt burdens and provide long-term reserves to low income, emerging market and developing countries.

The IMF was asked to establish a new resilience and sustainability trust (RST) in addition to enhanced allocations for the poverty reduction and growth trust (PRGT) to provide long-term financing to help low-income countries and vulnerable middle-income countries to achieve macroeconomic stability. The new RST will be channelized through the PRGT. The Rome declaration committed the G20 to IMF governance reform under the 16th general review of quotas including the new quota formula by December 2023.

The two-pillar solution to address the tax challenges arising from the digitalization of the economy and the OECD/G20 inclusive framework on base erosion and profit sharing represents a historic agreement that will establish a more stable and fairer international tax system. The Rome declaration asked the OECD/G20 to swiftly develop the model rules and multilateral instruments envisaged under the detailed implementation plan.

Health and environment were high-focus sectors for the Rome summit. Extensive COVID-19 immunization was recognized as a global public good. The global goal was to vaccinate 40 per cent of the population in all countries by the end of 2021, and 70 per cent by mid-2022. The ACT-Accelerator including COVAX was extended to 2022 as also the formation of a multilateral leaders' task force on COVID-19. The G20 committed itself to expand the provision and access to vaccines. A joint finance-health task force to work out the modalities of establishing a financial facility for pandemic prevention, preparedness and response was established. There was also focus on other areas of health care, like primary health care services, and universal health coverage.

On environment, the G20 committed to collectively plant one trillion trees to combat land degradation. The commitment to the initiative of reducing land degradation under the Saudi Presidency found continued support. The decade 2021-2030 will be the UN decade on ecosystem restoration. On sustainable development also, the commitments to the 2030 SDG agenda and the Addis Ababa action agenda were reiterated. The G20 remained committed to hold the global average temperature well below 2 degrees C and to pursue efforts to limit it to 1.5 degrees C above pre-industrial levels. They also committed themselves to a successful COP 26, reducing greenhouse gas emissions and adopting circular carbon economy. The G20 action plan introduced a pillar dedicated to protecting the planet. The International Energy Forum was asked to facilitate a dialogue between producers and consumers to bolster efficiency of energy markets.

The other areas that were discussed included gender equality and women's empowerment, employment and social protection, education, migration and forced displacement, and transportation and travel. The G20 committed itself to take the global agenda forward in each of these areas. The ILO, the International Organization on Migration, the United Nations High Commissioner for Refugees, and the international institutions working in these sectors would be collaborating in taking the agenda forward. The G20 also reaffirmed its endeavour to restart international travel in a safe and orderly manner consistent with the work of the WHO, the International Civil Aviation Organization, the International Maritime Organization and the OECD.

The Financial Stability Board was asked to strengthen the non-bank financial intermediation (NBFI) sector. The ongoing work on central bank digital currencies and their implications on the international monetary system was to be continued. On trade and investment, the Rome summit said it would take forward the Riyadh initiative on the future of the WTO to undertake necessary reform of the WTO, through the 12th WTO ministerial conference (MC12). Commitments were made to extend the global infrastructure hub mandate until the end of 2024, and building on the G20 infrastructure investors dialogue. On productivity, the G20 looked at digital transformation and productivity recovery as also to good corporate governance.

Financial inclusion, digital economy, and higher education also figured prominently in the G20 Rome leaders statement. The global partnership for financial inclusion, (GPFI) undertaking the work of the 2020 financial inclusion annual plan was extended support for engaging with MSME's. The G20 innovation league was sought to be promoted, multilateral cooperation in ICT security was strengthened. On tourism and culture, the G20 supported a sustainable recovery of the tourism sector, and adopted the G20 guidelines for the future of tourism. Commitments were also made to promote culture with a key role to be played by UNESCO. The anti-corruption agenda was reiterated with support to the 2022-2024 anti-corruption action plan and the G20 high level principles on corruption. The G20 anti-corruption accountability report was adopted. Full support was extended to the financial action task force's ongoing work on anti-money laundering and countering the financing of terrorism. FATF-style regional bodies were also encouraged to be promoted.

India's views at the Rome G20

India, represented by Prime Minister Modi, reiterated its full support for the financial action task force (FATF) and recognized that effective implementation of the measures to combat money laundering, terrorist financing, and proliferation were essential to build confidence in financial markets, ensure a sustainable recovery and protect the integrity of the financial system.

Prime Minister Modi participated in a session on 'climate change and environment' which was followed by a discussion on sustainable development. The G20 leaders committed themselves to providing USD 100 billion to counter climate change and for ending international financing for all new coal plants by the end of 2021. India's pitch in the climate talks largely centred around promoting renewable energy and controlling emissions through energy transition. The Green Grids Initiative—One Sun, One World, One Grid (GGI-OSOWOG) was launched immediately after the G20 summit at the COP 26 leaders' summit. India said that achieving its climate goals may be linked to issues like its membership to the nuclear suppliers group, which was held up due to China's opposition. India pushed for membership of the NSG for adequate availability of raw material for nuclear supply and several other associated concerns around cost of power for climate transition from coal to nuclear.

Prime Minister Modi participated in the summit on global supply chain resilience convened by the US President on the sidelines of G20, wherein he pitched India as the trusted source in the IT and pharmaceutical supply chains and underlined the critical requirements for improving global supply chains. He also expressed India's keenness to participate in the clean technology supply chain.

India also gave a strong message in the health sector discussions in agreeing to the strengthening of the World Health Organization, to fast track the process for emergency use authorization (EUA) for COVID-19 vaccines. India also said that it was ready to produce over five billion COVID vaccine doses by the end of 2021 to help the world fight against the pandemic. The Union Commerce Minister and India's Sherpa to the G20 said that "it was decided that the recognition of the COVID vaccines which were deemed to be safe and efficacious will be mutually accepted subject to national and privacy laws that countries may have."

Conclusion

On 30 November 2021, the Italian Presidency came to an end and the baton was picked up by Indonesia to lead the G20 economies. The Italian government focused on People, Planet and Prosperity and worked for 12 months until the leaders' summit convening 175 events, 20 ministerial meetings in various cities, two special meetings of G20 leaders on global health and Afghanistan, six Sherpas' meetings, 62 working groups and 60 finance track meetings.

It is important to understand how the world leaders viewed the Rome Summit 2021. Italy's Prime Minister Mario Draghi said, "The summit was a success" adding that cooperation is essential on issues like climate, health, and poverty. Prime Minister Draghi said "The form of cooperation we know best is multilateralism" and called the G20 members to act swiftly together. The declaration reaffirmed the crucial role of multilateralism and international cooperation in overcoming multiple global challenges arising from the COVID-19 pandemic.

President Biden said he encountered a 'real eagerness' for American leadership in confronting global challenges during his meetings with world leaders. "We helped lead what happened here. The United States of America is the most critical part of this entire agenda, and we did it". The American President said there was "no substitute" for meeting in person and working through disagreements. Further, he said "I am proud that the G20 endorsed the global minimum tax. This is something the USA has been driving for over a year, building momentum up to this achievement. And this is an incredible win for all our countries. Instead of nations competing against one another to attract investments by bottoming out corporate tax rates, this set a minimum floor of 15 per cent to ensure that giant corporations begin to pay their share no matter where they are headquartered, instead of hiding profits overseas. We also agreed to establish a fund in the future that countries can draw on to help prevent, if necessary, and respond to the next pandemic. The USA and the European Union have agreed to negotiate the world's first trade agreement based on how much carbon is in a product."

In conclusion, it can be said that the G20 Rome summit was a success—consensus was achieved on several issues: the global minimum tax; setting up of a global body to respond to future pandemics; and a global vaccination target of 40 per cent population by the end of 2021. Further, the G20 enabled rallying the forces of future global ecological protection.

5

Prime Minister Modi in UNGA, G20 and BRICS

"Only reformed multilateralism with a reformed United Nations at its centre can meet the aspirations of humanity."

—**Prime Minister Modi**[1]

Prime Minister Modi[2] has been a vocal supporter of multilateralism and institutional mechanisms in global governance. He has tried to re-establish the multilateral world order at a time when the USA had pulled out of the Paris Climate Agreement, and the trans-Pacific Partnership, stressing on America First policies. India's positions have consistently been to work with all stakeholders and global institutions.

In the 75th year of the United Nations, Prime Minister Modi said, *"Only reformed multilateralism with a reformed United Nations can meet the aspirations of humanity"*. He called on members of United Nations to pledge for reforms in the world body to make it more representative to reflect today's realities and give a voice to stakeholders. The path to achieve sustainable peace and prosperity is through multilateralism. Prime Minister Modi said the United Nations was originally born from the furies of the Second World War and India, as a founding signatory, was part of the noble vision reflecting India's own philosophy "Vasudhaiva Kutumbakam" which sees all creation as one family. The fury of the pandemic provides the context for its rebirth and reform.

From 2020 to 2022, Prime Minister Modi has made 'reformed

multilateralism' a part of India's foreign policy, making repeated calls in several fora—the United Nations General Assembly, UNECOSOC, the Shanghai Cooperation Organization (SCO), BRICS meetings in 2020, G7 Summit in 2021, and in the World Economic Forum.

The three major themes of the Reformed Multilateralism are:

- An urgent need to complete the process of decision-making in the Security Council
- Positioning of development issues at the forefront of the work of the UN
- Transforming the UN into a multi-stake holder body to respond effectively to the challenge it faces.

Prime Minister Modi at UNGA

Prime Minister Modi addressed the 74th and 75th sessions of UNGA in 2019 and 2020. In his addresses, he presented India's development vision along with the Indian approach to global challenges of climate change, combating terrorism and other issues.

In 2018, Prime Modi received the Champion of Earth for policy leadership from the United Nations Environment Program (UNEP). He had pledged to eliminate single-use plastic in India by 2022 and for the pioneering work in championing the International Solar Alliance and new areas of cooperation on environmental action. The award was conferred by the United Nations Secretary-General Antonio Guterres who said the *"World needs bold leadership and I thank India for setting an example."*

Prime Minister Modi has said, "What is needed today is a comprehensive approach which covers everything from education to values, and from lifestyle to developmental philosophy. What we need is a global people's movement to bring about behavioural change."

India's vision for climate change envisaged increasing the share of non-fossil fuel, and by 2022 to increase renewable energy capacity to much beyond 175 GW, and later up to 450 GW. India prepared plans to make the transport sector green through e-mobility. India also worked to considerably increase the proportion of the bio-fuel blend in petrol and diesel and provided clean cooking gas to 150 million families. The Jal Jeevan Mission for water conservation, rainwater harvesting, and development of water resources was highly focused on covering 150 million homes by 2024.

Nearly 80 countries joined the India-led initiative of the International Solar Alliance. The alliance initiative provides a platform for governments and the private sector opportunities for cooperation in the area of technology innovation to develop low carbon pathways for industry. India also led the efforts for a coalition for disaster resilient infrastructure. A people's movement to end the use of single-use plastic was launched and was highly successful.

In his address to the 75th session of UNGA, Prime Minister Modi said, "Reform in the responses, in the processes, in the character of the United Nations is the need of the hour. It is a fact that the faith and respect that the United Nations enjoys in India are unparalleled. However, it is also true that the people of India have been waiting for a long time for the completion of the reforms of the United Nations. Today, people of India are concerned whether this reform process will ever reach its logical conclusion. For how long will India be kept out of the decision-making structures of the United Nations?"

In his address to the 76th session of UNGA, Prime Minister Modi focused on fighting the pandemic, and said from his experience, democracy can deliver all-inclusive equitable development. He focused on the Atma Nirbhar Bharat (Self Reliant India) campaign. Further, he emphasised on a rule-based world order in Maritime Security which was promoted by India in its Presidency of the United Nations Security Council.

Prime Minister Modi at G20

Prime Minister Modi has addressed the G20 summit meetings from 2014 to 2021 on a range of issues.

In the Brisbane G20 summit in 2014, he made a strong pitch against black money. India said there were many rigidities in international tax laws and the past tax treaties also did not facilitate easy exchange of information. Prime Minister Modi built consensus in the G20 for inclusion of a clause in the Communiqué that would make it difficult for tax havens to give complete tax exemption to companies. India's concerns on black money and tax avoidance have been taken onboard at the G20. The G20 Communiqué said that 'we endorse the finalized common reporting standard for automatic exchange of tax information on a reciprocal basis which will provide a step-change in our ability to tackle and deter cross-border tax evasion. We will begin exchanging information automatically between each other and with other countries by 2017 or end 2018' said the G20 communiqué. The development assumed significance in the case of India as it was facing difficulties in getting information on cases of suspected tax evasion from other countries, especially Switzerland. Soon the global protocol was adopted by Switzerland and also Mauritius with which India had worked to revise the bilateral treaty due to concerns of money laundering. The exchange of information with a confidentiality clause would allow governments to obtain detailed account information from their financial institutions on an annual basis.

The G20 endorsed the global common reporting standard for automatic exchange of tax information on a reciprocal basis committing itself to 'transparency of tax payer-specific rulings found to construe harmful tax practices.' Prime Minister Modi also took up the issue of black money in his bilateral meetings with Japanese Prime Minister Shinzo Abe and BRICS leaders wherein he called for close cooperation on unaccounted money stashed abroad, saying that it also posed security challenges.

In the Antalya summit in 2015, in the session on Inclusive Growth, Global Economy, Growth Strategies, Employment and Investment Strategies, Prime Minister Modi called on the multilateral development banks to enlarge their capital base and support infrastructure needs of developing countries. He welcomed the new multilateral financing institutions like the New Development Bank. He called upon the G20 to align its efforts with the UN Sustainable Development Goals, particularly the goal of elimination of all poverty by 2030. He welcomed the G20's focus on women and youth, and called for additional efforts to promote labour mobility and skill portability. In the session on enhancing resilience, Prime Minister Modi called for effective supervision, better use of technology and enhanced cyber security. He called for IMF reforms and general review of quotas ratified in 2010. India supported the base erosion and profit sharing package, the automatic exchange of information initiative and the international efforts to implement common reporting standards based on automatic exchange of tax information. Prime Minister Modi called on the G20 to promote transparency and integrity, citing India's zero tolerance policy on corruption and black money, greater international cooperation for return of illicit money to the country of origin, addressing the barriers of excessive banking secrecy and effective counter terrorism financing tools.

At the Antalya summit, Prime Minister Modi addressed issues of trade and energy. He called for a transparent, equitable, non-discriminatory, and rule-based global trading system as an essential feature for the world economy. He supported a liberalized multilateral trade regime ahead of regional trade agreements. He also called for an increase in labour mobility and skill portability. For clean energy, he said India had set itself a goal of 175 GW of renewable energy by 2022, cut back on subsidies on fossil fuel and imposed carbon cess on coal, while working on clean coal technology. India had set itself a target of 40 per cent of energy through non-fossil fuel. Prime Minister Modi called for an increase in research and development in clean and renewable energy, reduction in cost, and universal access through technology transfer and financial support.

Prime Minister Modi intervened in the session on Global Challenges—Terrorism and Refugee Crisis in which he said terrorism was the principal global challenge and that there were countries that still used terrorism as an instrument of state policy. He called for a comprehensive global framework for security to combat terrorism, urging the world to speak in one voice and act in unison against terrorism without any political considerations isolating those who support and sponsor terrorism. Prime Minister Modi called for a comprehensive convention on international terrorism by restructuring the international legal framework to deal with the challenges of terrorism. All efforts must be made to prevent supply of arms to terrorists, disrupt terrorist movements and curb and criminalize terrorist financing. Global cooperation in securing cyber space and minimizing the use of the internet and social media for terrorist activities was recommended. Prime Minister Modi also called on the G20 to address the refugee crisis with an estimated 60 million people in need of protection worldwide.

In the Buenos Aires G20 summit in 2018, Prime Minister Modi highlighted India's flagship programs of PMJDY, MUDRA, and Start-up India at the opening session. India's steps to modernize the economy, promote inclusive growth, and promote micro small-medium enterprises through the refinance agency MUDRA were highlighted. Further he cited Start-up India as an initiative to promote start-ups, generate employment, and create wealth.

At the Buenos Aires G20 summit, Prime Minister Modi presented a nine-point agenda on fugitive economic offenders seeking global cooperation to comprehensively deal with fugitive economic offenders. Cooperation in legal processes such as freezing of the proceeds of crime, early return of the offenders and efficient treatment of the proceeds of crime should be enhanced and streamlined. India also called for joint efforts by the G20 countries to form a mechanism that denied entry and safe havens to fugitive economic offenders. India suggested that the Financial Action Task Force (FATF) should be called upon to assign priority and focus to establishing international cooperation that lends to timely and comprehensive exchange of information between competent authorities and financial intelligence units. India also advocated setting up of a common platform for sharing experiences and best practices including successful cases of extradition, gaps in existing systems of extradition and legal assistance. It said the G20 forum should consider initiating work on locating properties of economic offenders who have a tax debt in the country of their residence for its recovery.

The BRICS leaders informal meetings have become a part of the G20 summit meetings and Prime Minister Modi addressed BRICS leaders in each of these meetings. The BRICS also pursued efforts for reform of multilateral institutions like the UN, WTO, UNFCC, IMF, and the World Bank, so as to maintain their relevance and reflect the realities of the current times. The Prime Minister suggested 'Reformed Multilateralism' in the BRICS meetings.

The G20 Osaka summit was Prime Minister Modi's 6th G20 summit. At the Osaka summit, he presented the '5-I' vision to maximize digital technology for social benefit. The '5-I's—inclusiveness, indigenization, innovation, investment in infrastructure and international cooperation. He said 'In the next five years, our target is to make India a five-trillion dollar economy. The social sector remains our top priority. Also, we will focus more on infrastructure development especially digital infrastructure.'

In the Osaka summit, at a meeting on digital economy, the Prime Minister of Japan underscored the importance of a 'Data flow with trust' concept, a move spearheaded by Japan that called for the creation of international rules enabling free movement of data across borders. Japan sought to standardize rules in global movement of data flows with better protection in personal information, intellectual property, and cyber security. Japan's contention was that digitally driven economies can spark innovation and encourage economic growth and a reliable set of rules for free flow of data are needed. The USA also supported Japan's plan, saying that the free flow of data is an integral part of the American digital economy's success, along with strong privacy and intellectual property protections and access to capital and innovation. India believed that the discussions and negotiations pertaining to data should be held within the context of the World Trade Organization (WTO) as 'data is the new form of wealth'. The issue became a major point of discord between the developed countries in the G20 and India and China on the other side. India's concerns on the digital divide were stated by the Commerce Minister as 'We believe all nations should appreciate that the digital divide within and across nations is a serious impediment for developing countries, can be overcome with timely support of training and creation of digital infrastructure. This is important for facilitating a level playing field in the digital economy for all countries to take equitable advantage of data free flow.'

At the BRICS leaders meeting on the margins of the G20 summit, Prime Minister Modi focused on three major challenges—recession and uncertainty in the world economy, one-sided decisions, and rivalry dominating over rule-based multilateral international trading systems and making development and progress inclusive and sustainable. He made five key recommendations, synergy between BRICS countries can lead to resolution of side effects of unilateral decisions, by emphasizing on multilateralism and business institutions and organizations for necessary reforms. For sustained economic growth, the required resources such as oil and gas are needed to be constantly available at low prices. Physical and social infrastructure and renewable energy programs of the member-countries should get more priority by the New Development Bank. India's initiative for a coalition for disaster resilient infrastructure will help in the development of an appropriate infrastructure to face natural calamities by the least developed and developing countries. Prime Minister Modi exhorted all nations to join this coalition. Further, he said the movement of skilled workers around the world should be easy. This will benefit countries where a large part of the population has crossed the working age. Prime Minister Modi called for a global conference on terrorism.

Prime Minister Modi chaired the informal summit of 'Russia-India-China' (RIC) leaders on the margins of the G20 Osaka Summit 2019. A similar trilateral meet was held on the margins of the Buenos Aires G20 summit also. The three nations, discussed enhancing cooperation in international forums, reforms and strengthening of multilateral institutions that had benefited the world including the United Nations, WTO and established global financial institutions. At the Buenos Aires summit, he attended a trilateral meet of the 'Japan-America-India' (JAI), a close partnership that is aimed towards realizing a free and open Indo-Pacific, in which the three nations shared their views on advancing a free, open, conclusive, and rule-based order in the Indo-Pacific region based on respect for international law and peaceful resolution of all differences. The USA said that the partnership with India is extremely good and extremely strong and stronger than ever. India's participation in JAI and RIC represented Prime Minister Modi's astute management of major power relations over the years.

At the G20 Riyadh summit, the Prime Minister congratulated the Kingdom of Saudi Arabia for its successful Presidency and for organizing the virtual summit 2020 despite the challenges of the COVID-19 pandemic. The summit under the Saudi Presidency with the theme "Realizing 21st Century Opportunities for All" focused on overcoming the pandemic, economic recovery and restoring jobs, and building an inclusive, sustainable, and resilient future. Prime Minister Modi called for a new global index for the post corona virus world that comprises four elements—creation of a vast talent pool, ensuring that technology reaches all segments of society, transparency in systems of governance, and dealing with Mother Earth in a spirit of trusteeship. Prime Minister Modi said that based on this, the G20 can lay the foundation for a new world. Further, he focused on multi-skilling and re-skilling to create a vast human talent pool.

At the G20 Rome summit, Prime Minister Modi addressed the sessions on Global economy and global health, Climate change and environment and Sustainable development. In the session on Global economy and global health, Prime Minister Modi put forward India's vision of 'One Earth-One Health' for the world to deal with such crises in the future. He spoke of India's role as the pharmacy to the world delivering medicines to 150 countries of the world, India's IT-BPO sector working round the clock to support the whole world without disruption by bringing work-from-anywhere norms, and extended support for the 15 per cent global corporate tax rate in making global financial architecture more fair. Prime Minister Modi committed India's seriousness in meeting global obligations with the manufacture of more than five billion vaccine doses over the next year which will go a long way in preventing the global transmission of corona.

At the session on Climate change and environment, Prime Minister Modi expressed full sensitivity towards climate mitigation and achieving 175 GW of renewable energy, 20 per cent ethanol blending in petrol by 2025, and net zero emission by Indian Railways by 2030. He further cited the neglect of climate finance by developed countries and said that without concrete progress on climate finance, pressurizing the developing countries for climate action was unjust. He suggested developed countries make available one per cent of their GDP to finance green projects in developing countries as part of the 'clean energy projects fund'. He also urged the G20 countries to create an institution of global standards in the field of green hydrogen to encourage its production and use.

At the session on Sustainable development, Prime Minister Modi laid great importance on SDGs in the post-recovery period particularly in LDCs and African countries. He said that India's development journey could offer many templates to other developing countries in digital connectivity, financial inclusion, and immunization of children, expressing willingness to share India's digital solutions as an open source available to entire humanity. He further emphasized that in the first year of 'Decade of Action' it is the G20's shared responsibility to extend the benefits of global recovery to all countries.

Prime Minister Modi at BRICS

Prime Minister Modi attended BRICS leaders' summit meetings from 2014 to 2022. In this period, 10 summit meetings were held from the 6th summit meeting in 2014 to the 15th summit meeting in 2022. In these BRICS summit meetings, Prime Minister Modi focused on the issues of strengthening BRICS economies and the effective implementation of the Sustainable Development agenda 2030.

Prime Minister Modi said India would continue to work closely with BRICS partners in the spirit of mutual trust, respect, and transparency. He suggested BRICS collaboration areas could be further expanded to include trade fairs; agriculture research; railway research; digital initiative; energy efficient technologies; cooperation between states, cities and local bodies; and promoting films and sports exchange.

In the period 2014 to 2022, BRICS was successful in establishing the New Development Bank and joint efforts were made for Quota and voice reform in the International Monetary Fund. Following the quota reforms, the share of BRICS countries in the IMF reached a total of 14.18 per cent. The BRICS leaders worked within the G20 agenda and supported the economic cooperation efforts undertaken by the G20. BRICS worked towards strengthening the Base erosion and profit shifting (BEPS), exchange of tax information on economic offenders, and capacity building of tax policies. In the education sector, the BRICS Network University was operationalized with the objective of engaging 12 universities of BRICS countries. The BRICS Energy research cooperation platform was another strong institution established under the aegis of BRICS.

Prime Minister Modi attended the 6th BRICS summit meeting in Fortaleza, Brazil, in July 2014. The summit resulted in the official inauguration of the New Development Bank to allow states to pool their resources for economic stabilization.

The 7th BRICS summit was held in the Russian city of Ufa in 2015 which was a joint summit with the Shanghai Cooperation Organization and the Eurasian Economic Union. The agreements of the New Development Bank and the BRICS Contingent reserve arrangement were operationalized. It was agreed that the New Development Bank would be lending in local currencies. The Ufa summit also discussed areas of BRICS economic cooperation. By 2016, the BRICS trade fair and the BRICS business council were also operationalized.

The 8th BRICS summit was held in Goa, India, with the Bay of Bengal Initiative for Multi-sectoral and economic cooperation (BIMSTEC) in 2016 under India's chairmanship. Prime Minister Modi called for a pro-active agenda for BRICS, covering a diverse range of subjects. He called for an intra-BRICS trade target worth USD 500 billion by 2020. The BRICS film festival and BRICS trade fair were held along with the leaders' summit. Prime Minister Modi said that India ratified the Paris Climate Agreement from 2 October 2016. BRICS leaders agreed to work together and act decisively against terrorism.

Prime Minister Modi said:

> *"Terrorism casts a long shadow on our development and economic prosperity. Its reach is now global. It has grown more lethal and adept at the use of technology. Our response to terrorism must, therefore, be nothing less than comprehensive. And we need to act both individually and collectively. Selective approaches to terrorist individuals and organizations will not only be futile but also counter-productive. There must be no*

distinction based on artificial and self-serving grounds. Criminality should be the only basis for punitive action against individuals and organizations responsible for carrying out terrorist acts. Terrorist funding, their weapons supply, training, and political support must be systematically cut off. In this respect, we need to deepen the security cooperation between our national security advisors."

The 9th BRICS summit was held at Xiamen, China, in 2017. There, Prime Minister Modi called for energy financing from the New Development Bank particularly in solar energy. He said India would be happy to work towards more focused capacity building engagement between BRICS and African countries in areas of skills, health, infrastructure, manufacturing, and connectivity.

Prime Minister Modi said:

"Renewable energy is particularly important on multiple counts. Recognizing this, India, together with France, launched a major international initiative—the International Solar Alliance (ISA) —in November 2015. It will bring together a coalition of 121 countries for mutual gain through enhanced solar energy utilisation. BRICS countries can work closely with ISA to strengthen the solar energy agenda. Our five countries have complementary skills and strengths to promote the use of renewable and solar energy. The NDB can also establish an effective link with ISA to support such cooperation. We would wish to see more clean energy funding, particularly in solar energy, from the NDB."

The 10th BRICS summit was held at Johannesburg, South Africa, in 2018. Prime Minister Modi identified lack of infrastructure financing resources in emerging market economies as a principal challenge. In this regard, he said physical and social infrastructure and renewable energy programs of the member-countries should get more priority by the New Development Bank. India's initiative for Coalition for disaster resilient infrastructure will help in the development of appropriate infrastructure to face natural calamities by the least developed and developing countries. He also called for a Global conference on terrorism.

The 11th BRICS summit was held at Brasilia, Brazil, in 2019. The theme was "BRICS: Economic Growth for an Innovative Future".

The 12th BRICS summit was to be held at Saint Petersburg in 2020 but was held in the virtual mode because of the COVID-19 pandemic. Prime Minister Modi labelled the BRICS Counter-terrorism strategy as an important achievement. He suggested that BRICS NSAs discuss a Counter-terrorism action plan. He said the main task of economic integration amongst BRICS lies in the hands of the private sector. Prime Minister Modi suggested that the BRICS Business council draw up a concrete plan to take our bilateral trade to the $ 500 billion target.

The 13th BRICS summit was held as a virtual conference under India's chairmanship. The theme was BRICS@15: Intra-BRICS Cooperation for Continuity, Consolidation and Consensus.

Prime Minister Modi, chairing the summit, said that

> *"India has received full cooperation from all BRICS partners and from everybody during this chairmanship and I am deeply grateful to all of you for this. The BRICS platform has witnessed several achievements in the last one-and-a-half decades. Today we are an influential voice for the emerging economies of the world. This platform has also been useful for focusing attention on the priorities of developing nations as well."*

BRICS has taken a collective position on 'Strengthening and reforming multilateral systems' and also adopted the BRICS Counter terrorism action plan. Prime Minister Modi also called for BRICS youth summits, BRICS Sports, and increase in exchanges amongst civil society organizations and think tanks to strengthen people-to-people contacts.

The 14th BRICS summit was held as a virtual summit in June 2022 hosted by China under the theme "Foster High-Quality BRICS Partnership, Usher in a New Era for Global Development". BRICS called for reforms of United Nations Security Council, revitalization of United Nations Economic and Social Council, reforms of WTO, and to work in solidarity with G20.

NOTES

1. Prime Minister Narendra Modi's speech at the United Nations Economic and Social Council on "Multilateralism after COVID-19: What kind of UN do we need at the 75th Anniversary?" 17 July 2022.
2. High-Level Dialogue of the United Nations Economic and Social Council (UNECOSOC) on "Multilateralism after COVID-19: What kind of UN do we need at the 75th Anniversary?" July 2020 www.pmo.gov.in

6

G20@2023: Reforming Multilateralism

Multilateralism in the G20 works through a number of international organizations and India has played an important role in the reforms in multilateral institutions.

Multilateralism in the G20 works through a number of international organizations including the United Nations, IMF, World Bank Group, OECD, WTO, ILO, FSB, and BIS contributing to the process. There are ministerial meetings, development working group meetings (DWG), employment working group meetings (EWG), global partnership for financial inclusion (GPFI), climate finance study group (CFSG) all of which contribute to the multilateral discussions.

There also exist G20 engagement groups like Business 20, Civil Society 20, Labour 20, Think 20, and Youth 20 which contribute extensively to the G20 processes. The ministerial groups comprise finance ministers and central bank governors, agriculture and water ministers, environment ministers, trade and investment ministers, anti-corruption ministers, tourism ministers, digital ministers, labour and employment ministers and health ministers.

India has played an important role in the reforms in multilateral institutions. It has supported the IMF's strictly limited gold sales in 2009-10. In the first phase of the IMF's exclusively off-market transactions to interested central banks and other official holders at market prices, the Fund sold 200 metric tons of gold to the Reserve Bank of India. India's influence was also seen in the Fund's flexible view in the liberalization and management of capital flows taking into account the specific country circumstances. Post the 2008 crisis, India's strong presence on the G20 enabled it to strongly push for quota reform in the IMF. The IMF quota reform represents the most significant achievement of the G20 in reforms in multilateral institutions.

The United Nations

The United Nations[1] celebrated its 75th anniversary in May 2020. Addressing member-nations, Secretary-General Guterres[2] launched the landmark report for the future of global cooperation, "Our Common Agenda". The report focused on new goals:

- The importance of protecting vulnerable groups is recognized through commitments to gender equality and leaving no one behind which include reinforcing social protections and promoting gender parity.
- Ensuring a more sustainable global economy was identified as a goal, with support for the poorest and a fairer international trading system.
- Climate action goals get special mention with commitments to limit warming to 1.5 degrees above pre-industrial levels, and net zero carbon emission by 2050, end fossil fuel subsidies, and a package of support for developing countries.
- US$ 50 billion vaccination plan, doubling the vaccine production and ensuring vaccines reach 70 per cent of the global population in the first half of 2022.

The United Nations proposed a summit of the future to set out a "New Agenda for Peace." The summit was to take into account the complex context of global governance with the goal of inclusive and networked multilateralism. Further, the United Nations proposed biennial high-level meetings at the level of heads of government and states between the G20, ECOSOC, international financial institutions and the United Nations Secretary-General. A futures lab to issue regular reports was to be created. The UN sought to embark on a Decade of Action —10 years—to make real progress to deliver the promise of a fairer future by 2030, with multilateralism at the heart of the process.

The United Nations called for the core values of the UN—development, peace and security and human rights—to be reaffirmed. Further, it recognized that the climate crisis posed an existential crisis and could be solved only if all of the international community worked together.

The United Nations said its impact on the daily lives of citizens had been meaningful and concrete. In its 75th anniversary year, members reinforced their collective commitment to the values and principles of multilateralism and their commitment to act with unity and solidarity. They said that multilateralism despite its weaknesses remained the only option for addressing humanity's present and future challenges.

By 2022, Secretary-General Guterres said that the 2030 Sustainable Development Goals agenda had been thrown off course with the pandemic and the impact of war in Ukraine. Further, the climate catastrophe is mounting by the day with global greenhouse emissions at their highest levels in human history and rising.

The United Nations adopted the Declaration to promote peace, prevent conflicts, abide by international law, ensure justice, place women and children at the centre, build trust, improve digital cooperation, ensure sustainable financing, boost partnerships and work with youth.

India chaired the UNSC in August 2021, the 75th year of UN, during which 14 outcome documents of which five were UNSC resolutions were adopted. India's chairmanship handled the key issues of maritime security, peacekeeping and counter-terrorism. Prime Minister Modi chaired a high-level meeting on "Enhancing Maritime Security—A Case for International Cooperation", the first time an Indian PM had chaired a UNSC session. A UN Convention on Law of Sea was adopted. Sessions were also chaired by the External Affairs minister and Foreign Secretary during this period.

The year 2021 also witnessed the USA returning to multilateralism with the rescinding of decisions to leave the WHO and the Paris Climate Agreement. The USA hosted a summit for democracy to meet the challenges of the 21st century in December 2021. President Biden called the defence of democracy the defining challenge of our times.

The International Monetary Fund

The Managing Director IMF said if there had been a time for multilateralism it was now. Multilateralism is the only way forward, she said to meet the shared challenges. The managing director highlighted that two emerging market countries, Indonesia and India, would be chairing the G20 one after another and India would lead the world in using the G20 as a platform for multilateral cooperation to address the common challenges of climate change and support the most vulnerable countries. In 2022, the International Monetary and Finance Committee made an overwhelming call to stop the war highlighting the adverse impacts of the war which had a global scope. There was no consensus on the communiqué given the objections raised by Russia and no communiqué was issued despite the overwhelming majority of the members supporting the elements of work to be done by the IMF.

The war in Ukraine has had a massive global impact slowing down global growth and raising inflation. Global growth is projected to slow down to 3.1 per cent in 2022 from 6.1 per cent in 2021. Global inflation has been projected at 5.7 per cent in 2022 in advanced economies and 8.7 per cent in emerging market economies. The prices of oil, wheat, and fertilizers have risen sharply and there are disruptions in the global manufacturing systems with car production having slowed down. Labour markets have tightened and rising inflation has meant that real wages have fallen. Interest hikes are witnessed across the global economy particularly in developing countries which have record debt levels. Global current account balances have also widened with the USA running a larger deficit and higher surpluses in China and the European Union.

The IMF has flagged the adverse impacts of a worsening of the war resulting in further deepening of the humanitarian crisis, increased social tensions, a resurgence of the pandemic, a worsening slowdown in China, high interest rates leading to widespread debt distress, and the ongoing climate emergency as areas that necessitate multilateral cooperation. The IMF has said multilateral efforts to respond to the humanitarian crisis prevent further economic fragmentation. Maintaining global liquidity, managing the debt crisis and ending the pandemic are essential. Given the international nature of these policy challenges, multilateral institutions remain critically important in providing safety nets, emergency liquidity, preventing crisis from spreading and for progress in orderly debt restructuring.

The G20's common framework for debt treatment in an orderly and coordinated manner jointly supported by the IMF and World Bank, also agreed to by the Paris Club, represented an important milestone for multilateral institutions. Further, the G20's commitments to the catastrophe containment and relief trust to provide debt service relief for COVID-19 and future shocks were to be monitored by the IMF and World Bank. There was commitment for a continued process of IMF governance reform under the 16th General review of quotas by December 2023. The Resilience and sustainability trust received financial commitments of USD 40 billion from 12 countries including China and Saudi Arabia.

The US Secretary of the Treasury said that the multilateral financial architecture must be strengthened to meet the challenges posed by climate, health, migration and fragility. The USA condemned in the strongest terms Russia's illegal, unprovoked war against Ukraine. The USA said that Russia's invasion was an assault on fundamental international rules and norms and threatened the core of the international order. It also said that international financial institutions must step in to help low-income countries respond to food and energy shocks caused by the war. The World Bank Group was urged to mobilize energy, ideas, public and private financing to raise global climate ambition as part of the work to achieve a net zero future. Further, the World Bank and WHO were urged to work together to accelerate vaccine deployment to reach global targets of vaccinating 70 per cent of the world. The USA sought enhanced efforts to address elevated debt burdens threatening low-income countries and emerging markets with the Common framework process effectively delivering comprehensive debt treatment.

The Governor of the People's Bank of China said that China had provided the largest amount of debt servicing amongst G20 countries under the Debt service suspension initiative (DSSI). Further, China supported the establishment of the Resilience and sustainability trust (RST). China said it had always been upholding and practising multilateralism, promoting global growth based on openness and innovation, supporting common development, actively addressing climate change, and facilitating green and low-carbon transition. China called on the IMF for timely completion of the 16th General review of quotas by December 2023 to effectively accomplish quota share realignment reflecting the relative shares in the global economy. China called on all countries to support the peace talks between Russia and Ukraine and all countries to take effective measures to maintain smooth functioning of global supply chains and defend the multilateral trading system.

The Governor of the Central Bank of Indonesia, called on the IMF to focus on surveillance and policy advice, address debt vulnerabilities, lead the support to vulnerable members, support a sustainable recovery and a quota increase under the 16th General review of quotas. On debt sustainability, Indonesia said that there was a need to step up the progress and operationalization of the common framework in a timely and orderly manner. On lending support for vulnerable members, Indonesia said that a comprehensive reform of the Poverty Reduction and Growth Trust along with the timely operationalization of the IMF's new financing facility—the Resilience and Sustainability Trust (RST) to meet members' structural transformation needs.

The Governor of the Central Bank of Japan said that Russian aggression against Ukraine was a unilateral attempt to change the status quo by force and a blatant violation of international law that undermines the foundations of international order. Japan said that multilateral cooperation based on law and trust is important. Japan said that it had played an important role in stabilizing the international monetary and financial system by supporting the rapid financing instrument. On debt issues, Japan called for an accurate debt sustainability analysis. On SDR channelling and the resilience and sustainability trust Japan pledged 20 per cent of its newly allocated SDRs to support vulnerable countries. On climate change, Japan asked the IMF to support members' efforts to achieve net zero status. Japan raised a number of procedural issues on the 16th General review of quotas.

The IMF had adopted policy reforms and funding packages to better support the recovery of low-income countries for the pandemic. In 2022, the IMF had recommended setting up new rules and guidelines for taking forward the DSSI and the Common framework as also continued financing for the Catastrophe containment and relief trust.

The World Trade Organization

The WTO's 12th ministerial conference (MC12) was held from June 2022 at Geneva. The MC12 outcome statement resolved to strengthen the rule-based, non-discriminatory multilateral trading system with the WTO at its core. The WTO reaffirmed the provisions for special and differential treatment for developing country members and LDC's as an integral part of the WTO and its agreements. The WTO reiterated that it would work towards necessary reform of the WTO and also address challenges in the dispute settlement system and those related to the appellate body. The MC12 witnessed several ministerial decisions on emergency response to food security, response to the COVID-19 pandemic, WFP exemption from export prohibitions and an agreement on fisheries subsidies.

The MC12 adopted important declarations, amongst them being the Ministerial declaration on the emergency response to food security. There were concerns about food security and the rising prices of food including fertilizers underscored the need for agri-food trade to flow, and reaffirmed the importance of not imposing restrictions in a manner inconsistent with relevant WTO provisions. The MC12 resolved to minimize trade distortions, keep them temporary and minimal and members should take note of the possible global ramifications in imposing such restrictions. Members with surplus food stocks were encouraged to release the surplus on international markets.

India recommended that WTO embrace a people first approach to trade and said that the MC12 should send a strong message that the rich care for the poor, vulnerable and marginalized people and that the world needed to come together for a better future. India reinforced the importance of "One Earth-One Health" in calling for global solidarity and collective action. India asked the global community to reach an agreement on sustainable fishing and not repeat the errors of the Uruguay round. Further, India presented the case for WTO reform as necessary, keeping development at its core, to be decided through a precise, transparent and inclusive process, upholding the basic principles and objectives of the WTO particularly consensus-based decision making. Further, India said that the WTO should not negotiate rules on non-trade related subjects like climate change, gender, etc., which fall within the domain of the other inter-governmental organizations.

The USA said that the MC12 presented an opportunity to work together to bring new life and new conversations to the WTO after two years of grappling with the corona virus pandemic. It referred to the Marrakesh declaration and agreement on which the WTO was founded in identifying widening inequality, economic insecurity, and incentives that degrade working and living conditions on the planet as key challenges. The USA said it was committed to the WTO and the WTO rules helped in maintaining the flow of global trade and fostered transparency in the measures taken by countries to respond to the crisis. It said that Russia's war against Ukraine had created a humanitarian disaster well beyond Ukraine's borders which had resulted in disruptions to the global supply and distribution of staple commodities, which exacerbate the effects of inflation and create the risk of food insecurity for millions. The USA had donated USD 1.5 billion to the World Food Program in the first four months of 2022. The USA urged all WTO members to commit at MC12 to exempt their donations to the World Food Program without any export restrictions. Further, the USA said it supported accommodations for the intellectual property rules for COVID vaccines to facilitate global health recovery. It said that multilateral institutions needed to work differently and better; to be more responsive, better at sharing information, and able to keep pace with 21st century demands. It urged the MC12 to engage in issues of the role of trade in addressing climate change.

Financial Stability Board

The Financial stability board was established in Basel, Switzerland, in 2009 following discussions in the Pittsburgh summit with the key mandate of reforming international financial regulation and supervision. The G20 called for strengthening the FSB in the Cannes summit 2011. The FSB plenary amended its charter on the following lines:

(a) The FSB should remain a flexible, responsible, member-driven, multi-institutional and multidisciplinary institution.
(b) The FSB to remain effective should preserve the nexus between the political level and regulatory policy making through the G20 and other stakeholders.
(c) The FSB role in standard setting should address regulatory gaps that pose a risk to financial stability.
(d) The FSB should also enhance implementation of monitoring capacity, establish relationships with institutional members and transparent communication.

The amended FSB charter was presented for endorsement of the G20, and has a representation from the G20 Troika countries, and five countries with the largest overall systemic importance. The amended charter of FSB was endorsed by G20 in the 2012 Los Cabos summit.

One of the important reports prepared by the FSB is the COVID-19: Policy Responses.[3] The FSB said the policy measures adopted in G20 member-countries fell under five broad categories:

(a) Lending and credit support to financial institutions through loan guarantee schemes so that they could continue lending
(b) Funding and liquidity support to ensure markets have adequate liquidity in domestic and foreign currency
(c) To support operations of the markets through volatility control mechanisms
(d) Operational and business continuity of financial organizations.
(e) Continuity of supervisory and regulatory activities.

The FSB laid down global principles in fighting the COVID-19 pandemic. These included sharing of information on a timely basis, using flexibility in formulating financial responses, temporarily reducing operational burdens on firms, roll back reforms that compromised the above objectives and coordinate the timely unwinding of temporary measures. The FSB principles said that international standards laid down in fighting the COVID-19 pandemic should be adopted by G20 to avoid unilateral action that would distort the level playing field and lead to market fragmentation. The FSB undertook a series of coordination steps with G20 for sharing of information on support to the financial sector and for coordinating support to ensure business continuity.

The FSB[4] in its 2022 July report to the G20 finance ministers and central bank governors had warned of lower growth, rising inflation and tighter global financial conditions. The issues of rising indebtedness across sovereign nations, non-financial corporates and households was seen. The FSB has also called for continuous assessment of impacts, interactions and trade-offs of policies affecting the financial sector.

The FSB's climate roadmap[5] sets out the progress made in addressing climate-related financing risks in the key areas of disclosures, data, vulnerability analysis and regulatory and supervisory approaches. There is a lot of focus on data quality which is an essential pre-requisite for assessment of vulnerabilities and development of new policy tools. The FSB is also collaborating with the Network for greening the financial system in these areas.

The FSB has undertaken an assessment of risks to financial stability from crypto assets. The FSB has clarified that so-called stable coins and other crypto assets should not operate in a regulatory free space and that crypto asset providers must meet all applicable regulatory, supervisory and oversight requirements.

OECD

The Organization for Economic Cooperation and Development was founded in 1961 with 38 member-countries, largely developed, to stimulate economic progress and world trade with headquarters in Paris, France. In 2013, the OECD[6] and G20 worked together and adopted a 15-point action plan to address base erosion and profit shifting (BEPS) as a key priority for tax reform. The OECD/G20 BEPS project aimed to create consensus-based international taxation rules to protect tax bases and ensure predictability to tax payers.

The OECD action plan[7] on base erosion and profit shifting said that globalization has resulted in large multi-national enterprises and a shift from country-specific operating models to global models. The MNE's operations were based on integrated supply chains that centralized functions at regional/global level. Digital products are often delivered on internet and production is located in distant geographical locations. Many governments had to cope with lesser tax revenue, as base erosion and profit shifting undermined the integrity of the tax system. Individuals and family-owned businesses were harmed by the distortions induced by BEPS. The G20 finance ministers called on the OECD to develop an action plan to address BEPS issues in a coordinated and comprehensive manner.

The OECD action plan recommended the following actions:

Action 1: Address the tax challenges of the digital economy

Action 2: Neutralize the effects of hybrid mismatch arrangements

Action 3: Strengthen controlled foreign company rules

Action 4: Limit base erosion via interest deductions and other financial payments

Action 5: Counter harmful tax practices more effectively, taking into account transparency and substance

Action 6: Prevent treaty abuse

Action 7: Prevent the artificial avoidance of permanent establishment status

Actions 8, 9, 10: Assure that transfer pricing outcomes are in line with value creation

Action 11: Establish methodologies to Collect and Analyse data on BEPS and Actions to Redress it

Action 12: Require Tax Payers to Disclose their aggressive tax planning arrangements

Action 13: Re-examine transfer pricing documentation

Action 14: Make dispute resolution mechanisms more effective

Action 15: Develop a multilateral instrument.

In 2021, over 130 countries agreed on plans for a new taxation policy—the Global minimum corporate tax. The OECD Secretary-General tax report[8] to G20 finance ministers was submitted in February 2022. The report outlined the developments in international tax reform and latest developments regarding the two-pillar agreement of 2021, as also the progress made in tax transparency and implementation of BEPS minimum standards and taxation of multinational companies. Further, the OECD undertook work to establish an inclusive framework to facilitate dialogue on implicit and explicit carbon pricing. The Secretary-General OECD said the technical design of the OECD/G20 inclusive framework on base erosion and profit shifting (BEPS) had been approved and would be deployed in 2023. The Global anti-base erosion rules are expected to be adopted after consultations by OECD by 2024.

The OECD said that in formulating the BEPS minimum standards and taxation of multinationals, tax challenges arising from digitalization continued to dominate the inclusive framework's work program. The inclusive framework covers the minimum reporting standard of 132 members. The reach of the multilateral convention to implement tax treaty related measures to prevent BEPS had expanded to 99 countries and covered 1,850 bilateral tax treaties. The OECD transfer pricing guidelines for multinational enterprises and tax administrations[9] were updated in 2021 December.

WHO

The World Health Organization was mandated by G20 leaders' commitment to build an equitable and effective Financial intermediary fund (FIF) for pandemic preparedness and response (PPR). The WHO Council on economics deliberated on the proposal and sent recommendations on the economics of health for all and the G20 health and development partnership[10] to the G20 leaders.

The Council for economics of health established in 2020 aims to reframe health for all as a public policy objective, and ensure national and global economies are well structured in a way to deliver this ambitious goal.

The G20 leaders' Rome communiqué said the following:

> *"We establish a G20 Joint Finance-Health Task Force aimed at enhancing dialogue and global cooperation on issues relating to pandemic PPR, promoting the exchange of experiences and best practices, developing coordination arrangements between finance and health ministries, promoting collective action, assessing and addressing health emergencies with cross-border impact, and encouraging effective stewardship of resources for pandemic preparedness and response (PPR) by early 2022, on modalities to establish a financial facility to be designed inclusively with the central coordination of the WHO, G20 driven and engaging from the outset low and middle-income countries, additional non-G20 partners and multilateral development banks, to ensure adequate and sustained financing for pandemic prevention, preparedness and response."* (G20 Leaders' Communiqué—Rome, 31 October 2021)

The Council for economics of health made recommendations on the financial intermediary fund (FIF) which covered issues of sustainability, innovation and multi-annual financing, sufficiency and scale, complementarity, additionality and effective evaluation, inclusivity and universality, transparency and accountability. The key recommendations are the following:

(a) Donors should commit themselves to a multi-year financing of the financial intermediary fund to focus on building core areas of programming. Long-term financing commitments should be made by donor countries. The FIF must promote innovative and blended financing mechanisms. An expert group on best practices to be created.

(b) The Pandemic preparedness response-financing gap has been evaluated at USD 10.5 billion/annum. The annual budget target for FIF should be USD 10.5 billion.

(c) The FIF should be complementary and additional and should not undermine the financing for existing urgent public health needs.

(d) The WHO should have a seat at the decision-making table and a central role in implementing the FIF rather than be a technical advisor.

(e) The FIF should establish accountability principles that are followed by donors and beneficiaries. The FIF should prioritize PPR investments.

The only global health initiative offering integrated, end-to-end solutions to fight the pandemic is the ACT-Accelerator. Dr. Ayoade Alakija was appointed as the WHO Special Envoy for the ACT-Acceleration in December 2021. The special envoy joined at a critical time when the global vaccination coverage targets have been missed and there are huge unvaccinated populations across the globe. The ACT-Accelerator has a total funding of USD 23.4 billion. A funding gap of USD 16 billion exists in the ACT-Accelerator financing and a USD 6.8 billion in-country delivery costs are necessary. The ACT-Accelerator has called for funding from developed countries. Only 10 per cent of the population in low-income countries have received at least one vaccine shot. The ACT-Accelerator Resource Mobilization Group led by Norway has drawn up 'fair share' of financing by rich countries calculated on the basis of size of their national economies. The middle-income countries were to self-finance USD 6.5 billion using domestic resources supported by multilateral development banks.

The significant achievements of the ACT-Accelerator include delivering over 1 billion COVID-19 vaccine doses via COVAX, procuring over 200 billion tests, USD 519 million medical oxygen, and USD 764 million personnel protective equipment.

Prime Minister Jonas Gahr Store of Norway[11] as co-chair of the ACT-Accelerator called on the world's leaders to join in acting urgently as it was seen time and again through the pandemic that no one was safe until everyone is. President Joko Widodo of Indonesia as G20 President said Indonesia had made strengthening global health architecture as one of the priority agenda. The strengthening capacity of developing countries must receive attention, must be empowered and should be part of the supply chain for medicines, vaccines and medical equipment. The theme is "Recover Together, Recover Stronger".

FAO

The Director-General, Food and Agriculture Organization, Mr. Qu Dongyu[12] made a statement on "Economic Impact of the War on Food Security" at the G20 finance ministers and central bank governors meeting on 15 July 2022. At this meeting, the Director-General said, *"Recent global events, from the COVID-19 pandemic to the climate crisis, multiple conflicts around the world and the war in Ukraine, have all heavily affected agrifood systems in multiple ways"*.

The FAO said that in 2021, up to 828 million people suffered from chronic hunger, and there was an increase of 46 million from 2020 compared to the 150 million from 2019 before the pandemic. The FAO food price index had touched 160 points in March 2022. Food import costs in 62 most vulnerable countries had increased to USD 24.6 billion affecting 1.79 billion people. The FAO called for solidarity and concentrated passion to help the most vulnerable first.

The FAO's package of measures include food aid, policies for increasing productivity, technological and social innovation to reduce market failures and scaling up of agrifood systems.

The FAO has developed a proposal for Global food import financing facility (FIFF)[13] which aims to assist countries with food purchases, implemented through the International Monetary Fund under the balance of payments mechanism. The FIFF would complement existing mechanisms of the UN system, would be strictly based on urgent needs and limited to low and lower-middle income countries.

The FAO has also observed a sharp hike in fertilizer prices which almost tripled since 2021. The Ukraine war affected the fertilizer market as Russia is a key producer of fertilizers. Many countries in Latin America, Europe, and Asia have import dependency of over 30 per cent on Russian fertilizers.

In the 2021 Rome summit, the FAO urged policy makers to find ways to feed the world and save the planet at the same time. Global food security remains high on the agenda of the G20, and the FAO has rolled out three initiatives—Hand in Hand initiative to improve agri-food potential of countries, Green Cities initiative to enhance urban environment and a G20 Green Garden was created in Rome to support the common agenda with Italy.

African Union

The African Union is made up of 55 member-states which represent all the countries of the African continent. The continental priorities are that the AU should focus on issues related to political affairs, peace and security, economic integration and reinforcing Africa's global voice.

The Italian Presidency enlarged the G20 to the African Union by extending an invitation to the foreign ministers meeting. The third edition of the "Encounter with Africa" was held along with the foreign ministers meeting in October 2021 in Rome. The chairperson of the African Union

Commission[14] flagged the issues of climate change, investment in peace and security in Africa and structuring projects of significant economic growth and inclusive development in Africa.

The African Union chairperson[15] also took part in the G20's "Compact with Africa" launched by the German Presidency in 2017 to create an enabling environment for investment and mobilizing the private sector from Germany and other G20 countries to invest in African projects. The African Union–European Union partnership post 2020 was proposed as a continent-to-continent partnership, with a crucial role for the African Union.

The African Union has flagged that African debt levels are rising, projected at 70 per cent of GDP in 2021 and fiscal deficit in 8.7 per cent. The African Union has said that although Africa has benefitted from the G20 debt service suspension initiative (DSSI), member states continue to be under pressure to maintain debt service payments, are on the verge of debt distress or are defaulting. The African Union has called that allocation of SDRs to Africa be increased from 5 per cent to 25-30 per cent to directly provide financing to African economies.

The African Union Development Agency–New Partnership for Africa's Development (AUDA–NEPAD) was established in June 2018 with the objective of incubating innovative programs in various fields including technology, research and development and knowledge management. The NEPAD has participated in G20 ministerial meetings and the G20 Africa partnership initiative.

NOTES

1. Omar Hilale, The Need for a Strenghtened Multilateral Approach to Confront COVID-19 and other Global Challenges, www.un.org
2. Gutteres., The Future of the UN: Time to Think Big, www.un.org
3. COVID-19: Policy Responses, www.fsb.org
4. FSB chair flags G20 growing challenges to financial stability, 12 July 2022, www.fsb.org
5. FSB Roadmap for Addressing Climate-Related Financial Risks, 7 July 2021, www.fsb.org
6. OECD/G20 Base Erosion and Profit Sharing Project, www.oecd-ilibrary.org
7. OECD, Action Plan on Base Erosion and Profit Sharing, www.oecd-ilibrary.org
8. OECD Secretary-General Tax Report to G20 Finance Ministers and Central Bank Governors, Indonesia, February 2022, www.oecd.org
9. OECD, OECD Transfer Pricing Guidelines for Multinational Enterprises and Tax Administrations 2022, www.oecd.org

10. WHO, Delivering on the G20 Leaders Commitment to Build an Equitable and Effective Financial Intermediary Fund (FIF) for Pandemic Preparedness and Response (PPR), WHO, 19 April 2022, www.who.int
11. WHO., ACT-Accelerator calls for fair share based financing of US$ 23 billion to end pandemic as global emergency in 2022, WHO 9 February 2022, www.who.in
12. FAO., G20: FAO says Global Threats to Agrifood Systems need complex approach, FAO, 10 July 2022, www.fao.org
13. FAO, Surging Food Prices: FAO calls for Import financing facility for poorer nations at G20 meeting, FAO 20 April 2022, www.fao.org
14. AU, Opening Remarks of the Chairperson of the African Union Commission H.E. Moussa Faki Mahamat at the ministerial 'Encounter with Africa' meeting in Italy, AU 8 October 2021, www.au.int
15. AU, Communique on the African Union Commission Chairperson visit to Germany., AU 31 October 2018, www.au.int

7

G20: Engagement Groups

The G20 Engagement Groups have become an integral part of the G20 schedule. Engagement Groups comprise non-officials, youth, scientists and civil society who provide recommendations to G20 on global policy challenges.

The Indonesian Presidency operationalized 10 engagement groups, some of which are discussed in this chapter.

Business 20

The B20, established in 2010, is the most prominent engagement group of the G20, comprising over 1,000 delegates from G20 countries including top executives of MNC's. The B20 will submit its final recommendations for spurring growth and development at the G20 summit in November 2022. The B20 operated six task forces with focus on trade and investment, energy, sustainability and climate, digitalization, finance and infrastructure, future of work and education, integrity and compliance, and women in business action council.

The B20's key message from the Rome summit was called "Reshaping the Future". The B20 called for unlocking the digital transformation, building skills for tomorrow, scaling up sustainable finance and supporting impact investing. The B20 recommended promotion of open trade, especially on vaccines, promotion of sustainable governance, increase transparency and fair competition. The B20 sought G20's actions on accelerating the net zero race, and fight climate change. Further the B20 said G20 should establish a global emergency governance for future crisis, reform the WTO and level the digital playing field.

The B20 called for empowerment of women and youth ensuring equal opportunities for all. This could be done by reducing the gender gap by giving women and youth secure employment post COVID-19, building more equal workspace cultures and increasing the number of women and youth in business leadership and entrepreneurship. The B20 recommended the gender gap be brought down from 26 per cent in 2021 to 19 per cent in 2025.

The B20 said there was a need for unlocking digital transformation and building skills for tomorrow. For this, it was important to provide connectivity as an essential service by increasing network coverage and capacity. Further, there was a need for expanding access to finance for unbanked and uninsured individuals through digital instruments and platforms. The B20 said there was a need to ensure a digital ready population by updating educational systems and upskilling/reskilling individuals. The B20 projected that internet connectivity should increase from 51 per cent in 2021 to 70 percent in 2024. The B20 called on the G20 to establish global emergency governance to ensure evidence-based decision-making during the crises.

The Indonesian B20 was headed by the chairman of the Indonesian Chamber of Commerce and Industry with priority areas of focus being trade and investment, energy, sustainability and climate, digitalization, finance and infrastructure, future of work and education, integrity and compliance and women in business action council. The B20 Indonesia reiterated its commitment to bring together global G20 business communities under one accord to recover stronger towards an inclusive, resilient and sustainable global economic growth.

Women 20

The Women 20 was established in 2015 to ensure due consideration of gender issues in G20, foster gender equality and promote women's empowerment. The Women 20 called on the G20 leadership to address inequalities, establish sustainable development policies, employ and fund strategies to support empowerment of women, with priority on tackling the structural barriers that negatively impact women and girls in their diversity.

Several key recommendations emanated from the Rome W20. These include placing gender equality at the heart of the budgeting decisions, ensure equal representation for women at all levels of decision making, collect, analyze and report on all areas identified using gender sensitive and disaggregated data, develop gender impact assessments and promote education by investing in infrastructure.

The key focus areas were cultural changes and gender stereotypes, health equality and gender medicine, women's entrepreneurship and finance, digital empowerment, labour, violence against women and girls and gender-based violence. Another important area was environmental sustainability. The W20 recommended ensuring safe access and use of digital technologies for all women and girls in G20 economies by 2026. Further, the W20 said, that the G20 work towards guaranteeing foundational digital skills for all women and girls of G20 members with pathways to future work and expertise in disruptive technologies by 2026. Another important aspect was to ensure that women hold equal leadership roles in digital fields in G20 economies by 2030.

Financial inclusion for women through legislation, inheritance rights, pensions, and insurance remains an important aspect of the W20 agenda. This coupled with facilitating access to finance and capacity building for all, in particular microenterprises, was an important thrust area. Financing women-owned and led SME's and scale-ups and incentivizing investors to invest more in women-founded and female/male co-founded employer companies was an important thrust area.

Creating new career opportunities for women, fostering standards and tools for remote working guaranteeing privacy, safety, security, work-life balance and right to disconnect from work were important features that emanated from the W20.

The W20 called on governments to formulate national plans to tackle gender stereo types within a period of three years and allocate funds for implementation. One of the important aspects was to develop lifelong learning programs and campaigns to address gender stereotypes in all professional fields from pre-school to tertiary education. Another important aspect was to build systemic awareness building measures to control sexism and gender biases by mobilizing key multipliers, media players and men and boys to take action on gender and equality.

The W20 called on the G20 to work towards more, better and equally paid jobs for women and establish a clear mechanism to monitor progress on commitments for gender equality.

Think 20

The Think 20 (T20) is an engagement group bringing together leading think tanks and research organizations worldwide. It serves as the ideas bank of G20 and aims to provide research-based policy recommendations for G20 leaders. The T20's vision is delivering for people, planet, and prosperity.

For the people, the T20 said, global health was the most urgent short-term priority. A 'One Health' approach to strengthen the preparedness of health systems worldwide while also addressing the long-term challenges of poverty and inequalities was a core theme of T20's push for people-centric policies.

The T20 discussed climate change issues as the greatest long-term challenge of our times. It called on the G20 to stimulate more coordinated global efforts to promote orderly energy transition without jeopardizing economic growth. Energy efficiency measures need to be pursued and the political momentum has to emanate from COP26. The T20 urged the IMF to include climate risk analysis in its surveillance activity and open a financing window through which balance of payments and fiscal support for climate efforts could be channelled. ESG gap financing policies for the next 10 years to be formulated and the G20 should ensure that developed and emerging markets are part of the strategy of design processes. The T20 recommended that an international hydrogen economy initiative (IHEI) with a secretariat at Rome should be set up for establishing collaborations with the green steel support policies in collaboration with the World Steel Association.

For prosperity to be achieved, the focus on people and planet is important. The T20 recommended coordinated policy measures in areas of tax policy and international trade to enable the benefits of digital transformation to be uniformly delivered. The T20 called on the G20 to explore convergence between the multilateral initiatives such as the G7 Building Back a Better World (B3W) initiative or the existing Belt and Road Initiative to build a sustainable economy. Infrastructure investments are part of the changing geopolitical order and consistency amongst the existing initiatives must be pursued. The T20 further said development of new digital infrastructure in emerging countries has significant spill over effects to achieve the well-being of an economy. The T20's vision for a changed world was based on cooperation, representation, inclusivity, and transparency as the guiding principles of multilateralism.

Youth 20

The Youth 20, with its first Y20 conference held in 2010, is an inclusive platform aimed at enabling young people to express their visions and ideas to the heads of state and government at the G20. The Y20 has been focused on issues of digitalization, innovation and future of work. It recommended multilateral cooperation to prevent emerging technology monopolizations for broadband access. Further, by 2025, digital literacy and competency framework in topics related to computer science, algorithmic fairness and digital rights could be incorporated into the informal educational frameworks for young people.

The Y20 discussed issues of developing digital rights and a free, open and safe digital space. The focus was on youth innovation and research hubs for entrepreneurship, fostering digital health, and developing a digital universal credential recognition. On youth access to employment, the Y20 said that providing equal employment opportunities and decrease in youth not in employment, education or training to 10 per cent by 2030 would be the stated objective. The Y20 also discussed issues of equality in the labour markets, financial inclusion, youth empowerment and social cohesion as important features of their agenda. Youth, education and green jobs was part of the Y20's agenda on sustainability, climate, and energy.

Civil 20

The Civil 20 was launched as an official G20 engagement group in 2013. The C20 is an engagement group of G20 covering more than 560 organizations and networks from more than 100 countries working for justice and sustainable development and fighting inequalities. The C20 as a vehicle for civil society engagement in the G20 process supported the demands of communities and ensured civil society voices are heard by governments. The Civil 20 has promoted Global solidarity for multilateralism by supporting an ambitious UN-centred International economic reconstruction and system reform summit, a universal tax convention and inter-governmental tax commission and a UN-led systematic, comprehensive and enforceable process for sovereign debt restructuring.

The C20 discussed the framework of human rights and was guided by the overarching principles of 'leave no one behind', gender transformative approach, comprehensive vision for real sustainability and policy coherence to link together the future of the planet and humankind. The C20 also said that protecting the peoples' and planet's existence was not enough if fundamental rights and freedoms are not ensured. The C20 recommended adoption of the UN Principles of Business on human rights by G20 members as well as policy legislation on preserving workers' rights.

The C20 said that it remains committed to advocating for the changes that communities need to create a just world for our people and planet. The C20 asked the G20 leaders to engage with civil society, respect the task of NGO's and activists, protect human rights and respect the rule of law. The C20 said that a better tomorrow could only be built with an active and vibrant global citizenry.

Urban 20

The Urban 20 is a city diplomacy initiative that brings together cities from G20 member-countries to discuss economic, climate and development issues. The Urban 20 was established in December 2017 during the Argentine Presidency at the One Planet Summit in Paris. The U20 initiative is convened by C40 cities and united cities and local governments. In 2022, the initiative is in its fifth year having previously been chaired by Buenos Aires, Tokyo, Riyadh and Rome.

The U20 called on G20 to make smart investments for a green and just recovery and accelerated climate action in COPs. The U20 said the G20 may support intermediary cities based on a symbiotic relationship between rural and urban areas and build cities with nature for climate resilience and transforming food systems.

The U20 said that it was important to strengthen local democracy, promote fiscal autonomy and foster local economic development.

Other Engagement Groups

In addition to the above engagement groups, the Indonesian Presidency also witnessed contributions by Parliament 20, Science 20, SAI-20 and

Labour 20. The Parliament 20 brought in a parliamentary dimension to global governance and raised awareness, building political support for international commitments. The Science 20 presented policy makers with consensus-based science driven recommendations formulated through task forces comprising of international experts. The Supreme Audit Institutions was an engagement group introduced by the Indonesian Presidency and played an important role in ensuring transparency and accountability in promoting cooperation among the G20 members. The Labour 20 convenes trade union leaders from G20 countries and provides an analysis and policy recommendations aimed at addressing labour-related issues.

Engagement Groups in the Indian Presidency

India has announced that 11 engagement groups would be operationalized in the Indian Presidency. The G20 engagement groups of the Indian Presidency would be Supreme Audit Institutions20 (SAI-20) headed by the Comptroller and Auditor General, Parliament20 headed by the Speaker of the Lok Sabha, Business20 headed by N. Chandrasekaran, Chairman, Tata Sons, Civic 20 headed by Mata Amritandamayi, Labour20 headed by Hiranmay Pandya, President, BMS, Science20 headed by Vijay P. Bhatkar, Chairman, Vijnana Bharati, Think20 headed by Sujan Chinoy, DG, MP-IDSA, Youth20 headed by Anmol Sovit, Women20 headed by Dr. Sandhya Purecha, chairperson, Sangeet Natak Akademy, Urban20 headed by Kirtikumar Parma, Mayor, Ahmedabad, and Startup20 headed by Dr. Chintan Vaishnav, Mission Director, Atal Innovation Mission.

The engagement groups in the Indian Presidency would represent continuity and change. The Startup20 would be the new engagement group in the Indian Presidency. This is based on the experience that start-ups act as catalysts for economic growth and development. They offer platforms and tools to foster collaboration and spur innovation across borders and facilitate economies in achieving SDG targets. The Startup-20 engagement group would recommend steps to G20 leaders to address growth challenges and other constraints.

8

Leadership at G20 Summits 2014-2022

"My aim for the G20 to send a clear signal for free markets and against isolation, and a clear commitment to the multilateral trading system."

"As the G20, we cannot ignore the challenge that climate change poses to all of us in the world."

—Angela Merkel

The Hamburg Summit 2017

Leadership at G20 summits is not easy and host nations had to deal with difficult guests and were often faced with the responsibility of balancing conflicting positions, particularly on climate change and trade. The G20 Hamburg summit 2017 posed significant leadership challenges for the four-time German Chancellor Angela Merkel. She is often called the "climate chancellor" for her strong advocacy of progressive global climate policies.

It was President Trump's first G20 summit. He was elected on the "America First" slogan and the USA had withdrawn from the Paris climate agreement. The future of global cooperation looked dismal as several other G20 member-Nations could follow the USA. To achieve any progress in climate change issues, she needed to deal with President Trump. A private dinner between the two leaders did not bring about the much-needed agreement. President Trump did not attend the G20 climate protection negotiations and instead attended a bilateral meeting with Russian President Vladimir Putin. As the Foreign Affairs[1] says, "Nothing was more excruciating for Merkel as having to deal with a USA under Trump." Further, the Hamburg summit 2017 witnessed violent protests with the "Welcome to Hell" anti-globalization march which was countered with use of police force. The Turkish President was banned from addressing a rally of Turkish nationals in Hamburg and said she was committing political suicide.

Despite overwhelming challenges, Angela Merkel proved she was a bulwark of reason and efficiency.[2] She worked silently with the highly professional Germany diplomatic corps to achieve consensus without the USA being on board. The G20 Communiqué adopted said that the Paris climate agreement was irreversible and that the G20 reaffirmed its strong commitment to the Paris climate agreement.

Angela Merkel[3] said, "Together we can achieve more". She called upon all sides to embrace compromise in the spirit of the G20 motto of the German Presidency, "Shaping an Inter-Connected World". Angela Merkel had succeeded in achieving consensus in the G20 on the following issues:

(a) Keeping the markets open around the world—Angela Merkel felt that markets must be kept open, and that they had played an important role in stabilizing national economies and financial markets even in 2008
(b) International trade based on clear rules—despite intensive discussions on trade, the G20 agreed to fight protectionism and unfair trade practices and adopt a rule-based international trading system as embodied by the World Trade Organization
(c) Resilient Financial System—Angela Merkel led the G20 Hamburg action plan which was adopted at the summit to promote greater inclusiveness, fairness, and equality.
(d) Better equipped to deal with pandemics—It was Angela Merkel's Presidency that witnessed the G20 health ministers meet for the first time, along with the WHO Director-General. Angela Merkel said that world was better equipped to deal with pandemics.
(e) Enabling Women to participate more fully—Angela Merkel led the initiative 'Skills4Girls' to promote opportunities and equal participation for women and girls in the digital economy.
(f) Accepting Responsibility for Africa—The G20 Africa partnership represented the challenges and opportunities in African countries.
(g) Climate Policy, no attempt to conceal dissent—Angela Merkel was successful in getting all the G20 members other than the USA to say that the Paris agreement was irreversible.

Introductory Statement by Federal Chancellor Angela Merkel at the G20 Summit opening session in Hamburg

We have already been working with some of you at the Retreat, but let me extend a warm welcome once again to all of you. Welcome to Germany!

This is the first time Germany is hosting the G20 Summit. We are delighted to be here in the maritime city of Hamburg. That's one reason why we chose a seafaring logo for our meeting. It's a reef knot. As the tension increases, the reef knot becomes tighter.

Our motto for this G20 Presidency is: "Shaping an interconnected world". Because we represent large parts of the world, there are of course millions of people following us now and hoping, with all their worries, fears and hardships that we can help solve their problems. And I believe we should work together here in precisely that spirit. I am also quite sure that everyone here will be trying hard to make sure we achieve good results.

To get us to this high point in our G20 Presidency, our Sherpas have already done a huge amount of work. And they're going to have to work through another night tonight, but that's just part of the job.

Many groups in our societies—young people, women, the business community, workers, academia and the scientific community and lots of international organisations—have given us a good deal of help to get good material and good foundations for our discussions here today. And so I would like to express my gratitude for all the hard work done in advance.

I would also like to extend a very warm welcome to our partners. We are delighted that Spain, Norway, the Netherlands, Singapore, APEC Chair Viet Nam, Guinea, Chair of the African Union, and the President of Senegal, representing NEPAD, are our guests here, and we welcome them warmly. They have already played a very intensive part in preparing this meeting.

We are all familiar with the major global challenges. We know that time is of the essence. That's why solutions can often only be found if we are willing to compromise, if we are flexible, without, however, and I say this quite deliberately, bending too much, because it is true that we can point to some differences.

After all, we represent two-thirds of the world's population, four-fifths of global GDP, and three-quarters of global trade. So those not here today are in fact right to expect us to do a decent job. The German side tried to take account of these issues in putting together the agenda, obviously with regard to the economy and trade, but also with regard to climate change and energy policy. Germany has made Africa a priority, because, speaking from the European perspective, we regard Africa as our neighbouring continent and we must do everything possible to take it forward. Health plays a central role.

We will be discussing all these issues, and of course also the role of women in a world in which they still don't have equality, in which they often have a harder time of things, while at the same time bearing the main responsibility for families and young people.

Thank you all for coming.

G20Skills4Girls was a major initiative of Chancellor Angela Merkel for promoting the participation of women in the digital economy. It sought to strengthen the G20 leaders' goal to reduce the gap in gender labour force participation rates by 25 per cent by 2025, and to recognize that digital skills are vital to participate in and succeed in the digital economy. A range of skills are needed, including: generic ICT skills; complementary ICT skills to perform new tasks associated with the use of ICT at work; specialist ICT skills to code, develop applications and manage networks; digital financial skills and leadership skills. Angela Merkel felt the need was to provide women and girls with tailored opportunities to develop relevant skills and to effectively use them. The exposure to women as positive role models in science, technology, engineering and mathematics (STEM) themed early grade reading materials, exposure to technology at an early age, education in digital technologies and the acquisition of digital skills that are especially important to encourage girls into STEM subjects to lay the foundations for life-long learning and to empower girls in the digital economy.

Chancellor Merkel also pushed for better information sharing in the fight against terrorism. She said the work of the Financial Action Task Force should be strengthened. She said that the logo of the G20 summit had a maritime flair like the host city, "the greater the pressure, the firmer the knot", and called for greater global cooperation. She was convinced that solutions were only possible on the basis of compromise. In many ways,

Chancellor Angela Merkel bridged deep divides between G20 member-countries to ensure that the Hamburg G20 Communiqué was adopted.

The Osaka Summit 2019

Japan's Prime Minister Shinzo Abe's Presidency of the G20 successfully navigated competing interests and tensions at the G20 Osaka summit[4] in 2019. The summit witnessed the USA–China trade war. British Prime Minister Theresa May's confrontation with the Russian President Vladimir Putin witnessed consensus and gave cause for optimism. The summit gave a strong message for strong, sustainable, balanced and inclusive economic growth alongside agreements to reform the World Trade Organization, agreements on digital innovation and e-commerce, financial inclusion for ageing populations, and marine plastics.

All the member-nations agreed to the leaders' statement on trade, investment and international order to keep the markets open and to realize a free, fair non-discriminatory trade environment. In the special session on digital economy, Prime Minister Shinzo Abe successfully launched the "Osaka Track" framework to encourage multilateral discussion on digital economy and cross-border data sharing. In the environment session, "Osaka Blue Ocean Vision" sought to reduce pollution in the oceans to zero by 2050. Despite the trade war between the USA and China, the discussions at Osaka were cordial.

India, along with South Africa and Indonesia, did not accept the Data free flow with trust (DFFT) initiative as it felt that the DFFT could further aggravate the digital divide. The Osaka Track sought to promote cross-border data flow seeking the removal of prohibitions on data localization and urged nations to negotiate new rules on data flows, and cloud computing. India felt data was the new form of wealth and needed to be stored in the native country than in any other.

In the run-up to the Osaka summit of June 2019, Prime Minister Shinzo Abe convened the international conference on the Future of Asia in May 2019. In this conference, he enunciated Japan's approach to the G20 Osaka summit.

The range of issues included (a) Preserving the free and fair-trading system calling on Asian nations to join forces to join the RCEP trade agreement, (b) DFFT and Osaka Track to ensure free flow of data with trust, and (c) Innovation and global environmental challenges, under which Japan was to hold the Green Innovation Summit.

Presidency Press Conference by Prime Minister Shinzo Abe[5] following the G20 Osaka Summit

29 June 2019

On Saturday, 29 June, Prime Minister Shinzo Abe held a presidency press conference at the G20 Osaka summit for approximately 25 minutes from 2:50 p.m. The overview of the press conference is as follows.

It was a great pleasure to welcome leaders from around the world to Osaka and host the G20 summit in Japan, which held the G20 presidency for the first time.

"The world can unite."

I made my best efforts as President of the summit with such conviction. It is difficult to find instant solutions to various challenges. Nevertheless, at this year's summit, we were able to demonstrate to the world, the strong will of the G20 countries in many fields.

I was focused on one thing: to lay out a sustainable growth path towards the future which is beneficial to all countries.

The world economy still faces downside risks due to trade tensions. The G20 shared the determination to take further actions and lead strong economic growth while paying attention to such circumstances.

Amid deepening globalization, concerns and dissatisfaction over the rapid changes are generating even interstate conflicts. In response to concerns over the precarious post-war free trading system, we need to firmly set principles that will guide the world economy going forward.

Free, fair, non-discriminatory, Open markets, level playing field. At this G20 summit, we were able to explicitly confirm such fundamental principles of free trade.

Meanwhile, the reform of the World Trade Organization (WTO) is unavoidable. It is a reality that the WTO has not necessarily been able to adapt to recent developments, including globalization and digitalization.

In an era of rapid evolution of Big Data, artificial intelligence (AI), and the fourth industrial revolution, we need to create new rules on data—a source of added value. This was an important theme at this year's summit.

At this summit, together with many leaders, including President Trump, President Xi Jinping, and President of the European Council Juncker, we declared the launch of the "Osaka Track," a process that aims to promote rule-making under the "Data free flow with trust" concept.

We will speedily advance international rule-making to ensure cross-border data free flow while protecting privacy and security. This will no doubt breathe new life into the WTO reform process.

The G20, which accounts for 80 per cent of the world economy, has a major responsibility towards sustainable growth. Global environmental issues cannot be tackled by the efforts of some countries alone, and must be addressed jointly by the world.

Building on the work done by the G20 Hamburg summit two years ago and the G20 Buenos Aires summit last year, it is important that the world take action together to achieve a virtuous cycle of the environment and growth. It is highly significant that the G20 was able to share this view at this summit.

Marine plastic litter is another issue which cannot be resolved by some countries alone. Under such circumstances, the fact that the G20 was able to unite and share the "Osaka Blue Ocean Vision," which aims to reduce additional pollution by marine plastic litter to zero by 2050, represents a major step forward towards resolving this issue.

We also agreed on a concrete implementation framework for achieving this vision. Japan will fully leverage its technologies and experience to support waste management and human resources development in developing countries and contribute to the global efforts to address this issue making the most of its characteristics.

Solutions to various issues facing the international community can be found when leaders speak to each other directly. This can also move the process forward for resolving interstate issues.

At my summit meeting with the European Union (EU), significant developments were made towards easing restrictions on safe agricultural and fishery products from Tohoku. I would like to once again express my appreciation to the many countries that support the reconstruction of the affected areas.

With regards to the USA-China trade friction, which is a matter of significant concern to the world, I had discussions with President Xi two days ago and with President Trump yesterday. I stated that it is extremely important that the world's largest and second largest economic powers build stable economic relations through constructive discussions.

Countries can move closer to agreement regarding such trade frictions and regional affairs if leaders take this opportunity of the G20 summit to meet with each other directly and hold frank discussions. Japan will fulfil this role as much as possible.

While globalization supports economic growth, it also in turn widens disparities. The G20 must address this squarely and ensure that the fruits of growth reach all corners of society.

Education enhancement is the greatest key to sustainable economic growth. I confirmed with the other G20 leaders our determination to aim for a world where all girls can have access to quality education for at least 12 years.

Japan will continue to play a role in expanding girls' and women's education in developing countries. Japan will provide opportunities for quality education and human resources education to at least four million women in developing countries for over three years by 2020.

In this world, where emphasis tends to be overly placed on confrontations, we look for common grounds and points of agreement. Under an approach unique to Japan, at this Osaka summit, the G20 unites and sends a strong message regarding global issues. This has provided a major impetus towards concrete actions.

Last, but not the least, I would like to express my sincere appreciation to the people of Osaka for their tremendous cooperation for holding this summit. Thank you very much for welcoming us with warm hospitality unique to Osaka, a city of humanity.

That is all from me.

The *Japan Times*, in a lead article, said "G20 wrestles with response if Putin shows up at Bali Summit."[6] The article says that the range of possible scenarios includes some leaders staying away, sending lower-level delegations or only dialling in from afar, and the meeting could very well end without a formal communiqué for the first time. Indonesia finds itself balancing between the G7 nations and Russia. The Indonesian authorities are expected to invite Russia and President Putin to the G20 summit meeting as a neutral host nation. The President of Indonesia did not mention the war in Ukraine in his welcome address.

Indonesia has called the attack on Ukraine 'unacceptable' but refused to name Russia. Indonesia has supported the UN resolution condemning the invasion and demanding that Russia withdraw. Indonesia justified its position as adherence to international law—the principle of sovereignty. Indonesia has abstained from the vote to expel Russia from the United Nations Human Rights Council. As the G20 Chair, Indonesia has rejected calls on not extending an invitation to Russia to attend the Bali summit 2022.

In the G20 finance ministers and central bank governors meeting in April 2022, when the Russian finance minister began speaking virtually, the US Treasury Secretary and other finance ministers walked out. The Canadian finance minister said that the world's democracies would not stand idly by in the face of continued Russian aggression and war crimes. The US Federal Reserve Chairman and European Central Bank President were amongst the officials who walked out of the meeting. Further, the American officials have made it clear that President Biden has asked that Russia be removed from the G20, and that the Americans would not be participating in meetings if the Russians are there.

President Widodo,[7] as G20 chair, has travelled to Russia choosing to contribute to the peace process. Indonesia also called for lifting the Ukraine grain crisis to ensure global supply chains function effectively. The United Nations facilitated the Ukraine and Russia landmark grain agreement aimed to relieve the global food crisis caused by blocked Black Sea grain deliveries. Twenty million tons of wheat will be exported under the agreement to help address the global food crisis and rising prices.

President Widodo has said that the President of China and the President of Russia plan to attend the G20 summit in Bali in November 2022, the first global summit since the war in Ukraine and the tensions over Taiwan.

Welcoming Speech of the President of the Republic of Indonesia at the opening of the 1st FMCBG Indonesia G20 Presidency 2022

17 February 2022, Jakarta, Indonesia

May peace be upon you. The Honourable Minister of Finance of the Republic of Indonesia, The Honourable Governor of Bank Indonesia, finance ministers and central bank governors of the G20 member-countries, heads of international financial institutions and international organizations,

Distinguished Guests, Ladies and Gentlemen.

As I mentioned at the IMF-World Bank annual meeting in 2018, the winter is coming. And now, a severe winter is INDEED coming. The pandemic is far from over, and the global economy is struggling. In this situation, no single country can recover alone. All countries are interconnected, no one is isolated.

The rise of a region would trigger the rise of other regions. On the other hand, the collapse of a region would result in the collapse of others. In this circumstance, it is not a high time for rivalry. It is not the time to create new tensions that could affect global recovery, let alone jeopardize world peace as we've currently seen in Ukraine. It is necessary that every party puts an end to rivalry and friction. We must focus on synergy and collaboration to save and build back the world we are living in, in order to bounce back and recover immediately.

Distinguished guests, ladies and gentlemen, we must face this global uncertainty with synergy and collaboration. We must work together to keep the rising inflation under control. We must anticipate the food scarcity and the increase of food price. We must overcome container scarcity and other logistics chain problems. We must prevent starvation. We have an obligation to also undertake several transformations. We must accelerate the transition process towards new economy.

We must expedite digital transformation that is equal and affordable.

And we must encourage the growth of micro, small and medium enterprises.

This meeting among finance ministers and central bank governors of the G20 member-countries must be able to formulate fiscal and monetary measures that are aligned with each other in resolving collective problems, the global problems. We must collaborate to overcome the global strategic problems with concrete and measurable outcomes so that the global economic growth would be more inclusive and sustainable.

Ladies and gentlemen, with the spirit of recovering together, and recover stronger, Indonesia encourages discussions on global priority agendas. We must strengthen our global health architecture.

We must facilitate and finance the transition towards a green economy as well as accelerate digital economic transformation. Indonesia is enthusiastic to play its role as the G20 presidency to contribute to the world. Indonesia would foster synergy and collaboration including that of among finance ministers and central bank governors of the G20 member-countries in formulating appropriate fiscal and monetary policies in order to solve world problems. I have high hopes on the finance ministers and central bank governors of the G20.

I wish this meeting would lead to concrete synergic and collaborative measures that can be undertaken in no time with tangible outcomes.

Recover together, recover stronger!

Thank you! May peace be upon you!

NOTES

1. Constanze Stelzemuller, 'The Singular Chancellor—The Merkel Model and Its Limits'., *The Foreign Affairs*, 20 April 2021
2. Jeffrey D. Sachs, "How Angela Merkel secured consensus, minus US, on key issues at G20"., *Hindustan Times*, 13 July 2017
3. Angela Merkel, "Together we can achieve more", press conference at the end of the G20 Summit., www.g20germany.de
4. Kazuhiko Tago, "Abe's Fragile success at G20", East Asia Forum, 18 July 2019., www.eastasiaforum.org
5. Speeches and statements by the Prime Minister., https://japan.kantei.go.jp/98_abe/statement/201906/_00002.html
6. Bloomberg., "G20 wrestles with response if Putin shows up at Bali", *Japan Times*, 6 April 2022., www.japantimes.co.jp
7. Ann Marie Murphy, Seton Hall University, "Ukraine war highlights differences between Indonesian and US Foreign Policy Frameworks", Economics, Politics and Public Policy in East Asia and Pacific, 5 August 2022, www.eastasiaforum.org

9

G20: The Bali Summit 2022

"In a significant moment for our country and citizens, President of Indonesia Joko Widodo will hand over the G20 Presidency to India at the closing ceremony of the Bali Summit. India will officially assume the G20 Presidency from 1 December 2022."

—Prime Minister Modi[1]

The 17th G20 heads of state and government summit was held on 15-16 November 2022 at Bali, Indonesia. The summit marked the pinnacle of the G20 process carried out under the Indonesian presidency in the year through ministerial meetings, working groups, and engagement groups. The Bali summit had the theme "Recover Together, Recover Stronger". Indonesian President Joko Widodo said that the Bali summit would provide an opportunity for some of the world's biggest powers to set aside their differences in order to focus on addressing the pressing global challenges. President Widodo said, "Indonesia seeks to bring the G20 together. We must avoid disunity. Peace and stability are key to recovery and rebuilding the global economy."

In the departure statement ahead of his visit to Bali for the G20 leader's summit, Prime Minister Modi said, "In a significant moment for our country and citizens, the President of Indonesia Joko Widodo, will hand over the G20 presidency to India at the closing ceremony of the Bali summit. India will be officially assuming the presidency from 1 December 2022. I will also extend my personal invitation to G20 members and other invitees to our G20 summit next year."

The G20 Bali summit was attended by leaders of Argentina, Australia, Canada, China, European Union, France, Germany, Italy, Japan, Saudi Arabia, South Africa, South Korea, Turkey, United Kingdom, and USA. Spain is a permanent invitee and special invitees for the Bali Summit included leaders of Cambodia, Fiji, the Netherlands, Rwanda, Senegal, Singapore, Suriname, and UAE. The Indonesian President invited the Ukrainian President to address the summit virtually while the Russian President and the leaders of Brazil and Mexico did not attend.

It is important to recap the year-long journey of the G20 Indonesian presidency which witnessed the following salient milestones:

December 1 2021: Indonesia assumed the G20 presidency from Italy

February 17-18, 2022: G20 finance ministers and central bank governors meeting at Jakarta

April 20, 2022: G20 finance ministers and central bank governors meeting in Washington DC

July 7-8, 2022: G20 foreign ministers meet in Bali

July 15-16, 2022: G20 finance ministers and central bank governors meet in Bali

August 24-25, 2022: Ministerial conference on women empowerment in Bali

September 1, 2022: Digital ministers meeting in Bali

September 1-2, 2022: Education ministers meeting in Bali

September 2, 2022: G20 Energy transition ministers meeting in Bali

September 12-13, 2022: G20 Culture ministers meeting, Borobudur

September 13-14, 2022: G20 Labour ministers meeting, Bali

September 21-23, 2022: G20 Trade, investment and industry ministers meeting, Labuan Bajo

September 27-29, 2022: G20 Agriculture ministers meeting in Bali

October 11, 2022: G20 Finance and agriculture ministers meeting in Washington DC

October 12-13, 2022: G20 Finance ministers and central bank governors meeting, Washington DC

October 27-28, 2022: G20 Health ministers meeting in Bali

The run up to the G20 leaders' summit was preceded by four meetings of finance ministers and central bank governors, foreign ministers, commerce and industry ministers, agriculture ministers, health ministers, labour ministers, energy ministers, culture ministers, education ministers and women empowerment ministers. Based on these multiple ministerial meetings, the agenda for the G20 Bali leaders' summit meeting was drawn up. Indonesia's G20 co-Sherpa Edi Prio Pambudi said that the Indonesian presidency witnessed indissoluble challenges and commendable achievements. With the world in transition, the Bali summit was a moment for G20 leaders to live up to the spirit of solidarity and collaboration and bring the world to a full recovery.

The G20 Bali summit agenda included Global Health architecture, Digital transformation and Sustainable energy transition. The G20 leaders engage in discussions in three sessions—Food and energy security, Health partnership for global infrastructure and Digital transformation. The summit also assessed the policy discussions conducted under the Indonesian presidency which covered 12 working groups and 10 engagement groups. A number of bilateral meetings were held on the sidelines of the summit, the most important being the one between the presidents of the USA and China.

The G20 Bali Leaders Declaration, adopted on 16 November 2022, is a broad-based, futuristic document in tune with the Indonesian presidency's G20 theme of "Recover Together, Recover Stronger." The Bali leaders declaration dealt with the global macroeconomic challenges, the issues of multilateral trade, food security, energy security, climate change issues, international taxation, investment, digital economy and debt restructuring.

The key features of the Bali G20 leaders' declaration are the following

- **Ukraine War:** Most G20 members strongly condemned the war in Ukraine and stressed that it was causing immense human suffering and exacerbating the existing fragilities in the global economy—constraining growth, increasing inflation, disrupting supply chains, heightening energy and food insecurity, and elevating financial stability risks. The G20 acknowledged that security issues can have significant consequences for the global economy.
- **Food Security:** The G20 expressed deep concerns on challenges to global food security exacerbated by current tensions and conflicts. The G20 members committed themselves to addressing food insecurity in developing and least developed countries. The G20

asked the FAO and the World Bank to build on the G20 Agricultural market information system (AMIS) and report by the 2023 spring meetings.

- **Climate Change:** The G20 reaffirmed the steadfast commitments to tackle climate change by strengthening the full and effective implementation of the Paris Agreement and the relevant outcomes of the COPs and CMAs. The G20 resolved to pursue efforts to limit the temperature increase to 1.5 degrees C through meaningful actions by all countries and legally binding instruments. The G20 will scale up efforts for deforestation, desertification, land degradation and drought to achieve the objectives of the 2030 Agenda for sustainable development.
- **Accessible Health Care:** The G20 members committed themselves to come together for strengthening national health systems, equitable access to pandemic countermeasures and welcomed the efforts of the ACT-A. The G20 also pledged to finance the new Financial intermediary fund for pandemic PPR (the Pandemic Fund) hosted by the World Bank and welcomed the pledges of USD 1.4 billion. Further recognizing the COVID-19 vaccine as a global public good, the G20 asked all WTO members to remain committed to a multi-sectoral 'One Health Approach'. The G20 said there was a need to build on the success of existing standards and digital COVID-19 certificates.
- **Digital Skills and Literacy:** The G20 encouraged international collaboration to further develop digital skills and literacy to better harness the impacts of digital transformation for women, girls, and people in vulnerable situations. The G20 endorsed the Financial inclusion framework on harnessing digitalization to increase productivity and foster a sustainable and inclusive economy.
- **Recover Together—Recover Stronger Policies:** The G20 committed to coordinated policy action for strong, sustainable and balanced growth, achieving price stability, and swiftly implement the OECD/G20 two-pillar international tax package. The G20 called for further pledges for the Resilience and sustainability trust (RST) and committed to step up efforts to implement the Common framework for debt treatment beyond the Debt service suspension initiative (DSSI).

On the margins of the G20 Bali summit, the NATO and G7 leaders issued a joint statement which said, "We condemn the barbaric missile attacks that Russia perpetrated on Ukrainian cities and civilian infrastructure on 15 November 2022. We discussed the explosion that took place in the eastern part of Poland near the border with Ukraine.... We reaffirm our steadfast support for Ukraine and the Ukrainian people in the face of ongoing Russian aggression, as well as our continued readiness to hold Russia accountable for its brazen attacks on Ukrainian communities, even as the G20 meets to deal with the wider impacts of the war."

Prime Minister Modi addressed the G20 session on Digital Transformation. In his address, he said technology has emerged as a major force multiplier in battling poverty and digital solutions can show the way to solve global challenges like climate change. He emphasized on making digital technology more inclusive so that meaningful change can be brought to the lives of the poor. Prime Minister Modi also mentioned India's technology-related efforts which have helped millions of Indians during the pandemic.

Prime Minister Modi held several important bilateral meetings on the sidelines of the G20 Bali summit. The bilateral meeting between him and US President Biden reviewed the continuing deepening of the India-USA strategic partnership including cooperation in future oriented sectors like critical and emerging technologies, advanced computing, artificial intelligence, etc. India and the USA have collaborated closely in new groupings such as Quad, I2U2, etc.

In his meeting with UK Prime Minister Rishi Sunak, the deliberations focused on the state of the wide-ranging India-UK Comprehensive strategic partnership and progress on the roadmap 2030 for future relations.

In his meeting with Australian Prime Minister Anthony Albanese, the two leaders expressed satisfaction at the excellent state of relations between the two countries under the Comprehensive strategic partnership and the high-level interactions taking place on a regular basis.

Prime Minister Modi also met the Prime Minister of Singapore, the President of France and the Chancellor of Germany during the Bali summit meetings. In these meetings, he reviewed the ongoing collaborations in diverse areas, and regional and global issues of mutual interest.

During the closing ceremony of the Bali summit, President Joko Widodo symbolically transferred the G20 presidency by handing over the gavel to Prime Minister Modi. In his closing remarks, President Joko Widodo said, "I want to extend my congratulations to India, which will take over the next G20 presidency. The mandate to safeguard and realize global recovery and strong and inclusive growth will now rest in the hands of His Excellency Prime Minister Narendra Modi".

Prime Minister Modi said "India is taking charge at a time when the world is simultaneously grappling with geopolitical tensions, economic slowdown, rising food prices and the long-term ill-effects of the pandemic. At such a time, the world is looking at the G20 with hope". Prime Minister Modi said that India's G20 presidency will be inclusive, ambitious, decisive and action-oriented. He referred to the Lifestyle for Environment (LiFE) campaign for the safe future of the planet. Further, he said that there is a need that the benefits of development are universal and all-inclusive. Global development is not possible without women's participation, and women-led development would be a priority issue in India's G20 agenda. Further, he said that the G20 would convey a strong message of peace and harmony. These priorities are fully embodied in the theme of India's G20 chairmanship—"One Earth, One Family, One Future". Prime Minister Modi invited all countries to participate in the unique celebration in India and together, he said the G20 would be a catalyst for global change.

A *Jakarta Post* editorial said, "Mission Accomplished", "a success on all counts"—the 17th G20 heads of state and government summit managed to defy the negative expectations, considering the palpable tensions between G20 member-countries on how to best respond to the war in Ukraine. The *Jakarta Post* further said, "The fruits of the Indonesian presidency can be summed up by the key deliverable: the sprawling 1,186-page G20 Bali leaders declaration, several communiqués, and chair summaries, as well as pages of notes and annexures dealing with the work produced throughout the year."

Indonesian authorities said they would seek to work with the new G20 Troika, to ensure the declaration was translated into action.

NOTE

1. PM's Departure Statement ahead of his visit to Bali for G20 Leaders' Summit, www.pmindia.gov.in, 14 November 2022

10

Logo, Theme and Website of India's G20 Leadership

Prime Minister Modi launched the Logo, Theme, and Website of India's G20 Leadership on 8 November 2022. The event marked the commencement of the roadmap for India's presidency of G20@2023.

Prime Minister Modi said:

> *"India's G20 presidency is coming at a time of crisis and chaos in the world. The world is going through the after effects of a disruptive once-in-a-century pandemic, conflicts, and a lot of economic uncertainty. The symbol of the lotus in the G20 logo is a representation of hope of these times. No matter how adverse the circumstances, the lotus still blooms. Even if the world is in crisis, we can still progress and make the world a better place.*
>
> *In Indian culture, both the goddesses of knowledge and of prosperity are seated on a lotus. This is what the world needs most today. Shared knowledge that helps us overcome our circumstances, and shared prosperity that reaches the last person at the last mile.*
>
> *In the G20@2023 logo, the Earth is placed on a lotus too. The seven petals of the lotus in the logo are also significant. They represent the seven continents. Seven is also the number of notes in the universal language of music. In music, when the seven notes come together, they create perfect harmony. But each note has its uniqueness. Similarly, the G20 aims to bring the world together in harmony while respecting diversity."*

Prime Minister Modi further enunciated that India's G20 logo reflects the notion of universal brotherhood. The G20 presidency represents not merely a diplomatic opportunity for India; it is a new responsibility and measure of the world's trust in India. While India strives for its progress, it also envisages global progress. Environment is a global cause for India and a personal effort. India's G20 mantra is "One Earth, One Family, One Future".

Prime Minister Modi also said that the G20 will not be confined to Delhi or a few places; every citizen, State government and political party should participate in it. "Each of our States has its own characteristics, beauty, heritage, culture and hospitality." Prime Minister Modi urged all citizens and intellectuals to come forward and be a part of India's G20@2023.

The values of democracy, sustainable development, yoga, and digital technology in development, removal of corruption, improving ease of doing business and ease of living can be a template for many countries. Women empowerment, women-led development and financial inclusion through the Jan Dhan accounts to reach the world through the Indian G20 residency.

Prime Minister Modi said India maintains close relations with developed countries and the developing countries. India's presidency of the G20 will be built with all the friends of the "Global South" who have been co-travellers for decades. It shall be India's endeavour that there is no first world or third world but only one world.

The G20@2023 would have 43 heads of delegations. The special invitees include Bangladesh, Egypt, Mauritius, the Netherlands, Nigeria, Oman, Singapore, Spain, and UAE.

The G20@2023 will deliberate on the issues of finance and technology for climate action, G20 collective action for SDGs, debt sustainability, digital public goods, just energy transitions and reform of multilateral systems. India's leadership will be spiritually elevating, culturally enriching, mentally rejuvenating and physically invigorating.

11

Conclusion

"India's G20 presidency will be inclusive and action oriented."

—**Prime Minister Modi**

Prime Minister Modi[1,2,3] said India's G20 presidency would be inclusive and action oriented. He also said that the world is looking to India with hope and priority will be given to women-led development. The novel ideas include the addition of a new engagement group Start-up20 to spur innovations across borders and facilitate in achieving the SDG targets and the Lifestyle for Future (LiFE) campaign for the future of the planet. The G20 presidency would showcase India's strengths in digital infrastructure, direct benefits transfer, digital health and pharmaceuticals.

The utilization of high-quality digital connectivity for financial inclusion and digital transformation will be presented. As part of the inclusive G20 approach, the Indian presidency will examine the challenges in realizing the 2030 Agenda for sustainable development and the Addis Ababa action agenda in a timely manner. For a women-led development model, the Indian presidency will examine issues of inclusive and quality education for girls, and women entrepreneurship through MSMEs as also access to leadership positions. India's zero tolerance for corruption approach would be discussed in the working group meetings. The Sherpa track, the Finance track and the engagement groups track have been clearly defined.

Several key takeaways from the Bali summit 2022 would continue to be relevant to the Indian presidency. After several G20 ministerial meetings ended without a joint declaration, the G20 leaders' summit adopted a declaration that said the majority members deplored the aggression by the Russian Federation in Ukraine and demanded its complete and unconditional withdrawal from the territory of Ukraine. Further, the leaders' declaration said the use or threat to use nuclear weapons is inadmissible.

The Bali summit also witnessed the first bilateral meeting between the Presidents of the USA and China. In pursuance of these discussions, the US Secretary of State will be visiting China.

Global economy, Food security and Climate change, establishment of the Pandemic fund, operationalization of the Resilience and sustainability trust in the International Monetary Fund and the Energy transition mechanism for Indonesia featured prominently in the leaders' declaration. The joint commitment that at least 30 per cent of the world's land and seas will be protected by 2030 will be kept as also continue the commitment to reduce land degradation by 50 per cent by 2040. The concrete and tangible agreements will need timely implementation. The President of France said reform of international organizations was a constant endeavour and France supported the entry of the African Union into the G20 to enhance representation for the global south.

Food security emerged as the biggest challenge in the G20 Bali summit. It will need the Turkey and UN-brokered Istanbul agreement signed on 22 July 2022 on the Safe transportation of grain and foodstuffs from Ukrainian ports and the MOU between Russia and the UN on promoting Russian food products and fertilizers to the world markets. Full and timely implementation will necessitate continued commitment by all stakeholders. The FAO and World Bank Group need to build on the G20 agricultural market information system and complete the mapping exercise on food security along with technical and systemic analysis by spring meetings 2023.

Energy security envisages to close gaps in energy access and to eradicate energy poverty. The Bali compact and the Bali energy transition roadmap will need focused implementation. The G20 said that it would support clean energy transitions for developing countries along with development of net zero and low emission power generation. Further, the G20 said it would implement the Glasgow climate pact and the outcomes of COP26/ COP27. Additional resource mobilization will be done for achieving the

Global biodiversity framework to address issues of reducing land degradation and conservation of global ocean and seas.

The Pandemic Fund has a financing gap of USD 10 billion until the Bali summit pledges of USD 1.4 billion have been received. The mobilization of additional resources is required in the Indian presidency as part of the health sector taskforce work plan for 2023.

The trade issues envisage deliberations in WTO on TRIPS agreement extension to cover the production and supply of COVID-19 drugs and therapeutics. The WTO reform would continue to be pursued in MC-13.

The finance track will be pursuing the commitment of continuing with the IMF quota reform and the new quota formula to be put in place by 15 December 2023. The operationalization of the Resilience and Sustainability Trust expeditiously will help low-income countries. To enable countries to Recover Together and Recover Stronger, financial commitments of USD 81.6 billion have been received against the stated goal of USD 100 billion. The Common Framework for DSSI would continue to be operationalized.

To conclude, I quote former Union Minister and G20 Sherpa, Suresh Prabhu,[4] "As every presidency has a prerogative to set its own agenda, there is scope for new priorities. India's target during its presidency should be to have some tangible outcomes. The advantage is Prime Minister Modi is well versed in global issues. India should shape a global agenda next year. There must be emphasis on engagement groups, which ultimately feed important inputs to leaders."

NOTES

1. Suhasini Haidar, "India's G20 Presidency will be inclusive, action oriented: Modi", *The Hindu*, 17 November 2022
2. Shantanu Nandan Sharma, "G20-23 Vision", *The Economic Times*, 13 November 2022
3. "Getting Ready", Editorial, *The Hindu*, 17 November 17, 2022
4. Suresh Prabhu, "India Should Shape a Global Agenda", *The Economic Times*, 13 November 2022

ANNEXURES

Summit Leader's Communiques: 2014-2022

(1) BRISBANE 2014

G20 LEADERS' COMMUNIQUÉ
Brisbane, November 16, 2014

1. Raising global growth to deliver better living standards and quality jobs for people across the world is our highest priority. We welcome stronger growth in some key economies. But the global recovery is slow, uneven and not delivering the jobs needed. The global economy is being held back by a shortfall in demand, while addressing supply constraints is key to lifting potential growth. Risks persist, including in financial markets and from geopolitical tensions. We commit to work in partnership to lift growth, boost economic resilience and strengthen global institutions.
2. We are determined to overcome these challenges and step up our efforts to achieve strong, sustainable and balanced growth, and to create jobs. We are implementing structural reforms to lift growth and private sector activity, recognising that well-functioning markets underpin prosperity. We will ensure our macroeconomic policies are appropriate to support growth, strengthen demand and promote global rebalancing. We will continue to implement fiscal strategies flexibly, taking into account near-term economic conditions, while putting debt as a share of GDP on a sustainable path. Our monetary authorities have committed to support the recovery and address deflationary pressures when needed, consistent with their mandates. We will be mindful of the global impacts of our policies and cooperate to manage spillovers. We stand ready to use all policy levers to underpin confidence and the recovery.

3. This year we set an ambitious goal to lift the G20's GDP by at least an additional two per cent by 2018. Analysis by the IMF-OECD indicates that our commitments, if fully implemented, will deliver 2.1 per cent. This will add more than US$2 trillion to the global economy and create millions of jobs. Our measures to lift investment, increase trade and competition, and boost employment, along with our macroeconomic policies, will support development and inclusive growth, and help to reduce inequality and poverty.

4. Our actions to boost growth and create quality jobs are set out in the Brisbane Action Plan and in our comprehensive growth strategies. We will monitor and hold each other to account for implementing our commitments, and actual progress towards our growth ambition, informed by analysis from international organisations. We will ensure our growth strategies continue to deliver and will review progress at our next meeting.

Acting together to lift growth and create jobs

5. Tackling global investment and infrastructure shortfalls is crucial to lifting growth, job creation and productivity. We endorse the Global Infrastructure Initiative, a multi-year work programme to lift quality public and private infrastructure investment. Our growth strategies contain major investment initiatives, including actions to strengthen public investment and improve our domestic investment and financing climate, which is essential to attract new private sector finance for investment. We have agreed on a set of voluntary leading practices to promote and prioritise quality investment, particularly in infrastructure. To help match investors with projects, we will address data gaps and improve information on project pipelines. We are working to facilitate long-term financing from institutional investors and to encourage market sources of finance, including transparent securitisation, particularly for small and medium-sized enterprises. We will continue to work with multilateral development banks, and encourage national development banks, to optimise use of their balance sheets to provide additional lending and ensure our work on infrastructure benefits low-income countries.

6. To support implementation of the Initiative, we agree to establish a Global Infrastructure Hub with a four-year mandate. The Hub will contribute to developing a knowledge-sharing platform and network

between governments, the private sector, development banks and other international organisations. The Hub will foster collaboration among these groups to improve the functioning and financing of infrastructure markets.

7. To strengthen infrastructure and attract more private sector investment in developing countries, we welcome the launch of the World Bank Group's Global Infrastructure Facility, which will complement our work. We support similar initiatives by other development banks and continued cooperation amongst them.

8. Trade and competition are powerful drivers of growth, increased living standards and job creation. In today's world we don't just trade final products. We work together to make things by importing and exporting components and services. We need policies that take full advantage of global value chains and encourage greater participation and value addition by developing countries. Our growth strategies include reforms to facilitate trade by lowering costs, streamlining customs procedures, reducing regulatory burdens and strengthening trade-enabling services. We are promoting competition, entrepreneurship and innovation, including by lowering barriers to new business entrants and investment. We reaffirm our longstanding standstill and rollback commitments to resist protectionism.

9. Our actions to increase investment, trade and competition will deliver quality jobs. But we must do more to address unemployment, raise participation and create quality jobs. We agree to the goal of reducing the gap in participation rates between men and women in our countries by 25 per cent by 2025, taking into account national circumstances, to bring more than 100 million women into the labour force, significantly increase global growth and reduce poverty and inequality.

10. We are strongly committed to reducing youth unemployment, which is unacceptably high, by acting to ensure young people are in education, training or employment. Our Employment Plans include investments in apprenticeships, education and training, and incentives for hiring young people and encouraging entrepreneurship. We remain focussed on addressing informality, as well as structural and long-term unemployment, by strengthening labour markets and having appropriate social protection systems. Improving workplace safety and health is a priority. We ask our labour

and employment ministers, supported by an Employment Working Group, to report to us in 2015.

11. We are committed to poverty eradication and development, and to ensure our actions contribute to inclusive and sustainable growth in low-income and developing countries. We commit to take strong practical measures to reduce the global average cost of transferring remittances to five per cent and to enhance financial inclusion as a priority. The G20 Food Security and Nutrition Framework will strengthen growth by lifting investment in food systems, raising productivity to expand food supply, and increasing incomes and quality jobs. We support efforts in the United Nations to agree an ambitious post-2015 development agenda. The G20 will contribute by strengthening economic growth and resilience.

Building a stronger, more resilient global economy

12. Strengthening the resilience of the global economy and stability of the financial system are crucial to sustaining growth and development. We have delivered key aspects of the core commitments we made in response to the financial crisis. Our reforms to improve banks' capital and liquidity positions and to make derivatives markets safer will reduce risks in the financial system. We welcome the Financial Stability Board (FSB) proposal as set out in the Annex requiring global systemically important banks to hold additional loss absorbing capacity that would further protect taxpayers if these banks fail. Progress has been made in delivering the shadow banking framework and we endorse an updated roadmap for further work. We have agreed to measures to dampen risk channels between banks and non-banks. But critical work remains to build a stronger, more resilient financial system. The task now is to finalise remaining elements of our policy framework and fully implement agreed financial regulatory reforms, while remaining alert to new risks. We call on regulatory authorities to make further concrete progress in swiftly implementing the agreed G20 derivatives reforms. We encourage jurisdictions to defer to each other when it is justified, in line with the St Petersburg Declaration. We welcome the FSB's plans to report on the implementation and effects of these reforms, and the FSB's future priorities. We welcome the progress made to strengthen the orderliness and predictability of the sovereign debt restructuring process.

13. We are taking actions to ensure the fairness of the international tax system and to secure countries' revenue bases. Profits should be taxed where economic activities deriving the profits are performed and where value is created. We welcome the significant progress on the G20/OECD Base Erosion and Profit Shifting (BEPS) Action Plan to modernise international tax rules. We are committed to finalising this work in 2015, including transparency of taxpayer-specific rulings found to constitute harmful tax practices. We welcome progress being made on taxation of patent boxes. To prevent cross-border tax evasion, we endorse the global Common Reporting Standard for the automatic exchange of tax information (AEOI) on a reciprocal basis. We will begin to exchange information automatically with each other and with other countries by 2017 or end-2018, subject to completing necessary legislative procedures. We welcome financial centres' commitments to do the same and call on all to join us. We welcome deeper engagement of developing countries in the BEPS project to address their concerns. We will work with them to build their tax administration capacity and implement AEOI. We welcome further collaboration by our tax authorities on cross-border compliance activities.

14. We endorse the 2015-16 G20 Anti-Corruption Action Plan that will support growth and resilience. Our actions are building cooperation and networks, including to enhance mutual legal assistance, recovery of the proceeds of corruption and denial of safe haven to corrupt officials. We commit to improve the transparency of the public and private sectors, and of beneficial ownership by implementing the G20 High- Level Principles on Beneficial Ownership Transparency.

Strengthening global institutions

15. The G20 must be at the forefront in helping to address key global economic challenges. Global economic institutions need to be effective and representative, and to reflect the changing world economy. We welcome the increased representation of emerging economies on the FSB and other actions to maintain its effectiveness. We are committed to maintaining a strong, quota-based and adequately resourced International Monetary Fund (IMF). We reaffirm our commitment in St Petersburg and in this light we are deeply disappointed with the continued delay in progressing the IMF quota and governance

reforms agreed in 2010 and the 15th General Review of Quotas, including a new quota formula. The implementation of the 2010 reforms remains our highest priority for the IMF and we urge the United States to ratify them. If this does not happen by year-end, we ask the IMF to build on its existing work and stand ready with options for next steps.

16. We need a strong trading system in an open global economy to drive growth and generate jobs. To help business make best use of trade agreements, we will work to ensure our bilateral, regional and plurilateral agreements complement one another, are transparent and contribute to a stronger multilateral trading system under World Trade Organization (WTO) rules. These rules remain the backbone of the global trading system that has delivered economic prosperity. A robust and effective WTO that responds to current and future challenges is essential. We welcome the breakthrough between the United States and India that will help the full and prompt implementation of the Trade Facilitation Agreement and includes provisions on food security. We commit to implement all elements of the Bali package and to swiftly define a WTO work programme on the remaining issues of the Doha Development Agenda to get negotiations back on track. This will be important to restore trust and confidence in the multilateral trading system. We agreed to discuss ways to make the system work better when we meet next year. We will continue to provide aid-for-trade to developing countries in need of assistance.

17. Increased collaboration on energy is a priority. Global energy markets are undergoing significant transformation. Strong and resilient energy markets are critical to economic growth. Today we endorse the G20 Principles on Energy Collaboration. We ask our energy ministers to meet and report to us in 2015 on options to take this work forward. Gas is an increasingly important energy source and we will work to improve the functioning of gas markets.

18. Improving energy efficiency is a cost-effective way to help address the rising demands of sustainable growth and development, as well as energy access and security. It reduces costs for businesses and households. We have agreed an Action Plan for Voluntary Collaboration on Energy Efficiency, including new work on the efficiency and emissions performance of vehicles, particularly heavy

duty vehicles; networked devices; buildings; industrial processes; and electricity generation; as well as work on financing for energy efficiency. We reaffirm our commitment to rationalise and phase out inefficient fossil fuel subsidies that encourage wasteful consumption, recognising the need to support the poor.

19. We support strong and effective action to address climate change. Consistent with the United Nations Framework Convention on Climate Change (UNFCCC) and its agreed outcomes, our actions will support sustainable development, economic growth, and certainty for business and investment. We will work together to adopt successfully a protocol, another legal instrument or an agreed outcome with legal force under the UNFCCC that is applicable to all parties at the 21st Conference of the Parties (COP21) in Paris in 2015. We encourage parties that are ready to communicate their intended nationally determined contributions well in advance of COP21 (by the first quarter of 2015 for those parties ready to do so). We reaffirm our support for mobilising finance for adaptation and mitigation, such as the Green Climate Fund.

20. We are deeply concerned with the humanitarian and economic impact of the Ebola outbreak in Guinea, Liberia and Sierra Leone. We support the urgent coordinated international response and have committed to do all we can to contain and respond to this crisis. We call on international financial institutions to assist affected countries in dealing with the economic impacts of this and other humanitarian crises, including in the Middle East.

21. We remain resolute in our commitment to lift economic growth, support job creation, promote development and build global confidence. We thank Australia for its leadership this year. We look forward to working together in 2015 under Turkey's presidency and to discussing progress at our next meeting in Antalya on 15-16 November 2015. We also look forward to meeting in China in 2016.

(2) ANTALYA 2015

Introduction

1. We, the Leaders of the G20, met in Antalya on 15-16 November 2015 to determine further collective actions towards achieving strong, sustainable and balanced growth to raise the prosperity of our people. We are firm in our resolve to ensure growth is robust and inclusive, and delivers more and better quality jobs. We recognize that advancing inclusive growth and entrenching confidence require the use of all policy tools and strong engagement with all stakeholders.

2. In pursuing our objectives, we have adopted a comprehensive agenda this year around the three pillars of decisive *implementation* of our past commitments to deliver on our promises, boosting *investments* as a powerful driver of growth and promoting *inclusiveness* in our actions so that the benefits of growth are shared by all. We have also enhanced our dialogue with low income developing countries as part of our implementation of this agenda.

Strengthening the Recovery and Lifting the Potential

3. Global economic growth is uneven and continues to fall short of our expectations, despite the positive outlook in some major economies. Risks and uncertainties in financial markets remain, and geopolitical challenges are increasingly becoming a global concern. In addition, a shortfall in global demand and structural problems continue to weigh on actual and potential growth.

4. We will continue to implement sound macroeconomic policies in a

cooperative manner to achieve strong, sustainable and balanced growth. Our monetary authorities will continue to ensure price stability and support economic activity, consistent with their mandates. We reiterate our commitment to implement fiscal policies flexibly to take into account near-term economic conditions, so as to support growth and job creation, while putting debt as a share of GDP on a sustainable path. We will also consider the composition of our budget expenditures and revenues to support productivity, inclusiveness and growth. We remain committed to promote global rebalancing. We will carefully calibrate and clearly communicate our actions, especially against the backdrop of major monetary and other policy decisions, to mitigate uncertainty, minimize negative spillovers and promote transparency. Against the background of risks arising from large and volatile capital flows, we will promote financial stability through appropriate frameworks, including by ensuring an adequate global financial safety net, while reaping the benefits of financial globalization. We reaffirm our previous exchange rate commitments and will resist all forms of protectionism.

5. We remain committed to achieving our ambition to lift collective G20 GDP by an additional 2 percent by 2018 as announced in Brisbane last year. Our top priority is timely and effective implementation of our growth strategies that include measures to support demand and structural reforms to lift actual and potential growth, create jobs, promote inclusiveness and reduce inequalities. We have made significant progress towards fulfilling our commitments since last year, implementing half of our multi-year commitments. Analysis by the IMF, OECD and World Bank Group indicates that our implementation so far represents more than one third of our collective growth ambition. Yet we also acknowledge that more needs to be done. We will strive more and take prompt action to expedite implementation of our remaining commitments. Going forward, we will continue to closely monitor the implementation of our commitments through the robust framework we developed this year. We will also continue reviewing and adjusting our growth strategies to ensure that they remain relevant to evolving economic conditions, policy priorities and structural challenges, in particular slow productivity growth, and that they remain consistent with our collective growth ambition. The Antalya Action Plan, comprising our

adjusted growth strategies and implementation schedules for key commitments, reflects our determination to overcome global economic challenges.

6. We are committed to ensure that growth is inclusive, job-rich and benefits all segments of our societies. Rising inequalities in many countries may pose risks to social cohesion and the well-being of our citizens and can also have negative economic impact and hinder our objective to lift growth. A comprehensive and balanced set of economic, financial, labour, education and social policies will contribute to reducing inequalities. We endorse the Declaration of our Labour and Employment Ministers and commit to implementing its priorities to make labour markets more inclusive as outlined by the G20 Policy Priorities on Labour Income Share and Inequalities. We ask our Finance, and Labour and Employment Ministers to review our growth strategies and employment plans to strengthen our action against inequality and in support of inclusive growth. Recognizing that social dialogue is essential to advance our goals, we welcome the B20 and L20 joint statement on jobs, growth and decent work.

7. Unemployment, underemployment and informal jobs are significant sources of inequality in many countries and can undermine the future growth prospects of our economies. We are focused on promoting more and better quality jobs in line with our G20 Framework on Promoting Quality Jobs and on improving and investing in skills through our G20 Skills Strategy. We are determined to support the better integration of our young people into the labour market including through the promotion of entrepreneurship. Building on our previous commitments and taking into account our national circumstances, we agree to the G20 goal of reducing the share of young people who are most at risk of being permanently left behind in the labour market by 15% by 2025 in G20 countries. We ask the OECD and the ILO to assist us in monitoring progress in achieving this goal. We will continue monitoring the implementation of our Employment Plans as well as our goals to reduce gender participation gap and to foster safer and healthier workplaces also within sustainable global supply chains.

8. We will address current opportunities and challenges brought into the labour markets through such issues as international labour mobility and the ageing of populations. Domestic labour mobility is

an important labour market issue in some G20 countries. We recognize and will further explore the potential of a flourishing silver economy. We further ask our Labour and Employment Ministers to report to us on progress made in 2016.

9. To provide a strong impetus to boost investment, particularly through private sector participation, we have developed ambitious country-specific investment strategies, which bring together concrete policies and actions to improve the investment ecosystem, foster efficient and quality infrastructure, including by the public sector, support small and medium sized enterprises (SMEs), and enhance knowledge sharing. Analysis by the OECD indicates that these strategies would contribute to lifting the aggregate G20 investment to GDP ratio, by an estimated 1 percentage point by 2018.

10. To improve our investment preparation, prioritization and execution processes, we have developed guidelines and best practices for public-private-partnership (PPP) models. We also considered alternative financing structures, including asset-based financing, and simple and transparent securitization to facilitate better intermediation for SMEs and infrastructure investment. Going forward, we call on our Ministers to continue their work to improve the investment ecosystem, promote long-term financing, foster institutional investors' involvement, support the development of alternative capital market instruments and asset-based financing models, and encourage Multilateral Development Banks (MDBs) to mobilize their resources, optimize their balance sheets, and catalyze private sector funding. We are advancing efforts and developing toolkits to unlock the ways and means for countries to better prepare, prioritize and finance infrastructure projects. We expect the Global Infrastructure Hub to make a significant contribution towards these endeavors. To help ensure a strong corporate governance framework that will support private investment, we endorse the G20/OECD Principles of Corporate Governance. We have placed a special focus on promoting long-term financing for SMEs, and we welcome the Joint Action Plan on SME Financing, the G20/OECD High-Level Principles on SME Financing as guidance, and the establishment of the private sector-led World SME Forum, a new initiative that will serve as a global body to facilitate the contributions of SMEs to growth and employment.

11. Global trade and investment continue to be important engines of economic growth and development, generating employment and contributing to welfare and inclusive growth. We note that global trade growth remains below pre-crisis levels. This is a result of both cyclical and structural factors. We therefore reaffirm our strong commitment to better coordinate our efforts to reinforce trade and investment, including through our Adjusted Growth Strategies. Inclusive Global Value Chains (GVCs) are important drivers of world trade. We support policies that allow firms of all sizes, particularly SMEs, in countries at all levels of economic development to participate in and take full advantage of GVCs and encourage greater participation and value addition by developing countries. We further reaffirm our longstanding commitment to standstill and rollback on protectionist measures and will remain vigilant by monitoring our progress. For this, we ask the WTO, OECD and UNCTAD to continue their reporting on trade and investment restrictive measures. We ask our Trade Ministers to meet on a regular basis and we agree on a supporting working group.

12. The WTO is the backbone of the multilateral trading system and should continue to play a central role in promoting economic growth and development. We remain committed to a strong and efficient multilateral trading system and we reiterate our determination to work together to improve its functioning. We are committed to working together for a successful Nairobi Ministerial Meeting that has a balanced set of outcomes, including on the Doha Development Agenda, and provides clear guidance to post-Nairobi work. We will also need to increase our efforts to implement all the elements of the Bali Package, including those on agriculture, development, public stock holding as well as the prompt ratification and implementation of the Trade Facilitation Agreement. We will continue our efforts to ensure that our bilateral, regional and plurilateral trade agreements complement one another, are transparent and inclusive, are consistent with and contribute to a stronger multilateral trade system under WTO rules. We emphasize the important role of trade in global development efforts and will continue to support mechanisms such as aid for trade in developing countries in need of capacity building assistance.

Enhancing Resilience

13. Strengthening the resilience of financial institutions and enhancing stability of the financial system are crucial to sustaining growth and development. To enhance the resilience of the global financial system, we have completed further core elements of the financial reform agenda. In particular, as a key step towards ending too-big-to-fail, we have finalized the common international standard on total-loss-absorbing-capacity (TLAC) for global systemically important banks. We also agreed to the first version of higher loss absorbency requirements for global systemically important insurers.

14. Critical work remains to build a stronger and more resilient financial system. In particular, we look forward to further work on central counterparty resilience, recovery planning and resolvability and ask the FSB to report back to us by our next meeting. We will continue to monitor and, if necessary, address emerging risks and vulnerabilities in the financial system, many of which may arise outside the banking sector. In this regard, we will further strengthen oversight and regulation of shadow banking to ensure resilience of market-based finance, in a manner appropriate to the systemic risks posed. We look forward to further progress in assessing and addressing, as appropriate, the decline in correspondent banking services. We will expedite our efforts to make further progress in implementing the over-the-counter (OTC) derivatives' reforms, including by encouraging jurisdictions to defer to each other, when it is justified in line with the St. Petersburg Declaration. Going forward, we are committed to full and consistent implementation of the global financial regulatory framework in line with the agreed timelines, and will continue to monitor and address uneven implementation across jurisdictions. We welcome the FSB's first annual report on the implementation of reforms and their effects. We will continue to review the robustness of the global regulatory framework and to monitor and assess the implementation and effects of reforms and their continued consistency with our overall objectives, including by addressing any material unintended consequences, particularly for emerging markets and developing economies (EMDEs).

15 To reach a globally fair and modern international tax system, we endorse the package of measures developed under the ambitious G20/OECD Base Erosion and Profit Shifting (BEPS) project.

Widespread and consistent implementation will be critical in the effectiveness of the project, in particular as regards the exchange of information on cross-border tax rulings. We, therefore, strongly urge the timely implementation of the project and encourage all countries and jurisdictions, including developing ones, to participate. To monitor the implementation of the BEPS project globally, we call on the OECD to develop an inclusive framework by early 2016 with the involvement of interested non-G20 countries and jurisdictions which commit to implement the BEPS project, including developing economies, on an equal footing. We welcome the efforts by the IMF, OECD, UN and WBG to provide appropriate technical assistance to interested developing economies in tackling the domestic resource mobilization challenges they face, including from BEPS. We acknowledge that interested non-G20 developing countries' timing of implementation may differ from other countries and expect the OECD and other international organizations to ensure that their circumstances are appropriately addressed in the framework. We are progressing towards enhancing the transparency of our tax systems and we reaffirm our previous commitments to information exchange on-request as well as to automatic exchange of information by 2017 or end-2018. We invite other jurisdictions to join us. We support the efforts for strengthening developing economies' engagement in the international tax agenda.

16. In support of our growth and resilience agenda, we remain committed to building a global culture of intolerance towards corruption through effectively implementing the 2015-2016 G20 Anti-Corruption Action Plan. We endorse the G20 High-Level Principles on Integrity and Transparency in the Private Sector which will help our companies comply with global standards on ethics and anti-corruption. Ensuring the integrity and transparency of our public sectors is essential. In this regard, we endorse the G20 Anti-Corruption Open Data Principles and the G20 Principles for Promoting Integrity in Public Procurement, and we welcome the ongoing work on asset disclosure frameworks. We will further work to strengthen international cooperation, including where appropriate and consistent with domestic legal systems, on civil and administrative procedures, as an important tool to effectively combat bribery and to support asset recovery and the denial of safe haven to corrupt officials and those

who corrupt them. We welcome the publication of our Implementation Plans on beneficial ownership transparency and will continue our efforts in this regard.

17. We remain deeply disappointed with the continued delay in implementing the IMF quota and governance reforms agreed in 2010. The 2010 reforms remain our highest priority for the IMF and we urge the United States to ratify these reforms as soon as possible. Mindful of the aims of the 2010 reforms, we ask the IMF to complete its work on an interim solution that will meaningfully converge quota shares as soon as and to the extent possible to the levels agreed under the 14th General Review of Quotas. The 14th Review should be used as a basis for work on the 15th Review, including a new quota formula. We reaffirm our commitment to maintaining a strong, quota-based and adequately resourced IMF. We reaffirm our agreement that the heads and senior leadership of all international financial institutions should be appointed through an open, transparent and merit-based process and we reiterate the importance of enhancing staff diversity in these organizations. We reaffirm that the Special Drawing Rights (SDR) basket composition should continue to reflect the role of currencies in the global trading and financial system and look forward to the completion of the review of the method of valuation of the SDR.

18. We welcome the progress achieved on the implementation of strengthened collective action and *paripassu* clauses in international sovereign bond contracts, which will contribute to the orderliness and predictability of sovereign debt restructuring processes. We ask the IMF, in consultation with other parties, to continue promoting the use of such clauses and to further explore market-based ways to speed up their incorporation in the outstanding stock of international sovereign debt. We look forward to the upcoming review of the IMF-WB Debt Sustainability Framework for Low-Income Countries. We acknowledge the existing initiatives aimed at improving sustainable financing practices, as stressed in the Addis Ababa Action Agenda. We also take note of the Paris Forum initiative, which contributes to further the inclusiveness by fostering dialogue between sovereign debtors and creditors.

Buttressing Sustainability

19. 2015 is a crucial year for sustainable development and we remain committed to ensuring our actions contribute to inclusive and sustainable growth, including in low income developing countries. The 2030 Agenda, including the Sustainable Development Goals (SDGs) and the Addis Ababa Action Agenda, sets a transformative, universal and ambitious framework for global development efforts. We are strongly committed to implementing its outcomes to ensure that no-one is left behind in our efforts to eradicate poverty and build an inclusive and sustainable future for all. We adopt the G20 and Low Income Developing Countries Framework to strengthen our dialogue and engagement on development. We will develop an action plan in 2016 to further align our work with the 2030 Agenda.

20. Our work this year supports key areas for sustainable development such as energy access, food security and nutrition, human resource development, quality infrastructure, financial inclusion and domestic resource mobilization. We endorse the G20 Action Plan on Food Security and Sustainable Food Systems, which underlines our commitment to improve global food security and nutrition and ensure the way we produce, consume and sell food is economically, socially and environmentally sustainable. We remain focused on promoting responsible investment in agriculture and food systems, improving market transparency, increasing incomes and quality jobs, and fostering sustainable productivity growth. We will pay particular attention to the needs of smallholder and family farmers, rural women and youth. We also commit to reducing food loss and waste globally. We welcome Expo Milano with the theme "Feeding the Planet – Energy for Life". We also welcome our Agriculture Ministers´ decision to establish a new platform to improve the way we and other countries can measure and reduce food loss and waste.

21. The private sector has a strong role to play in development and poverty eradication. Through our G20 Call on Inclusive Business we stress the need of all stakeholders to work together in order to promote opportunities for low income people and communities to participate in markets as buyers, suppliers and consumers. Our G20 National Remittance Plans developed this year include concrete actions towards our commitment to reduce the global average cost of transferring remittances to five percent with a view to align with the

SDGs and Addis Ababa Action Agenda. We are promoting financial inclusion by helping to open up access to payments, savings, credit and other services. We welcome the continued work on financial inclusion within the Global Partnership for Financial Inclusion (GPFI).

22. We remain focused on the G20 Principles on Energy Collaboration and welcome our Energy Ministers' first meeting ever. Recognizing that globally over 1.1 billion people lack access to electricity and 2.9 billion rely on the traditional use of biomass for cooking, we endorse the G20 Energy Access Action Plan: Voluntary Collaboration on Energy Access, the first phase of which focuses on enhancing electricity access in Sub-Saharan Africa where the problem is most acute. The Plan aims to strengthen G20 coordination and establishes a long-term voluntary cooperation framework that can be applied to other regions over time, recognising that energy access is a critical factor to foster development. In this first phase, we will cooperate and collaborate with African countries and relevant regional and international organizations on policy and regulatory environments, technology development and deployment, investment and finance, capacity building, regional integration and cooperation, taking into consideration national needs and contexts.

23. We recognize that actions on energy, including improving energy efficiency, increasing investments in clean energy technologies and supporting related research and development activities will be important in tackling climate change and its effects. We endorse the G20 Toolkit of Voluntary Options for Renewable Energy Deployment. We also highlight the progress made this year by participating countries in taking forward our collaboration on energy efficiency and agree to further support on a voluntary basis the 2015 outcomes of existing work streams on efficiency and emissions performance of vehicles, particularly heavy duty vehicles, networked devices, buildings, industrial processes and electricity generation, as well as financing for energy efficiency. We will continue to promote transparent, competitive and well-functioning energy markets, including gas markets. We stress the importance of diversification of energy sources and continued investments for increased energy security. We reaffirm our commitment to rationalise and phase-out inefficient fossil fuel subsidies that encourage wasteful consumption, over the medium term, recognising the need to support the poor. We

will endeavour to make enhanced progress in moving forward this commitment. We ask our Energy Ministers to report back on energy collaboration again in 2016 on the continued implementation of the G20 Principles on Energy Collaboration.

24. Climate change is one of the greatest challenges of our time. We recognize that 2015 is a critical year that requires effective, strong and collective action on climate change and its effects. We reaffirm the below 2°C goal as stated in the Lima Call for Action. We affirm our determination to adopt a protocol, another legal instrument or an agreed outcome with legal force under the UNFCCC that is applicable to all Parties. Our actions will support growth and sustainable development. We affirm that the Paris agreement should be fair, balanced, ambitious, durable and dynamic. We underscore our commitment to reaching an ambitious agreement in Paris that reflects the principle of common but differentiated responsibilities and respective capabilities, in light of different national circumstances. We reaffirm that UNFCCC is the primary international intergovernmental body for negotiating climate change. We welcome that over 160 Parties including all G20 countries have submitted their Intended Nationally Determined Contributions (INDCs) to the UNFCCC, and encourage others to do so in advance of the Paris Conference. We are prepared to implement our INDCs. We will instruct our negotiators to engage constructively and flexibly in the coming days to discuss key issues, among other things, mitigation, adaptation, finance, technology development and transfer and transparency in order to arrive at Paris with a way forward. We commit to work together for a successful outcome of the COP21.

25. The scale of the ongoing refugee crisis is a global concern with major humanitarian, political, social and economic consequences. There is a need for a coordinated and comprehensive response to tackle this crisis, as well as its long term consequences. We commit to continue further strengthening our support for all efforts to provide protection and assistance and to find durable solutions for the unprecedented numbers of refugees and internally displaced persons in various parts of the world. We call upon all states to contribute to responding to this crisis, and share in the burdens associated with it, including through refugee resettlement, other forms of humanitarian admission, humanitarian aid and efforts to ensure that refugees can access

services, education and livelihood opportunities. We underline the need to address the root causes of displacement. We highlight, in this regard, the importance of political solutions to conflicts and increased cooperation for development. We also recognize the importance of creating conditions to enable refugees and internally displaced persons to safely and voluntarily return to their homes. We will work with other states to strengthen our long term preparedness and capacity to manage migration and refugee flows. We invite all states according to their individual capacities to scale up their assistance to relevant international organizations in order to enhance their capabilities to assist affected countries in dealing with this crisis. We encourage the private sector and individuals to also join in the international efforts to respond to the refugee crisis.

26. We are living in an age of Internet economy that brings both opportunities and challenges to global growth. We acknowledge that threats to the security of and in the use of ICTs, risk undermining our collective ability to use the Internet to bolster economic growth and development around the world. We commit ourselves to bridge the digital divide. In the ICT environment, just as elsewhere, states have a special responsibility to promote security, stability, and economic ties with other nations. In support of that objective, we affirm that no country should conduct or support ICT-enabled theft of intellectual property, including trade secrets or other confidential business information, with the intent of providing competitive advantages to companies or commercial sectors. All states in ensuring the secure use of ICTs, should respect and protect the principles of freedom from unlawful and arbitrary interference of privacy, including in the context of digital communications. We also note the key role played by the United Nations in developing norms and in this context we welcome the 2015 report of the UN Group of Governmental Experts in the Field of Information and Telecommunications in the Context of International Security, affirm that international law, and in particular the UN Charter, is applicable to state conduct in the use of ICTs and commit ourselves to the view that all states should abide by norms of responsible state behaviour in the use of ICTs in accordance with UN resolution A/C.1/70/L.45. We are committed to help ensure an environment in which all actors are able to enjoy the benefits of secure use of ICTs.

Conclusion

27. We remain resolute to continue our collective action to lift actual and potential growth of our economies, support job creation, strengthen resilience, promote development and enhance inclusiveness of our policies. We thank Turkey for its G20 Presidency and hosting a successful Antalya Summit this year. We look forward to our next meeting in Hangzhou in September 2016 under the Chinese Presidency. We also look forward to meeting in Germany in 2017.

(3) HANGZHOU 2016

G20 LEADERS' COMMUNIQUÉ: HANGZHOU SUMMIT
Hangzhou, September 5, 2016

1. We, the Leaders of the G20, met in Hangzhou, China on 4-5 September 2016.
2. We met at a time when the global economic recovery is progressing, resilience is improved in some economies and new sources for growth are emerging. But growth is still weaker than desirable. Downside risks remain due to potential volatility in the financial markets, fluctuations of commodity prices, sluggish trade and investment, and slow productivity and employment growth in some countries. Challenges originating from geopolitical developments, increased refugee flows as well as terrorism and conflicts also complicate the global economic outlook.
3. We also met at a time of continued shifts and profound transformations in the configuration of the global economic landscape and dynamics for growth. With these transformations come challenges and uncertainties as well as opportunities. The choices we make together will determine the effectiveness of our response to the challenges of today and help to shape the world economy of the future.
4. We believe that closer partnership and joint action by G20 members will boost confidence in, foster driving forces for and intensify cooperation on global economic growth, contributing to shared prosperity and better well-being of the world.
5. We are determined to foster an innovative, invigorated,

interconnected and inclusive world economy to usher in a new era of global growth and sustainable development, taking into account the 2030 Agenda for Sustainable Development, the Addis Ababa Action Agenda and the Paris Agreement.

6. In this context, we, the G20, as the premier forum for international economic cooperation, forge a comprehensive and integrated narrative for strong, sustainable, balanced and inclusive growth, and thereby adopt the attached package of policies and actions - the Hangzhou Consensus - based on the following:

Vision. We will strengthen the G20 growth agenda to catalyze new drivers of growth, open up new horizons for development, lead the way in transforming our economies in a more innovative and sustainable manner and better reflect shared interests of both present and coming generations.

Integration. We will pursue innovative growth concepts and policies by forging synergy among fiscal, monetary and structural policies, enhancing coherence between economic, labor, employment and social policies as well as combining demand management with supply side reforms, short-term with mid- to long-term policies, economic growth with social development and environmental protection.

Openness. We will work harder to build an open world economy, reject protectionism, promote global trade and investment, including through further strengthening the multilateral trading system, and ensure broad-based opportunities through and public support for expanded growth in a globalized economy.

Inclusiveness. We will work to ensure that our economic growth serves the needs of everyone and benefits all countries and all people including in particular women, youth and disadvantaged groups, generating more quality jobs, addressing inequalities and eradicating poverty so that no one is left behind.

Strengthening Policy Coordination

7. Our growth must be shored up by well-designed and coordinated policies. We are determined to use all policy tools - monetary, fiscal and structural - individually and collectively to achieve our goal of strong, sustainable, balanced and inclusive growth. Monetary policy

will continue to support economic activity and ensure price stability, consistent with central banks' mandates, but monetary policy alone cannot lead to balanced growth. Underscoring the essential role of structural reforms, we emphasize that our fiscal strategies are equally important to supporting our common growth objectives. We are using fiscal policy flexibly and making tax policy and public expenditure more growth-friendly, including by prioritizing high-quality investment, while enhancing resilience and ensuring debt as a share of GDP is on a sustainable path. Furthermore, we will continue to explore policy options, tailored to country circumstances that the G20 countries may undertake as necessary to support growth and respond to potential risks including balance sheet vulnerability. We reiterate that excess volatility and disorderly movements in exchange rates can have adverse implications for economic and financial stability. Our relevant authorities will consult closely on exchange markets. We reaffirm our previous exchange rate commitments, including that we will refrain from competitive devaluations and we will not target our exchange rates for competitive purposes. We will carefully calibrate and clearly communicate our macroeconomic and structural policy actions to reduce policy uncertainty, minimize negative spillovers and promote transparency.

8. We are making further progress towards the implementation of our growth strategies, but much more needs to be done. Swift and full implementation of the growth strategies remains key to supporting economic growth and the collective growth ambition set by the Brisbane Summit, and we are prioritizing our implementation efforts. In the light of this, we launch the Hangzhou Action Plan and have updated our growth strategies, including new and adjusted macroeconomic and structural policy measures that can provide mutually-supportive benefits to growth. We will also strive to reduce excessive imbalances, promote greater inclusiveness and reduce inequality in our pursuit of economic growth.

Breaking a New Path for Growth

9. Our growth, to be dynamic and create more jobs, must be powered by new driving forces. While reaffirming the importance of addressing shortfalls in global demand to support short-term growth, we believe it is also imperative to address supply side constraints so

as to raise productivity sustainably, expand the frontier of production and unleash mid- to long-term growth potential.

10. We recognize that in the long run, innovation is a key driver of growth for both individual countries and the global economy as a whole. We are committed to tackling one of the root causes of weak growth by taking innovation as a key element of our effort to identify new growth engines for individual countries and the world economy, which will also contribute to creating new and better jobs, building a cleaner environment, increasing productivity, addressing global challenges, improving people's lives and building dynamic, cooperative and inclusive innovation ecosystems. We thus endorse the G20 Blueprint on Innovative Growth as a new agenda encompassing policies and measures in and across the areas of innovation, the new industrial revolution and the digital economy. In this context, we recognize the importance of structural reforms. We will act on the recommendations of the Blueprint in accordance with our national circumstances and in line with our vision for leadership, partnership, openness, inclusiveness, creativity, synergy and flexibility.

11. We commit to important cross-cutting actions related to multi-dimensional partnerships, supporting developing countries and improving skills and human capital. We will set up a G20 Task Force supported by the OECD and other relevant international organizations to take forward the G20 agenda on innovation, new industrial revolution and digital economy, subject to the priorities of the respective future G20 presidencies, ensuring continuity and consistency with the results so far, and promoting synergies with other G20 workstreams.

12. To achieve innovation-driven growth and the creation of innovative ecosystems, we support dialogue and cooperation on innovation, which covers a wide range of domains with science and technology innovation at its core. We deliver the G20 2016 Innovation Action Plan. We commit to pursue pro-innovation strategies and policies, support investment in science, technology and innovation (STI), and support skills training for STI—including support for the entry of more women into these fields—and mobility of STI human resources. We support effort to promote voluntary knowledge diffusion and technology transfer on mutually agreed terms and conditions.

Consistent with this approach, we support appropriate efforts to promote open science and facilitate appropriate access to publicly funded research results on findable, accessible, interoperable and reusable (FAIR) principles. In furtherance of the above, we emphasize the importance of open trade and investment regimes to facilitate innovation through intellectual property rights (IPR) protection, and improving public communication in science and technology. We are committed to foster exchange of knowledge and experience by supporting an online G20 Community of Practice within the existing Innovation Policy Platform and the release of the 2016 G20 Innovation Report.

13. To seize the opportunity that the new industrial revolution (NIR) presents for industry, particularly manufacturing and related services, we deliver the G20 New Industrial Revolution Action Plan. We commit to strengthen communication, cooperation and relevant research on the NIR, facilitate small and medium-sized enterprises (SMEs) to leverage benefits from the NIR, address employment and workforce skill challenges, encourage more cooperation on standards, adequate and effective IPR protection in line with existing multilateral treaties to which they are parties, new industrial infrastructure, and support industrialization, as committed in the action plan. We also support industrialization in developing countries, especially those in Africa and Least Developed Countries (LDCs). We are committed to supporting our workforces throughout this transition and to ensuring that the benefits of the NIR extend to all, including women, youth and disadvantaged groups. We call for cooperation to maximize the benefits and mitigate the negative impact of the expected technological and industrial changes. In all these initiatives, the G20 will take into consideration the different opportunities and challenges for developing and developed countries.

14. To unleash the potential of digital economy, we deliver the G20 Digital Economy Development and Cooperation Initiative, which builds on our work begun in Antalya. We aim to foster favorable conditions for its development and to address digital divide, including through expanded and better and affordable broadband access, flow of information for economic growth, trust and security, while ensuring respect for privacy and personal data protection, investment in the ICT sector, entrepreneurship, digital transformation, e-commerce

cooperation, enhanced digital inclusion and development of micro, small and medium-sized enterprises (MSMEs). We reaffirm paragraph 26 in the Antalya Communique, commit to offer policy support for an open and secure environment and recognize the key role of adequate and effective IPR protection and enforcement to the development of the digital economy. We welcome the efforts made by the OECD, IMF, national and other international organizations on the measurement of the digital economy, and recognize that further relevant research and exchange are needed.

15. We reiterate the essential role of structural reforms in boosting productivity and potential output, as well as promoting innovative growth in G20 countries. We deliver the Enhanced Structural Reform Agenda, noting that the choice and design of structural reforms are consistent with countries' specific economic conditions. We endorse the nine priority areas of structural reforms and a set of guiding principles identified in the Agenda to provide high-level and useful guidance to members, while allowing them to account for their specific national circumstances. We also support the quantitative framework consisting of a set of indicators, which will be improved over time, to help monitor and assess our efforts and progress with structural reforms and challenges. We are putting in place an integrated strategy for growth with short, medium and long-term measures. We will ensure that the Enhanced Structural Reform Agenda and the relevant elements of the Blueprint on Innovative Growth are well articulated.

More Effective and Efficient Global Economic and Financial Governance

16. Our growth, to be resilient, must be underpinned by effective and efficient global economic and financial architecture. We will continue our work in this regard.

17. We endorse the G20 Agenda Towards A More Stable and Resilient International Financial Architecture. We will continue to improve the analysis and monitoring of capital flows and management of risks stemming from excessive capital flow volatility. We look forward to the IMF's review of country experiences and emerging issues in handling capital flows by year-end. We note the ongoing work on the review of the OECD Code of Liberalization of Capital Movements.

We support work to further strengthen the Global Financial Safety Net (GFSN), with a strong, quota-based and adequately resourced IMF at its center, equipped with a more effective toolkit, and with more effective cooperation between the IMF and regional financing arrangements (RFAs), respecting their mandates. In this respect, we welcome the upcoming CMIM-IMF joint test run. We support maintaining access to bilateral and multilateral borrowing agreements between members and the IMF, in line with the objective of preserving the IMF's current lending capacity, and call for broad participation of the IMF membership, including through new agreements. We welcome the entry into effect of the 2010 IMF quota and governance reform and are working towards the completion of the 15th General Review of Quotas, including a new quota formula, by the 2017 Annual Meetings. We reaffirm that any realignment under the 15th review in quota shares is expected to result in increased shares for dynamic economies in line with their relative positions in the world economy, and hence likely in the share of emerging market and developing countries as a whole. We are committed to protecting the voice and representation of the poorest members. We support the World Bank Group to implement its shareholding review according to the agreed roadmap, timeframe and principles, with the objective of achieving equitable voting power over time. We underline the importance of promoting sound and sustainable financing practices and will continue to improve debt restructuring processes. We support the continued effort to incorporate the enhanced contractual clauses into sovereign bonds. We support the Paris Club's discussion of a range of sovereign debt issues, and the ongoing work of the Paris Club, as the principal international forum for restructuring official bilateral debt, towards the broader inclusion of emerging creditors. We welcome the admission of the Republic of Korea and the decision of Brazil to join the Paris Club. We welcome China's continued regular participation in Paris Club meetings and intention to play a more constructive role, including further discussions on potential membership. Following the IMF's decision, we welcome the inclusion of the RMB into the Special Drawing Right (SDR) currency basket on October 1st. We support the ongoing examination of the broader use of the SDR, such as broader reporting in the SDR and the issuance of SDR-denominated bonds, as a way to enhance resilience. In this context, we take note of the recent issuance of SDR bonds by the

World Bank in China's interbank market. We welcome further work by the international organizations to support the development of local currency bond markets, including intensifying efforts to support low-income countries.

18. Building an open and resilient financial system is crucial to supporting sustainable growth and development. To this end, we remain committed to finalizing remaining critical elements of the regulatory framework and to the timely, full and consistent implementation of the agreed financial sector reform agenda, including Basel III and the total-loss-absorbing-capacity (TLAC) standard as well as effective cross-border resolution regimes. We reiterate our support for the work by the Basel Committee on Banking Supervision (BCBS) to finalize the Basel III framework by the end of 2016, without further significantly increasing overall capital requirements across the banking sector, while promoting a level playing field. We welcome the second annual report of the Financial Stability Board (FSB) on implementation and effects of reforms, and will continue to enhance the monitoring of implementation and effects of reforms to ensure their consistency with our overall objectives, including by addressing any material unintended consequences. We will continue to address the issue of systemic risk within the insurance sector. We welcome the work towards the development of an Insurance Capital Standard (ICS) for internationally active insurers. We are committed to full and timely implementation of the agreed over-the-counter (OTC) derivatives reform agenda, and we will remove legal and regulatory barriers to the reporting of OTC derivatives to trade repositories and to authorities' appropriate access to data. We encourage members to close the gap in the implementation of the Principles for Financial Market Infrastructures and welcome the reports by the Committee on Payments and Market Infrastructures, International Organization of Securities Commissions and FSB on enhancing central counterparty resilience, recovery planning and resolvability. Recognizing the importance of effective macroprudential policies in limiting systemic risks, we welcome the joint work by the IMF, FSB and Bank for International Settlements (BIS) to take stock of international experiences with macroprudential frameworks and tools and to help promote effective macroprudential policies. We welcome the FSB consultation on proposed policy recommendations to address

structural vulnerabilities from asset management activities. We will continue to closely monitor, and if necessary, address emerging risks and vulnerabilities in the financial system, including those associated with shadow banking, asset management and other market-based finance. We will continue to address, through the FSB-coordinated action plan, the decline in correspondent banking services so as to support remittances, financial inclusion, trade and openness. We look forward to further efforts to clarify regulatory expectations, as appropriate, including through the review in October by the Financial Action Task Force (FATF) of the guidance on correspondent banking. We call on G20 members, the IMF and WBG to intensify their support for domestic capacity building to help countries improve their compliance with global anti-money laundering and countering the financing of terrorism (AML/CFT) and prudential standards. We endorse the G20 High-level Principles for Digital Financial Inclusion, the updated version of the G20 Financial Inclusion Indicators and the Implementation Framework of the G20 Action Plan on SME Financing. We encourage countries to consider these principles in devising their broader financial inclusion plans, particularly in the area of digital financial inclusion, and to take concrete actions to accelerate progress on all people's access to finance.

19. We will continue our support for international tax cooperation to achieve a globally fair and modern international tax system and to foster growth, including advancing on-going cooperation on base erosion and profits shifting (BEPS), exchange of tax information, tax capacity-building of developing countries and tax policies to promote growth and tax certainty. We welcome the establishment of the G20/OECD Inclusive Framework on BEPS, and its first meeting in Kyoto. We support a timely, consistent and widespread implementation of the BEPS package and call upon all relevant and interested countries and jurisdictions that have not yet committed to the BEPS package to do so and join the framework on an equal footing. We also welcome the progress made on effective and widespread implementation of the internationally agreed standards on tax transparency and reiterate our call on all relevant countries including all financial centers and jurisdictions, which have not yet done so to commit without delay to implementing the standard of automatic exchange of information by 2018 at the latest and to sign and ratify the Multilateral Convention

on Mutual Administrative Assistance in Tax Matters. We endorse the proposals made by the OECD working with G20 members on the objective criteria to identify non-cooperative jurisdictions with respect to tax transparency. We ask the OECD to report back to the finance ministers and central bank governors by June 2017 on the progress made by jurisdictions on tax transparency, and on how the Global Forum will manage the country review process in response to supplementary review requests of countries, with a view for the OECD to prepare a list by the July 2017 G20 Leaders' Summit of those jurisdictions that have not yet sufficiently progressed toward a satisfactory level of implementation of the agreed international standards on tax transparency. Defensive measures will be considered against listed jurisdictions. We encourage countries and international organizations to assist developing economies in building their tax capacity and acknowledge the establishment of the new Platform for Collaboration on Taxation by the IMF, OECD, UN and WBG. We support the principles of the Addis Tax Initiative. We recognize the significant negative impact of illicit financial flows on our economies and we will advance the work of the G20 on this theme. We emphasize the effectiveness of tax policy tools in supply-side structural reform for promoting innovation-driven, inclusive growth, as well as the benefits of tax certainty to promote investment and trade and ask the OECD and IMF to continue working on the issues of pro-growth tax policies and tax certainty. In this connection, China would make its own contribution by establishing an international tax policy research center for international tax policy design and research.

20. Financial transparency and effective implementation of the standards on transparency by all, in particular with regard to the beneficial ownership of legal persons and legal arrangements, is vital to protecting the integrity of the international financial system, and to preventing misuse of these entities and arrangements for corruption, tax evasion, terrorist financing and money laundering. We call on the FATF and the Global Forum to make initial proposals by the Finance Ministers and Central Bank Governors Meeting in October on ways to improve the implementation of the international standards on transparency, including on the availability of beneficial ownership information of legal persons and legal arrangements, and its international exchange.

21. We recognize that, in order to support environmentally sustainable growth globally, it is necessary to scale up green financing. The development of green finance faces a number of challenges, including, among others, difficulties in internalizing environmental externalities, maturity mismatch, lack of clarity in green definitions, information asymmetry and inadequate analytical capacity, but many of these challenges can be addressed by options developed in collaboration with the private sector. We welcome the G20 Green Finance Synthesis Report submitted by the Green Finance Study Group (GFSG) and the voluntary options developed by the GFSG to enhance the ability of the financial system to mobilize private capital for green investment. We believe efforts could be made to provide clear strategic policy signals and frameworks, promote voluntary principles for green finance, expand learning networks for capacity building, support the development of local green bond markets, promote international collaboration to facilitate cross-border investment in green bonds, encourage and facilitate knowledge sharing on environmental and financial risks, and improve the measurement of green finance activities and their impacts.

22. Recognizing the detrimental effects of corruption and illicit finance flows on equitable allocation of public resources, sustainable economic growth, the integrity of the global financial system and the rule of law, we will reinforce the G20's efforts to enhance international cooperation against corruption, while fully respecting international law, human rights and the rule of law as well as the sovereignty of each country. We endorse the G20 High Level Principles on Cooperation on Persons Sought for Corruption and Asset Recovery and welcome Chinese initiative to establish in China a Research Center on International Cooperation Regarding Persons Sought for Corruption and Asset Recovery in G20 Member States, which will be operated in line with international norms. We commit to continue the G20 Denial of Entry Experts Network. Consistent with our national legal systems, we will work on cross-border cooperation and information sharing between law enforcement and anti-corruption agencies and judicial authorities. We call for ratification by all the G20 members of the United Nations Convention Against Corruption and welcome the launch of the second cycle of its review mechanism. We will endeavor to apply effectively the extradition,

mutual legal assistance and asset recovery provisions of the above Convention and other applicable international conventions. We endorse the 2017-2018 G20 Anti-Corruption Action Plan to improve public and private sector transparency and integrity, implementing our stance of zero tolerance against corruption, zero loopholes in our institutions and zero barriers in our actions. We ask the Anti-Corruption Working Group to develop an implementation plan before the end of 2016 as a flexible framework to carry this work forward with renewed high-level attention and urgency. We also welcome outcomes of the London Anti-Corruption Summit in May 2016 and the OECD Ministerial Meeting in March 2016.

23. In line with the G20 Principles on Energy Collaboration, we reaffirm our commitment to building well-functioning, open, competitive, efficient, stable and transparent energy markets, fostering more effective and inclusive global energy architecture to better reflect the changing realities of the world's energy landscape, and shaping an affordable, reliable, sustainable and low greenhouse gas (GHG) emissions energy future while utilizing energy sources and technologies. We stress that continued investment in energy projects and better regional interconnection, particularly in sustainable energy projects, remains critically important to ensuring future energy security and preventing economically destabilizing price spikes. We endeavor to work with Sub-Saharan and Asia-Pacific countries to improve universal access to affordable, reliable, clean, sustainable and modern energy services, particularly by addressing barriers to electricity access. We encourage members to significantly improve energy efficiency based on the specific needs and national circumstances of each member and promote energy conservation through appropriate lifestyle changes. We will explore innovative collaborative arrangements for international cooperation on energy efficiency. We endorse the G20 Voluntary Collaboration Action Plan on Energy Access, the G20 Voluntary Action Plan on Renewable Energy and the G20 Energy Efficiency Leading Programme issued by the G20 energy ministers and ask them to meet regularly to follow up on the implementation of these plans.

24. We reaffirm the importance of energy collaboration towards a cleaner energy future and sustainable energy security with a view to fostering economic growth. We welcome the progress on the voluntary

international collaboration on energy efficiency in six key areas, taking into consideration the policies outlined in the Energy Efficiency Leading Programme and in line with national circumstances, including in heavy duty vehicles, and improving the efficiency of these vehicles. We also reaffirm our commitment to rationalize and phase-out inefficient fossil fuel subsidies that encourage wasteful consumption over the medium term, recognizing the need to support the poor. We welcome G20 countries' progress on their commitments and look forward to further progress in the future. Further, we encourage G20 countries to consider participating in the voluntary peer review process. Given that natural gas is a less emission-intensive fossil fuel, we will enhance collaboration on solutions that promote natural gas extraction, transportation, and processing in a manner that minimizes environmental impacts. We stress the importance of diversification of energy sources and routes.

Robust International Trade and Investment

25. Our growth, to be strong, must be reinforced by inclusive, robust and sustainable trade and investment growth. We note with concern the slow growth in trade and investment globally and commit to enhance an open world economy by working towards trade and investment facilitation and liberalization. We recognize the importance of economic diversification and industrial upgrading in developing countries to benefit from more open global markets. We endorse the outcome of the G20 Trade Ministers Meeting held in Shanghai on 9-10 July, and welcome the establishment of the G20 Trade and Investment Working Group (TIWG). We commit to further strengthen G20 trade and investment cooperation.

26. We reaffirm our determination to ensure a rules-based, transparent, non-discriminatory, open and inclusive multilateral trading system with the World Trade Organization playing the central role in today's global trade. We reiterate our commitment to shape the post-Nairobi work with development at its center and commit to advancing negotiations on the remaining DDA issues as a matter of priority, including all three pillars of agriculture (i.e. market access, domestic support and export competition), non-agricultural market access, services, development, Agreement on Trade-Related Aspects of Intellectual Property Rights (TRIPs) and rules. We also note that a

range of issues may be of common interest and importance to today's economy, and thus may be legitimate issues for discussions in the WTO, including those addressed in regional trade arrangements (RTAs) and by the B20. We will work together with all WTO members with a sense of urgency and solidarity and with a view to achieving positive outcomes of the MC11 and beyond and we will work together to further strengthen the WTO.

27. We commit to ratify the Trade Facilitation Agreement by the end of 2016 and call on other WTO members to do the same. We note the important role that bilateral and regional trade agreements can play in liberalizing trade and in the development of trade rules, while recognizing the need to ensure they are consistent with WTO rules. We commit to working to ensure our bilateral and regional trade agreements complement the multilateral trading system, and are open, transparent, inclusive and WTO-consistent. WTO-consistent plurilateral trade agreements with broad participation can play an important role in complementing global liberalization initiatives. G20 Environmental Goods Agreement (EGA) participants welcome the landing zone achieved in the WTO EGA negotiations, and reaffirm their aim to redouble efforts to bridge remaining gaps and conclude an ambitious, future-oriented EGA that seeks to eliminate tariffs on a broad range of environmental goods by the end of 2016, after finding effective ways to address the core concerns of participants.

28. We reiterate our opposition to protectionism on trade and investment in all its forms. We extend our commitments to standstill and rollback of protectionist measures till the end of 2018, reaffirm our determination to deliver on them and support the work of the WTO, UNCTAD and OECD in monitoring protectionism. We emphasize that the benefits of trade and open markets must be communicated to the wider public more effectively and accompanied by appropriate domestic policies to ensure that benefits are widely distributed.

29. We endorse the G20 Strategy for Global Trade Growth, under which the G20 will lead by example to lower trade costs, harness trade and investment policy coherence, boost trade in services, enhance trade finance, promote e-commerce development, and address trade and development. We welcome the World Trade Outlook Indicator released by the WTO as an important leading indicator of global trade. We endorse the G20 Guiding Principles for Global Investment

Policymaking, which will help foster an open, transparent and conductive global policy environment for investment.

30. We also support policies that encourage firms of all sizes, in particular women and youth entrepreneurs, women-led firms and SMEs, to take full advantage of global value chains (GVCs), and that encourage greater participation, value addition and upward mobility in GVCs by developing countries, particularly low-income countries (LICs).We welcome the B20's interest to strengthen digital trade and other work and take note of it's initiative on an Electronic World Trade Platform (eWTP).

31. We recognize that the structural problems, including excess capacity in some industries, exacerbated by a weak global economic recovery and depressed market demand, have caused a negative impact on trade and workers. We recognize that excess capacity in steel and other industries is a global issue which requires collective responses. We also recognize that subsidies and other types of support from government or government-sponsored institutions can cause market distortions and contribute to global excess capacity and therefore require attention. We commit to enhance communication and cooperation, and take effective steps to address the challenges so as to enhance market function and encourage adjustment. To this end, we call for increased information sharing and cooperation through the formation of a Global Forum on steel excess capacity, to be facilitated by the OECD with the active participation of G20 members and interested OECD members. We look forward to a progress report on the efforts of the Global Forum to the relevant G20 ministers in 2017.

Inclusive and Interconnected Development

32. Our growth, to be strong, sustainable and balanced, must also be inclusive. We are committed to ensuring the benefits of our growth reach all people and maximize the growth potential of developing and low-income countries. In this context, we place sustainable development high on the G20 agenda.

33. We pledge to enhance policy coherence on sustainable development and reaffirm our commitment to further align our work with the universal implementation of the 2030 Agenda for Sustainable Development and the Addis Ababa Action Agenda on financing for

development, based on the comparative advantage and the added value of the G20 and in accordance with our national circumstances, while acknowledging that the global follow-up and review of the 2030 Agenda is a UN-led process. We commit to contributing to the implementation of the 2030 Agenda by setting an example through bold, transformative collective and intended national actions in a wide range of areas. By endorsing the G20 Action Plan on the 2030 Agenda for Sustainable Development which also includes high-level principles, we reaffirm our commitment to achieve the ambition of the 2030 Agenda. We note the Addis Tax Initiative, welcome the establishment of the Technology Facilitation Mechanism and stress the importance of enhanced cooperation on technologies to achieving sustainable development.

34. We welcome the Hangzhou Comprehensive Accountability Report on G20 Development Commitments, which reflects our progress already made over the period of 2014-2016.

35. We launch the G20 Initiative on Supporting Industrialization in Africa and LDCs to strengthen their inclusive growth and development potential through voluntary policy options including: promoting inclusive and sustainable structural transformation; supporting sustainable agriculture, agri-business and agro-industry development; deepening, broadening and updating the local knowledge and production base; promoting investment in sustainable and secure energy, including renewables and energy efficiency; exploring ways to develop cooperation on industrial production and vocational training and sustainable and resilient infrastructure and industries; supporting industrialization through trade in accordance with WTO rules; and leveraging domestic and external finance and supporting equitable access to finance - with a focus on women and youth; and promoting science, technology and innovation as critical means for industrialization.

36. We will continue our work on addressing cross-border financial flows derived from illicit activities, including deliberate trade misinvoicing, which hampers the mobilization of domestic resources for development, and welcome the communication and coordination with the World Customs Organization for a study report in this regard following the Hangzhou Summit.

37. We acknowledge the important role of inclusive business in

development, and welcome the establishment of the G20 Global Platform on Inclusive Business and its future actions. We welcome the G20 Inclusive Business Report for the 2016 Summit.

38. We will fulfill our collective commitment to achieve a successful 18th replenishment of the International Development Association, as well as 14th replenishment of the African Development Fund.

39. We reaffirm our commitment to promote investment with focus on infrastructure in terms of both quantity and quality. We welcome the Joint Declaration of Aspirations on Actions to Support Infrastructure Investment by 11 multilateral development banks (MDBs), including their announcements of quantitative ambitions for high-quality infrastructure projects within their respective institutional mandates as well as their efforts to maximize the quality of infrastructure projects, strengthen project pipelines, collaborate further among existing and new MDBs, strengthen the enabling environment for infrastructure investment in developing countries, as well as catalyze private resources. We stress the importance of quality infrastructure investment, which aims to ensure economic efficiency in view of life-cycle cost, safety, resilience against natural disaster, job creation, capacity building, and transfer of expertise and know-how on mutually agreed terms and conditions, while addressing social and environmental impacts and aligning with economic and development strategies. We welcome the MDB Response to the G20 MDB Balance Sheet Optimization Action Plan and call for further implementation of the Action Plan. We note that infrastructure connectivity is key to achieving sustainable development and shared prosperity. We endorse the Global Infrastructure Connectivity Alliance launched this year to enhance the synergy and cooperation among various infrastructure connectivity programs in a holistic way. We ask the WBG to serve as the Secretariat of the Alliance, working closely with the Global Infrastructure Hub (GIH), OECD, other MDBs, and interested G20 members to support its activities. We endorse the G20/OECD Guidance Note on Diversification of Financial Instruments for Infrastructure and SMEs and we welcome the Annotated Public-Private Partnership (PPP) Risk Allocation Matrices completed by the GIH to help developing countries better assess infrastructure risks. We support the effective implementation of the G20/OECD Principles of Corporate Governance and G20/OECD High-level Principles on

SME Financing and look forward to the revision of the assessment methodology of the G20/OECD Principles of the Corporate Governance, which will be informed by an FSB peer review on corporate governance.

40. Generating quality employment is indispensable for sustainable development and is at the center of the G20's domestic and global agenda. We will work to ensure the benefits from economic growth, globalization and technological innovation are widely shared, creating more and better jobs, reducing inequalities and promoting inclusive labor force participation. We endorse the strategies, action plans and initiatives developed by G20 labor and employment ministers to enhance the growth and development agenda by taking effective actions to address changes in skill needs, support entrepreneurship and employability, foster decent work, ensure safer workplaces including within global supply chains and strengthen social protection systems. We endorse Sustainable Wage Policy Principles. We recognize entrepreneurship is an important driver for job creation and economic growth, reinforce our commitments in the G20 Entrepreneurship Action Plan, and welcome China's contribution in the establishment of an Entrepreneurship Research Center on G20 Economies. We also endorse the G20 Initiative to Promote Quality Apprenticeship with policy priorities of increasing the quantity, quality and diversity of apprenticeships. We will further develop the G20 employment plans in 2017 to address these commitments and monitor progress in a systemic and transparent manner in achieving the G20 goals especially on youth employment and female labor participation. We recognize strengthened labor market institutions and policies can support productivity and promote decent work, and therefore higher, sustainable wage growth, in particular for the low-income workers. We recognize the importance of addressing opportunities and challenges brought into the labor market through labor migration as well-managed migration can bring potential benefits to economies and societies.

41. The G20 will continue to prioritize its work on food security, nutrition, sustainable agricultural growth and rural development as a significant contribution to implementing the 2030 Agenda for Sustainable Development. We endorse the outcome of the G20 Agriculture Ministers Meeting and encourage our agriculture ministers to meet

regularly to jointly facilitate sustainable agricultural development and food value chains, including through technological, institutional and social innovation, trade and responsible investment, as a means of food security, rural development and poverty alleviation. We support increasing efforts in this regard by the agricultural scientific and private sectors and welcome the opening of the First G20 Agricultural Entrepreneurs Forum. We recognize the role of family farmers and smallholder agriculture in development, and welcome the Good Practices on Family Farming and Smallholder Agriculture that identifies a set of policies, programs and tools that can prove useful to G20 members and beyond. We welcome the contribution by programs and initiatives that promote sustainable agricultural development, including the Global Agriculture and Food Security Program.

Further Significant Global Challenges Affecting the World Economy

42. The outcome of the referendum on the UK's membership of the EU adds to the uncertainty in the global economy. Members of the G20 are well positioned to proactively address the potential economic and financial consequences stemming from the referendum. In the future, we hope to see the UK as a close partner of the EU.

43. We reiterate our commitment to sustainable development and strong and effective support and actions to address climate change. We commit to complete our respective domestic procedures in order to join the Paris Agreement as soon as our national procedures allow. We welcome those G20 members who joined the Agreement and efforts to enable the Paris Agreement to enter into force by the end of 2016 and look forward to its timely implementation with all its aspects. We affirm the importance of fulfilling the UNFCCC commitment by developed countries in providing means of implementation including financial resources to assist developing countries with respect to both mitigation and adaptation actions in line with Paris outcomes. We reaffirm the importance of the support provided by the Green Climate Fund. We welcome the G20 Climate Finance Study Group report on "Promoting Efficient and Transparent Provision and Mobilization of Climate Finance to Enhance Ambition of Mitigation and Adaptation Actions". We look forward to successful

outcomes in related multilateral fora, including the Montreal Protocol and the International Civil Aviation Organization.

44. Worldwide massive forced displacement of people, unprecedented since the Second World War, especially those generated from violent conflicts, is a global concern. We reiterate our call in Antalya for global concerted efforts in addressing the effects, protection need and root causes of refugee crisis to share in the burden associated with it. We call for strengthening humanitarian assistance for refugees and refugee resettlement, and we invite all states, according to their individual capacity, to scale up assistance to relevant international organizations in order to enhance their capabilities to assist affected countries, intensifying efforts to find durable solutions, in particular for protracted refugee situations, and in this regard, strengthening the contribution of development assistance to host communities. We support the international efforts to respond to the ongoing crisis and note the upcoming high-level meetings which will take place during the UN General Assembly. We note the World Bank's effort to work with other international organizations and its shareholders to develop a global crisis response platform to provide support to refugees and host communities in both low and middle income countries. The G20 will continue to address forced displacement in 2017 with a view to developing concrete actions. The G20 will also examine migration issues in 2017.

45. We strongly condemn terrorism in all forms and manifestations, which poses serious challenges to international peace and security and endangers our ongoing efforts to strengthen the global economy and ensure sustainable growth and development. We reaffirm our solidarity and resolve in the fight against terrorism in all its forms and wherever it occurs. We will tackle all sources, techniques and channels of terrorist financing, including extortion, taxation, smuggling of natural resources, bank looting, looting of cultural property, external donation, and kidnapping for ransom. In confronting terrorism, we remain committed to effectively exchanging information, freezing terrorist assets, and criminalizing terrorist financing. We call for the swift, effective and universal implementation of the FATF standards and of the provisions of the UN Security Council resolution 2253 worldwide. We welcome the progress achieved by the FATF in the implementation of its new

Consolidated Strategy on Combating Terrorist Financing and call for effective implementation of its operational plan. We call on the FATF to reflect by March 2017 on ways to progress in strengthening its traction capacity and enhanced effectiveness of the network of FATF and FATF-style regional bodies.

46. Antimicrobial resistance (AMR) poses a serious threat to public health, growth and global economic stability. We affirm the need to explore in an inclusive manner to fight antimicrobial resistance by developing evidence-based ways to prevent and mitigate resistance, and unlock research and development into new and existing antimicrobials from a G20 value-added perspective, and call on the WHO, FAO, OIE and OECD to collectively report back in 2017 on options to address this including the economic aspects. In this context, we will promote prudent use of antibiotics and take into consideration huge challenges of affordability and access of antimicrobials and their impact on public health. We strongly support the work of the WHO, FAO and the OIE and look forward to a successful high-level meeting on AMR during the UN General Assembly. We look forward to the discussion under the upcoming presidency for dealing with these issues.

47. We reaffirm that the G20's founding spirit is to bring together the major economies on an equal footing to catalyze action. Once we agree, we will deliver.

48. We thank China for hosting a successful Hangzhou Summit and its contribution to the G20 process, and look forward to meeting again in Germany in 2017 and in Argentina in 2018.

(4) HAMBURG 2017

G20 GERMANY 2017
HAMBURG

G20 LEADERS' DECLARATION: SHAPING AN INTERCONNECTED WORLD
July 8, 2017, Hamburg

We, the Leaders of the G20, met in Hamburg, Germany on 7-8 July 2017 to address major global economic challenges and to contribute to prosperity and well-being.

Mastering the challenges of our age and shaping an interconnected world is the common goal of the G20 as our premier forum for international economic cooperation. The G20 revealed its strength during the global economic and financial crisis some ten years ago when it played a crucial role in stabilising economies and financial markets. What was true then continues to hold: We can achieve more together than by acting alone.

Progressing our joint objective in the G20 – strong, sustainable, balanced and inclusive growth – remains our highest priority.

Globalisation and technological change have contributed significantly to driving economic growth and raising living standards across the globe. However, globalisation has created challenges and its benefits have not been shared widely enough. By bringing together developed and emerging market economies, the G20 is determined to shape globalisation to benefit all people. Most importantly, we need to better enable our people to seize its opportunities.

We are resolved to tackle common challenges to the global community, including terrorism, displacement, poverty, hunger and health threats, job creation, climate change, energy security, and inequality including gender inequality, as a basis for sustainable development and stability. We will continue to work together with others, including developing countries, to address these challenges, building on the rules-based international order.

Expanding on the results of previous presidencies, in particular the 2016 G20 Summit in Hangzhou, we decide today to take concrete actions to advance the three aims of building resilience, improving sustainability and ....

Sharing the Benefits of Globalisation

Prospering Global Economy: Current growth prospects are encouraging, though the pace of growth is still weaker than desirable. We reaffirm our commitment to international economic and financial cooperation to further strengthen growth and safeguard against downside risks. We will continue to use all policy tools – monetary, fiscal and structural – individually and collectively to achieve our goal of strong, sustainable, balanced and inclusive growth, while enhancing economic and financial resilience. Monetary policy will continue to support economic activity and ensure price stability, consistent with central banks' mandates. Fiscal policy will be used flexibly and be growth-friendly while ensuring debt as a share of GDP is on a sustainable path. We reinforce our commitment to structural reforms. We reaffirm our previous exchange rate commitments. We will strive to reduce excessive global imbalances in a way that supports global growth. We will promote greater inclusiveness, fairness and equality in our pursuit of economic growth and job creation. To these ends, we endorse the Hamburg Action Plan.

Trade and Investment: International trade and investment are important engines of growth, productivity, innovation, job creation and development. We will keep markets open noting the importance of reciprocal and mutually advantageous trade and investment frameworks and the principle of non-discrimination, and continue to fight protectionism including all unfair trade practices and recognise the role of legitimate trade defence instruments in this regard. We will strive to ensure a level playing field, in particular by promoting a favourable environment for trade and investment in this regard. We further reaffirm the importance of transparency for predictable and mutually beneficial trade relations. To this end, we value the monitoring activities by the WTO, UNCTAD and OECD within their existing mandates. We commit to further strengthen G20 trade and investment cooperation. We call on the OECD, WTO, World Bank Group and IMF to continue their work to better understand trade impacts and report back to G20 Leaders in 2018.

We recognise that the benefits of international trade and investment have not been shared widely enough. We need to better enable our people to seize the opportunities and benefits of economic globalisation. We agree to exchange experiences on the mitigation of the adjustment costs of trade and investment liberalisation and technological change, and on appropriate domestic policies, as well as to enhance international cooperation towards inclusive and sustainable global growth.

We underline the crucial role of the rules-based international trading system. We note the importance of bilateral, regional and plurilateral agreements being open, transparent, inclusive and WTO-consistent, and commit to working to ensure they complement the multilateral trade agreements. We welcome the entry into force of the WTO Trade Facilitation Agreement and call for its full implementation including technical assistance to developing countries. We commit to work together with all WTO members to make the eleventh WTO Ministerial Conference a success. To further improve the functioning of the WTO, we will cooperate to ensure the effective and timely enforcement of trade rules and commitments as well as improve its negotiating, monitoring and dispute settlement functions.

International investment can play an important role in promoting inclusive economic growth, job creation and sustainable development, and requires an open, transparent and conducive global policy environment. We will seek to identify strategies to facilitate and retain foreign direct investment.

Excess Capacities: Recognising the sustained negative impacts on domestic production, trade and workers due to excess capacity in industrial sectors, we commit to further strengthening our cooperation to find collective solutions to tackle this global challenge. We urgently call for the removal of market-distorting subsidies and other types of support by governments and related entities. Each of us commits to take the necessary actions to deliver the collective solutions that foster a truly level playing field. Therefore, we call on the members of the Global Forum on Steel Excess Capacity, facilitated by the OECD, as mandated by the Hangzhou Summit, to fulfil their commitments on enhancing information sharing and cooperation by August 2017, and to rapidly develop concrete policy solutions that reduce steel excess capacity. We look forward to a substantive report with concrete policy solutions by November 2017, as a basis for tangible and swift policy action, and follow-up progress reporting in 2018.

Sustainable Global Supply Chains: Global Supply Chains can be an important source of job creation and balanced economic growth. However challenges for achieving an inclusive, fair and sustainable globalisation remain. In order to achieve sustainable and inclusive supply chains, we commit to fostering the implementation of labour, social and environmental standards and human rights in line with internationally recognised frameworks, such as the UN Guiding Principles on Business and Human Rights and the ILO Tripartite Declaration of Principles concerning Multinational Enterprises and Social Policy. Those countries that adhere to the OECD Guidelines for Multinational Enterprises (OECD MNE Guidelines) commit to fostering them and welcome others to follow.

We will work towards establishing adequate policy frameworks in our countries such as national action plans on business and human rights and underline the responsibility of businesses to exercise due diligence. We will take immediate and effective measures to eliminate child labour by 2025, forced labour, human trafficking and all forms of modern slavery. We welcome the Vision Zero Fund for to prevent work-place related deaths and injuries and encourage enterprises and others to join.

We emphasise that fair and decent wages as well as social dialogue are other key components of sustainable and inclusive global supply chains. We support access to remedy and, where applicable, non-judicial grievance mechanisms, such as the National Contact Points for the OECD MNE Guidelines (NCPs). We will encourage multinational companies to conclude international framework agreements as appropriate. Recognising the ongoing work of the Global Partnership for Financial Inclusion (GPFI), we promote better access to financing, technology, and training facilities that help improve the capacity of micro, small and medium enterprises to integrate into sustainable and inclusive global supply chains.

Harnessing Digitalisation: Digital transformation is a driving force of global, innovative, inclusive and sustainable growth and can contribute to reducing inequality and achieving the goals of the 2030 Agenda for Sustainable Development. To this end, we need to bridge digital divides along multiple dimensions, including income, age, geography and gender. We will strive to ensure that all our citizens are digitally connected by 2025 and especially welcome infrastructure development in low-income countries in that regard. We will promote digital literacy and digital skills in all forms of education and life-long learning. We recognise that information and communication technology (ICT) plays a crucial role in modernizing and increasing efficiency in public administration. We recognise the important role that SMEs and start-ups play in the development of a full range of new and innovative business models and will promote better access to financial resources and services and a more entrepreneurial friendly environment.

We aim to foster favourable conditions for the development of the digital economy and recognise the need to ensure effective competition to foster investment and innovation. We will continue to promote effective cooperation of all stakeholders and encourage the development and use of market- and industry-led international standards for digitised production, products and services that are based on the principles of openness, transparency and consensus and standards should not act as barriers to trade, competition or innovation. They can promote interoperability and security in the use of ICT.

Trust in digital technologies requires effective consumer protection, intellectual property rights, transparency, and security in the use of ICT. We support the free flow of information while respecting applicable legal frameworks for privacy, data protection and intellectual property rights. The G20 Roadmap for Digitalisation will help us guide our future work.

We are committed to help ensure a secure ICT environment in which all sectors are able to enjoy its benefits and reaffirm the importance of collectively addressing issues of security in the use of ICTs.

We will constructively engage in WTO discussions relating to E-commerce and in other international fora with responsibilities related to various aspects of digital trade to foster digital economy development and trade. We will sustain and improve, as appropriate, predictable and transparent frameworks on digital trade. Intensified and concerted action is needed to enhance the ability of developing and least developed countries to more fully engage in digital trade.

Boosting Employment: Well-functioning labour markets contribute to inclusive and cohesive societies and resilient economies. Digitalisation offers the opportunity for creating new and better jobs, while at the same time raising challenges regarding skills, social protection and job quality.

We therefore recognise the need to educate and train people with the necessary skills for the future of work, the importance of opportunities to re- and upskill throughout their working lives, and assist them to successfully adapt to change, in accordance with each member´s domestic social framework.

Acknowledging the increasing diversity of employment, we will assess its impact on social protection and working conditions and continue to monitor global trends, including the impact of new technologies, demographic transition, globalisation and changing working relationships on labour markets. We will promote decent work opportunities during the transition of the labour market. We look forward to a continuous exchange on national experiences and practices.

We recognise the important role of vocational education and training, including quality apprenticeship in integrating young people into the labour market. In this regard, we acknowledge that it is particularly effective when it provides coordinated high quality school- and work-based learning and when it is built on cooperation among governments, business communities and social partners.

Building Resilience

Resilient Global Financial System: An open and resilient financial system, grounded in agreed international standards, is crucial to supporting sustainable growth. We remain committed to the finalisation and timely, full and consistent implementation of the agreed G20 financial sector reform agenda. We will work to finalise the Basel III framework without further significantly increasing overall capital requirements across the banking sector, while promoting a level playing field. We will continue to closely monitor and, if necessary, address emerging risks and vulnerabilities in the financial system. We emphasise the considerable progress made towards transforming shadow banking into resilient market based finance since the financial crisis and welcome the FSB assessment of the monitoring and policy tools available to address risks from shadow banking. We support the FSB's work to analyse the effects of financial regulatory reforms and the structured framework for post-implementation evaluation. Acknowledging that malicious use of ICT could endanger financial stability, we welcome the progress of the FSB's work and look forward to a stock-take report in October 2017.

International Financial Architecture: We need strong, effective and representative global economic and financial institutions to underpin growth and sustainable development. As laid out in the Hamburg Action Plan, we will continue to improve the system underpinning international capital flows and emphasise the need to promote sound and sustainable financing practices. We will enhance the international financial architecture and the global financial safety net with a strong, quota-based and adequately resourced IMF at its centre. We look forward to the completion of the 15th General Review of IMF Quotas, including a new quota formula, by the Spring Meetings 2019 and no later than the Annual Meetings 2019, and support ongoing work to further enhance the effectiveness of its lending toolkit. We endorse the MDBs' Joint Principles and Ambitions on Crowding-In Private Finance ("Hamburg Principles and Ambitions") and welcome their work on optimising balance sheets and boosting investment in infrastructure and connectivity.

International Tax Cooperation and Financial Transparency: We will continue our work for a globally fair and modern international tax system and welcome international cooperation on pro-growth tax policies. We remain committed to the implementation of the Base Erosion and Profit Shifting (BEPS) package and encourage all relevant jurisdictions to join the Inclusive Framework. We look forward to the first automatic exchange of financial account information under the Common Reporting Standard (CRS) in September 2017. We call on all relevant jurisdictions to begin exchanges by September 2018 at the latest. We commend the recent progress made by jurisdictions to meet a satisfactory level of implementation of the agreed international standards on tax transparency and look forward to an updated list by the OECD by our next Summit reflecting further progress made towards implementation. Defensive measures will be considered against listed jurisdictions. We continue to support assistance to developing countries in building their tax capacity. We are also working on enhancing tax certainty and with the OECD on the tax challenges raised by digitalisation of the economy. As an important tool in our fight against corruption, tax evasion, terrorist financing and money laundering, we will advance the effective implementation of the international standards on transparency and beneficial ownership of legal persons and legal arrangements, including the availability of information in the domestic and cross-border context.

Safeguarding against Health Crises and Strengthening Health Systems: The G20 has a crucial role in advancing preparedness and responsiveness against global health challenges. With reference to the results of the G20 health emergency simulation exercise, we emphasise the value of our ongoing, trust-building, cross-sectoral cooperation. We recall universal health coverage is a goal adopted in the 2030 Agenda and recognize that strong health systems are important to effectively address health crises. We call on the UN to keep global health high on the political agenda and we strive for cooperative action to strengthen health systems worldwide, including through developing the health workforce. We recognise that implementation of and compliance with the International Health Regulations (IHR 2005) is critical for efficient prevention, preparedness and response efforts. We strive to fully eradicate polio. We also acknowledge that mass movement of people can pose significant health challenges and encourage countries and International Organisations to strengthen cooperation on the topic. We support the WHO´s central coordinating role, especially for capacity building and response to health emergencies, and we encourage full implementation of its emergency reform. We advocate for sufficient and sustainable funding to strengthen global health capacities, including for rapid financing mechanisms and the WHO's Health Emergencies Programme. Furthermore, we see a need to foster R&D preparedness through globally coordinated models as guided by the WHO R&D Blueprint, such as the Coalition for Epidemic Preparedness Innovations (CEPI).

Combatting Antimicrobial Resistance (AMR): AMR represents a growing threat to public health and economic growth. To tackle the spread of AMR in humans, animals and the environment, we aim to have implementation of our National Action Plans, based on a One-Health approach, well under way by the end of 2018. We will promote the prudent use of antibiotics in all sectors and strive to restrict their use in veterinary medicine to therapeutic uses alone. Responsible and prudent use of antibiotics in food producing animals does not include the use for growth promotion in the absence of risk analysis. We underline that treatments should be available through prescription or the veterinary equivalent only. We will strengthen public awareness, infection prevention and control and improve the understanding of the issue of antimicrobials in the environment. We will promote access to affordable and quality antimicrobials, vaccines and diagnostics, including through efforts to preserve existing therapeutic options. We highlight the importance of fostering R&D, in particular for priority pathogens as identified by the WHO and tuberculosis. We call for a new international R&D Collaboration Hub to maximise the impact of existing and new anti-microbial basic and clinical research initiatives as well as product development. We invite all interested countries and partners to join this new initiative. Concurrently, in collaboration with relevant experts including from the OECD and the WHO, we will further examine practical market incentive options.

Improving Sustainable Livelihoods

Energy and Climate: A strong economy and a healthy planet are mutually reinforcing. We recognise the opportunities for innovation, sustainable growth, competitiveness, and job creation of increased investment into sustainable energy sources and clean energy technologies and infrastructure. We remain collectively committed to mitigate greenhouse gas emissions through, among others, increased innovation on sustainable and clean energies and energy efficiency, and work towards low greenhouse-gas emission energy systems. In facilitating well-balanced and economically viable long-term strategies in order to transform and enhance our economies and energy systems consistent with the 2030 Agenda for Sustainable Development, G20 members will collaborate closely. Recalling the G20 Principles on Energy Collaboration, we regard energy security as one of the guiding principles for the transformation of our energy systems, and we will continue to work on open, flexible, and transparent markets for energy commodities and technologies. We welcome international cooperation on the development, deployment, and commercialisation of sustainable and clean energy technologies and support financing by Multilateral Development Banks to promote universal access to affordable, reliable, sustainable and clean energy.

We take note of the decision of the United States of America to withdraw from the Paris Agreement. The United States of America announced it will immediately cease the implementation of its current nationally-determined contribution and affirms its strong commitment to an approach that lowers emissions while supporting economic growth and improving energy security needs. The United States of America states it will endeavour to work closely with other countries to help them access and use fossil fuels more cleanly and efficiently and help deploy renewable and other clean energy sources, given the importance of energy access and security in their nationally-determined contributions.

The Leaders of the other G20 members state that the Paris Agreement is irreversible. We reiterate the importance of fulfilling the UNFCCC commitment by developed countries in providing means of implementation including financial resources to assist developing countries with respect to both mitigation and adaptation actions in line with Paris outcomes and note the OECD's report "Investing in Climate, Investing in Growth". We reaffirm our strong commitment to the Paris Agreement, moving swiftly towards its full implementation in accordance with the principle of common but differentiated responsibilities and respective capabilities, in the light of different national circumstances and, to this end, we agree to the G20 Hamburg Climate and Energy Action Plan for Growth as set out in the Annex.

Leading the Way towards Sustainable Development: The adoption of the 2030 Agenda represented a milestone towards global sustainable development. We call on countries to work with stakeholders to strive towards its ambitious and integrated implementation and timely realisation in accordance with national circumstances. We commit to further align our actions with the 2030 Agenda for Sustainable Development and its integral part, the Addis Ababa Action Agenda on Financing for Development, domestically and internationally, including in support of developing countries and the provision of public goods.

Building on the G20's Action Plan on the 2030 Agenda for Sustainable Development, the Hamburg Update emphasises our collective and concrete commitments. We support the central role of the high-level political forum on sustainable development and other key UN processes towards achieving the Sustainable Development Goals. We will also engage in voluntary peer learning on the implementation of the 2030 Agenda and call upon others to join this important exercise as a complementary action towards Voluntary National Reviews.

The Annual Progress Report documents for the first time progress on selected prior G20 commitments on the implementation of the 2030 Agenda. Recognising the importance of financial inclusion as a multiplier for poverty eradication, job creation, gender equality, and women's empowerment, we support the ongoing work of the Global Partnership for Financial Inclusion and welcome the 2017 G20 Financial Inclusion Action Plan. We note the UN Secretary-General´s proposal to establish an International Finance Facility for education taking into account other existing initiatives, such as the Global Partnership for Education and Education Cannot Wait, and look forward to examining it in further detail under Argentina's Presidency with a view to making recommendations on it.

Women's Empowerment: Enhanced equal access to the labour market, property, quality employment and financial services for women and men are fundamental for achieving gender equality and full realisation of their rights as well as a prerequisite for sustainable and inclusive growth. We are making progress in achieving our 2014 Brisbane commitment to reduce the gender gap in labour force participation by 25 percent by 2025 but agree that more needs to be done. We also commit to take further action to improve the quality of female employment and eliminate employment discrimination, and reduce gender compensation gaps and provide women with protection from all forms of violence. We will improve women´s access to labour markets through provision of quality education and training, supporting infrastructure, public services and social protection policies and legal reforms, where appropriate.

Digitalisation and access to ICT serve as powerful catalysts for the economic empowerment and inclusion of women and girls. Access to STEM (Science, Technology, Engineering and Mathematics) related trainings and occupations is therefore key to establish an enabling environment for women's empowerment. We welcome the launch of the #eSkills4Girls initiative to promote opportunities and equal participation for women and girls in the digital economy, in particular in low income and developing countries (see Annex).

In order to scale up support for women´s entrepreneurship, we welcome the launch of the Women Entrepreneurs Financing Initiative (We-Fi), housed at the World Bank Group (see Annex). The We-Fi will support ongoing G20 efforts to reduce barriers to financial inclusion and increase women´s access to capital, markets and technical assistance as well as contribute to achieving the goals of the G20 Africa Partnership and the G20 Entrepreneurship Action Plan. We will also establish a Business Women Leaders' Taskforce, which will, in close cooperation with the W20 and B20, bring together business women from G20 countries to examine ways to increase women's participation in the economy and will make recommendations at next year's summit on the implementation of G20 commitments regarding the economic empowerment of women.

Towards Food Security, Water Sustainability and Rural Youth Employment: Water is an essential and precious resource. In order to achieve food security, we are committed to increase agricultural productivity and resilience in a sustainable manner, while aiming to protect, manage and use efficiently water and water-related ecosystems. In order to harness the potential of ICT, we stress the need for strengthened cooperation on ICT in agriculture and underline the importance of access to high-speed digital services for farmers and of adequately serving rural areas. To enhance transparency in global food markets, we call for a strengthening of the Agricultural Market Information System (AMIS) and an active engagement of its entire membership. We underline that making markets function better can contribute to reducing food price volatility and enhance food security. It is vital for farmers to be profitable and, along with consumers, have access to national, regional and international markets.

We launch the G20 Initiative for Rural Youth Employment in developing countries with a focus on Africa. This Initiative will, in alignment with developing countries' strategies, contribute to creating 1.1 million new jobs by 2022 and to providing innovative skills development programmes for at least 5 million young people over the next five years. Recognising the famine in some areas of South Sudan and risk of famine in Somalia, Yemen and North-Eastern Nigeria, we are more than ever committed to act with the required urgency, supporting UN agencies and other humanitarian and development organisations in a coordinated and comprehensive response to save lives and support conditions for sustainable development. We recognise the contributions made by different G20 members in line with the UN appeal for humanitarian assistance which represents over two thirds of the funding received for immediate requirements. We will further strengthen our humanitarian engagement and reaffirm our commitment to addressing the underlying causes of recurrent and protracted crises.

Resource Efficiency and Marine Litter: We launch two initiatives to contribute to the implementation of the 2030 Agenda and to reflect our commitment to sustainable development, as outlined in the Annexes. The G20 Resource Efficiency Dialogue will exchange good practices and national experiences to improve the efficiency and sustainability of natural resource use across the entire life cycle, and to promote sustainable consumption and production patterns. The G20 Marine Litter Action Plan seeks to prevent and reduce marine litter, including by considering its socio-economic aspects.

Assuming Responsibility

Africa Partnership: We launch the G20 Africa Partnership in recognition of the opportunities and challenges in African countries as well as the goals of the 2030 Agenda. Our joint efforts will foster sustainable and inclusive economic growth and development, in response to the needs and aspirations of African countries, contributing to create decent employment particularly for women and youth, thus helping to address poverty and inequality as root causes of migration. The Partnership includes related initiatives, such as #eSkills4Girls, Rural Youth Employment, African Renewable Energy and facilitates investment Compacts, as outlined in the Annex.

We welcome the outcomes of the G20 Africa Partnership Conference in Berlin, which highlighted the need for joint measures to enhance sustainable infrastructure, improve investment frameworks as well as support education and capacity building. Individual priorities for "Investment Compacts" were put forward by Côte d'Ivoire, Ethiopia, Ghana, Morocco, Rwanda, Senegal and Tunisia. Led by the respective African countries, the African Development Bank, IMF and WBG as well as the G20 and other partners, these Compacts aim to mobilise private investment as well as promote efficient use of public funding.

We are ready to help interested African countries and call on other partners to join the initiative. We support the goals of the Partnership through complementary initiatives as well as encourage the private sector to seize African economic opportunities in supporting sustainable growth and employment creation.

Based on equal partnership, we strongly welcome African ownership and commit to align our joint measures with regional strategies and priorities, in particular the African Union's Agenda 2063 and its Programme for Infrastructure Development in Africa (PIDA). The African Union and its specialised agency, the New Partnership for Africa's Development (NEPAD), are important partners in its implementation and monitoring.

Stepping up Coordination and Cooperation on Displacement and Migration: The world is experiencing historic levels of migration and forced displacement. While migration is influenced by many political, social and economic developments, the main drivers of forced displacement include conflicts, natural disasters as well as human rights violations and abuses. Migration and forced displacement trends are of major relevance for countries of origin, transit and destination. The social and economic benefits and opportunities of safe, orderly and regular migration can be substantial. Forced displacement and irregular migration in large movements, on the other hand, often present complex challenges.

We support those countries that choose to develop pathways for migration, underline the importance of nationally determined integration and endorse the G20 Policy Practices for the Fair and Effective Labour Market Integration of Regular Migrants and Recognised Refugees. We emphasise the sovereign right of states to manage and control their borders and in this regard to establish policies in their own national interests and national security, as well as the importance that repatriation and reintegration of migrants who are not eligible to remain be safe and humane. We commit to countering migrant smuggling and trafficking in human beings and we are determined to take action against people smugglers and traffickers.

We seek to address the root causes of displacement. We call for concerted global efforts and coordinated and shared actions, in particular with respect to countries and communities that are under high social, political and financial pressure, and for combining both an emergency approach and a long-term one. To this end, we acknowledge the importance of establishing partnerships with countries of origin and transit. We will promote sustainable economic development in those countries.

We commit to addressing the distinct needs of refugees and migrants, in particular close to their region of origin and, when applicable, to enable them to return home safely. At the same time, we place special emphasis on vulnerable groups, including women at risk and children, particularly those unaccompanied, and to protecting the human rights of all persons regardless of their status.

We call for improving the governance of migration and providing comprehensive responses to displacement and recognise the need to develop tools and institutional structures accordingly. Therefore, we look forward to the outcome of the UN process towards Global Compacts on Refugees and for Safe, Orderly and Regular Migration, both envisaged to be adopted in 2018. We emphasise the need for monitoring global displacement and migration, as well as its economic consequences. To this end, we ask the OECD, in cooperation with ILO, IOM and UNHCR, to update us annually on trends and policy challenges.

Fighting Corruption: We remain committed to fighting corruption, including through practical international cooperation and technical assistance, and will continue to fully implement the G20 Anti-Corruption Action Plan 2017-18. We endorse four sets of High Level Principles aimed at fostering integrity in the public and private sector. By endorsing the High Level Principles on the Liability of Legal Persons, we commit to ensuring that not only individual perpetrators but also companies benefitting from corruption can be held liable. We commit to organising our public administrations to be more resilient against corruption. We will intensify our fight against corruption related to illegal trade in wildlife and wildlife products. Wildlife trafficking is a threat to the planet's biodiversity, economic development, and, among others, health and security, and is facilitated by high levels of corruption, which the G20 cannot tolerate. We also endorse the High Level Principles on Countering Corruption in Customs and publish a guide on requesting international cooperation in civil and administrative proceedings. We will continue our work to address integrity in sports and urge international sports organisations to intensify their fight against corruption by achieving the highest global integrity and anti-corruption standards. In this respect, we strive for a common understanding regarding corruption risks in bids to host major sport events. We are also committed to fighting corruption in contracts, including in the natural resources sector. We call for ratification and implementation by all G20 members of the UN Convention against Corruption and for a strong involvement in its review process.

We thank Germany for hosting a successful Hamburg Summit and its contribution to the G20 process, and look forward to meeting again in Argentina in 2018, in Japan in 2019 and in Saudi Arabia in 2020.

(5) BUENOS AIRES 2018

G20

ARGENTINA 2018

BUILDING CONSENSUS FOR FAIR AND SUSTAINABLE DEVELOPMENT

G20 LEADERS' DECLARATION: BUILDING CONSENSUS FOR FAIR AND SUSTAINABLE DEVELOPMENT

December 1, 2018

1. Ten years since the first G20 Leaders' Summit we met in Buenos Aires, Argentina, on 30 November-1 December 2018 to build consensus for fair and sustainable development through an agenda that is people-centred, inclusive and forward-looking.

2. This year we have focused on the following pillars: the future of work, infrastructure for development, a sustainable food future and a gender mainstreaming strategy across the G20 agenda.

3. We have addressed our agenda promoting dialogue and the search for common ground. Building consensus requires the commitment of the society as a whole. Our discussions have been enriched by our engagement with stakeholder communities.

4. We welcome the strong global economic growth while recognizing it has been increasingly less synchronized between countries and some of the key risks, including financial vulnerabilities and geopolitical concerns, have partially materialized. We also note current trade issues. We reaffirm our pledge to use all policy tools to achieve strong, sustainable, balanced and inclusive growth, and safeguard against downside risks, by stepping up our dialogue and actions to enhance confidence. Monetary policy will continue to support economic activity and ensure price stability, consistent with central banks' mandates. Fiscal policy should rebuild buffers where needed, be used

flexibly and be growth-friendly, while ensuring public debt is on a sustainable path. Continued implementation of structural reforms will enhance our growth potential. We reaffirm the exchange rate commitments made by the Finance Ministers and Central Bank Governors last March. We endorse the Buenos Aires Action Plan.

5. We renew our commitment to work together to improve a rules-based international order that is capable of effectively responding to a rapidly changing world.

6. Transformative technologies are expected to bring immense economic opportunities, including new and better jobs, and higher living standards. The transition, however, will create challenges for individuals, businesses and governments. Policy responses and international cooperation will help ensure that the benefits of the technological transformation are widely shared. We endorse the Menu of Policy Options for the Future of Work which we will draw on, considering individual country circumstances, to: harness technology to strengthen growth and productivity; support people during transitions and address distributional challenges; secure sustainable tax systems; and ensure that the best possible evidence informs our decision-making.

7. We remain committed to building an inclusive, fair and sustainable Future of Work by promoting decent work, vocational training and skills development, including reskilling workers and improving labour conditions in all forms of employment, recognizing the importance of social dialogue in this area, including work delivered through digital platforms, with a focus on promoting labour formalization and making social protection systems strong and portable, subject to national law and circumstances. We will continue to foster cognitive, digital and entrepreneurship skills, and encourage the collection and exchange of good practices. We will promote increasing labour force participation of underrepresented as well as vulnerable groups, including persons with disabilities. We will implement policies to improve the employment situation of young people, consistent with the G20 Antalya Youth Goal. We will take actions to eradicate child labour, forced labour, human trafficking and modern slavery in the world of work, including through fostering sustainable supply chains. We will endeavor to further create enabling conditions for resource mobilization from public, private and

multilateral resources, including innovative financial mechanisms and partnerships, such as impact investment for inclusive and sustainable growth, in line with the G20 Call on Financing for Inclusive Business.

8. Access to education is a human right and a strategic public policy area for the development of more inclusive, prosperous, and peaceful societies. We underline the importance of girls´ education. To equip our citizens to reap the benefits of societal and technological innovations we will promote coordination between employment and equitable quality education policies, so we can develop comprehensive strategies that promote key competences such as learning to learn, foundation and digital skills, in a lifelong learning perspective from early childhood. We acknowledge the need to foster evidence-based innovative pedagogies and methods for all levels of education.

9. To maximize the benefits of digitalization and emerging technologies for innovative growth and productivity, we will promote measures to boost micro, small and medium enterprises and entrepreneurs, bridge the digital gender divide and further digital inclusion, support consumer protection, and improve digital government, digital infrastructure and measurement of the digital economy. We reaffirm the importance of addressing issues of security in the use of ICTs. We support the free flow of information, ideas and knowledge, while respecting applicable legal frameworks, and working to build consumer trust, privacy, data protection and intellectual property rights protection. We welcome the G20 Repository of Digital Policies to share and promote the adoption of innovative digital economy business models. We recognize the importance of the interface between trade and the digital economy. We will continue our work on artificial intelligence, emerging technologies and new business platforms.

10. Infrastructure is a key driver of economic prosperity, sustainable development and inclusive growth. To address the persistent infrastructure financing gap, we reaffirm our commitment to attract more private capital to infrastructure investment. To achieve this, we endorse the Roadmap to Infrastructure as an Asset Class and the G20 Principles for the Infrastructure Project Preparation Phase. We are taking actions to achieve greater contractual standardization,

address data gaps and improve risk mitigation instruments. In line with the Roadmap, we look forward to progress in 2019 on quality infrastructure.

11. Building on the G20 Food Security and Nutrition Framework, we reaffirm our commitment to tackling the challenges of food security, which is crucial to achieving a world free of hunger and all forms of malnutrition. We will promote dynamism in rural areas and sustainable agriculture, conscious of the importance of sustainable soil, water and riverbanks management supported by individual countries voluntarily, taking into consideration the specific needs of family and small-holder farmers. We encourage the voluntary use and sharing of innovative as well as traditional agricultural practices and technologies. We highlight the importance of collaboration among public and private stakeholders to strengthen risk management, facilitate adaptation to a changing environment, protect biodiversity and provide effective responses to reduce the impacts of extreme weather on agriculture. We will increase efforts to engage with the private sector, the scientific community and all other relevant stakeholders to enhance value addition, productivity, efficiency, sustainability and upgrading in Agro-Food Global Value Chains and encourage initiatives to reduce food loss and waste.

12. Gender equality is crucial for economic growth and fair and sustainable development. We are making progress in achieving our Brisbane commitment to reduce the gender gap in labour force participation rates by 25% by 2025 but affirm that more needs to be done. We will continue to promote initiatives aimed at ending all forms of discrimination against women and girls and gender- based violence. We commit to promoting women's economic empowerment, including by working with the private sector, to improve labour conditions for all, such as through access to quality and affordable care infrastructure and parental leave, and reducing the gender pay gap. We also commit to promote women's access to leadership and decision-making positions, the development of women and girls' digital skills and increasing their participation in STEM (Science, Technology, Engineering and Mathematics) and high-tech sectors. We welcome the continued implementation of the Women Entrepreneurs Financing Initiative (We-Fi), and we thank the Business Women Leaders' Taskforce for its work. Drawing from

this experience, we will consider how to better engage with women entrepreneurs.

13. Mobilizing sustainable finance and strengthening financial inclusion are important for global growth. We welcome the Sustainable Finance Synthesis Report 2018, which presents voluntary options to support deployment of sustainable private capital. We endorse the G20 Financial Inclusion Policy Guide, which provides voluntary policy recommendations to facilitate digital financial services, taking into account country contexts and the Global Partnership for Financial Inclusion Roadmap which outlines a process to streamline its work program and structure.

14. We launch the G20 Initiative for Early Childhood Development and stand ready to join all stakeholders in enhancing quality and sustainably financed early childhood programs that consider the multidimensional approach of ECD as means of building human capital to break the cycle of intergenerational and structural poverty, and of reducing inequalities, specially where young children are most vulnerable.

15. We encourage the activities of World Health Organization (WHO), together with all relevant actors, to develop an action plan for implementation of health-related aspects of SDGs by 2030. We commend the progress made by the international community in developing and implementing National and Regional Action Plans on Anti-Microbial Resistance (AMR) based on One-Health approach. We recognize the need for further multi-sectoral action to reduce the spread of AMR, as it is increasingly becoming a global responsibility. We note the work done by the Global AMR R&D Hub and, drawing on this, we look forward to further examine practical market incentives. We will tackle malnutrition, with a special focus on childhood overweight and obesity, through national, community-based and collaborative multi-stakeholder approaches. We reaffirm the need for stronger health systems providing cost effective and evidence-based intervention to achieve better access to health care and to improve its quality and affordability to move towards Universal Health Coverage (UHC), in line with their national contexts and priorities. This may encompass, where appropriate, scientifically proven traditional and complementary medicine, assuring the safety, quality and effectiveness of health services. We will continue to

strengthen core capacities required by International Health Regulations (IHR, 2005) for prevention, detection and response to public health emergencies, while recognizing the critical role played by WHO in this regard. We are committed to ending HIV/AIDS, tuberculosis and malaria, and look forward to a successful 6° replenishment of the Global Fund in 2019.

16. We note the 2018 G20 Annual International Migration and Displacement Trends and Policies Report prepared by the OECD in cooperation with ILO, IOM and UNHCR. We will consider how to continue the dialogue on these issues under the next presidency.

17. Large movements of refugees are a global concern with humanitarian, political, social and economic consequences. We emphasize the importance of shared actions to address the root causes of displacement and to respond to growing humanitarian needs.

18. We reaffirm our commitment to leading the transformation towards sustainable development and support the 2030 Agenda as the framework for advancing this goal and the G20 Action Plan. The Buenos Aires Update outlines the G20 current collective and concrete actions towards achieving that Agenda, recognizing that South-South and triangular cooperation have an important role to implement it. We underline our continued support to the G20 Africa Partnership, including the multidimensional approach of ECD, Compact with Africa, and other relevant initiatives. We reaffirm our commitment to addressing illicit financial flows that have a detrimental effect on domestic resources mobilization and will continue to take stock of progress. We endorse the G20 High Level Principles on Sustainable Habitat through Regional Planning.

19. A strong economy and a healthy planet are mutually reinforcing. We note the latest IPCC Special Report on the Impacts of Global Warming of 1.5 degrees centigrade. We recognize the importance of comprehensive adaptation strategies, including investment in infrastructure that is resilient to extreme weather events and disasters. In this sense, we support actions and cooperation in developing countries, especially those that are particularly vulnerable, including small island states such as those in the Caribbean. We discussed long-term low greenhouse gas emission development strategies and alignment of international finance flows. We also shared countries´ experiences and considered the 2018-2019 work program on

adaptation, acknowledging that each country may chart its own path to achieving a low emission future. We look forward to successful outcomes of the UNFCCC COP24, and to engage in the Talanoa Dialogue.

20. Signatories to the Paris Agreement, who have also joined the Hamburg Action Plan, reaffirm that the Paris Agreement is irreversible and commit to its full implementation, reflecting common but differentiated responsibilities and respective capabilities, in light of different national circumstances. We will continue to tackle climate change, while promoting sustainable development and economic growth.

21. The United States reiterates its decision to withdraw from the Paris Agreement, and affirms its strong commitment to economic growth and energy access and security, utilizing all energy sources and technologies, while protecting the environment.

22. We recognize the crucial role of energy in helping shape our shared future and we encourage energy transitions that combine growth with decreasing greenhouse gas emissions towards cleaner, more flexible and transparent systems, and cooperation in energy efficiency. We recognize the opportunities for innovation, growth, and job creation through increased investment into cleaner and sustainable energy sources—including renewables, technologies and infrastructure. We acknowledge the role of all energy sources and technologies in the energy mix and different possible national paths to achieve cleaner energy systems under the term 'transitions'. We will promote energy security, sustainability, resilience, efficiency, affordability and stability, acknowledging that there are varied sources of energy and technological advances to achieve a low emissions future. We continue to promote universal energy access by eradicating energy poverty, cooperating to provide displaced people and disaster-impacted and remote areas with access to it, and through enhanced implementation of G20 regional plans.

23. Strong and effective international financial institutions help underpin growth and sustainable development. We reaffirm our commitment to further strengthening the global financial safety net with a strong, quota-based, and adequately resourced IMF at its centre. We are committed to concluding the 15th General Review of Quotas including a new quota formula by the Spring Meetings and no later

than the Annual Meetings of 2019. We call on the IMF and World Bank to work with borrowers and creditors to improve the recording, monitoring and transparent reporting of public and private debt obligations. We look forward to the IMF review of programme conditionality and the review of its debt limits policy.

24. We will continue to monitor cross border capital flows and deepen our understanding of the available tools, so we can harness their benefits while also managing the risks and enhancing resilience. We will continue to take steps to address debt vulnerabilities in low income countries by supporting capacity building in public debt and financial management, and strengthening domestic policy frameworks. We will work towards enhancing debt transparency and sustainability, and improving sustainable financing practices by borrowers and creditors, both official and private, including infrastructure financing. We support ongoing work by the IMF, WBG and Paris Club on LICs debt and the continued efforts of the Paris Club towards the broader inclusion of emerging creditors. We welcome the final report of the G20 Eminent Persons Group on Global Financial Governance.

25. An open and resilient financial system, grounded in agreed international standards, is crucial to support sustainable growth. We remain committed to the full, timely and consistent implementation and finalization of the agreed financial reform agenda, and the evaluation of its effects. We will continue to monitor and, if necessary, tackle emerging risks and vulnerabilities in the financial system; and, through continued regulatory and supervisory cooperation, address fragmentation. We look forward to continued progress on achieving resilient non-bank financial intermediation. We will step up efforts to ensure that the potential benefits of technology in the financial sector can be realized while risks are mitigated. We will regulate crypto-assets for anti-money laundering and countering the financing of terrorism in line with FATF standards and we will consider other responses as needed. We thank Mr. Mark Carney for his service as FSB Chair and we welcome the appointment of Mr. Randal K Quarles, as Chair of the FSB and of Mr. Klaas Knot, as Vice Chair.

26. We will continue our work for a globally fair, sustainable, and modern international tax system based, in particular on tax treaties and transfer pricing rules, and welcome international cooperation to

advance pro-growth tax policies. Worldwide implementation of the OECD/G20 Base Erosion and Profit Shifting package remains essential. We will continue to work together to seek a consensus-based solution to address the impacts of the digitalization of the economy on the international tax system with an update in 2019 and a final report by 2020. We welcome the commencement of the automatic exchange of financial account information and acknowledge the strengthened criteria developed by the OECD to identify jurisdictions that have not satisfactorily implemented the tax transparency standards. Defensive measures will be considered against listed jurisdictions. All jurisdictions should sign and ratify the multilateral Convention on Mutual Administrative Assistance in Tax Matters. We continue to support enhanced tax certainty and tax capacity building in developing countries, including through the Platform for Collaboration on Tax.

27. International trade and investment are important engines of growth, productivity, innovation, job creation and development. We recognize the contribution that the multilateral trading system has made to that end. The system is currently falling short of its objectives and there is room for improvement. We therefore support the necessary reform of the WTO to improve its functioning. We will review progress at our next Summit.

28. Recalling our commitments from Hangzhou and Hamburg, we welcome the concrete policy solutions developed by the Global Forum on Steel Excess Capacity (GFSEC), facilitated by the OECD. We call on all members to implement the Berlin and Paris GFSEC Ministerial recommendations and commitments. We look forward to a substantive report by June 2019.

29. We remain committed to prevent and fight corruption and lead by example. We agree on the new action plan 2019-2021 and endorse Principles on Preventing Corruption and Ensuring Integrity in State-Owned Enterprises and on Preventing and Managing Conflicts of Interest in the Public Sector. These will foster transparency and integrity in the public and private sectors. We will continue practical cooperation to fight corruption including in line with our G20 commitments. We will further explore the links between corruption and other economic crimes and ways to tackle them, including through cooperation on the return of persons sought for such offences

and stolen assets, consistent with international obligations and domestic legal systems. We ask relevant international organizations to report back to us on those issues during the next presidency. We call for the effective implementation by all G20 countries of the UN Convention Against Corruption, including the criminalization of the bribery of foreign public officials, and note the work towards possible adherence to the OECD Convention on Combating Bribery of Foreign Public Officials in International Business Transactions.

30. We reaffirm our strong condemnation of terrorism in all its forms and manifestations. We commit to the full implementation of The Hamburg G20 Leaders Statement on Countering Terrorism. We will step up our efforts in fighting terrorist and proliferation financing, and money laundering. We urge the digital industry to work together to fight exploitation of the internet and social media for terrorist purposes.

31. We thank Argentina for its G20 Presidency and for hosting the successful Buenos Aires Summit and we look forward to our next meetings in Japan in 2019 and in Saudi Arabia in 2020.

(6) OSAKA 2019

G20
2019
JAPAN

G20 OSAKA LEADERS' DECLARATION
Osaka, Japan, June 29, 2019

Preamble

1. We, the Leaders of the G20, met in Osaka, Japan on 28-29 June 2019 to make united efforts to address major global economic challenges. We will work together to foster global economic growth, while harnessing the power of technological innovation, in particular digitalization, and its application for the benefit of all.

2. Building on work done by previous presidencies, we will strive to create a virtuous cycle of growth by addressing inequalities and realize a society where all individuals can make use of their full potential. We are resolved to build a society capable of seizing opportunities, and tackling economic, social and environmental challenges, presented today and in the future, including those of demographic change.

3. We will further lead efforts to foster development and address other global challenges to pave the way toward an inclusive and sustainable world, as envisioned in the 2030 Agenda for Sustainable Development.

Global Economy

4. Global growth appears to be stabilizing, and is generally projected to pick up moderately later this year and into 2020. This recovery is supported by the continuation of accommodative financial conditions and stimulus measures taking effect in some countries. However,

growth remains low and risks remain tilted to the downside. Most importantly, trade and geopolitical tensions have intensified. We will continue to address these risks, and stand ready to take further action.

5. We reaffirm our commitment to use all policy tools to achieve strong, sustainable, balanced and inclusive growth, and safeguard against downside risks, by stepping up our dialogue and actions to enhance confidence. Fiscal policy should be flexible and growth-friendly while rebuilding buffers where needed and ensuring debt as a share of GDP is on a sustainable path. Monetary policy will continue to support economic activity and ensure price stability, consistent with central banks' mandates. Central bank decisions need to remain well communicated. Continued implementation of structural reforms will enhance our growth potential. We also reaffirm the exchange rate commitments made by our Finance Ministers and Central Bank Governors in March 2018.

6. Global current account imbalances have narrowed in the aftermath of the global financial crisis, notably in emerging and developing economies and they have become increasingly concentrated in advanced economies. However, they remain large and persistent, and stock positions continue to diverge. In assessing external balances, we note the importance of monitoring all components of the current account, including services trade and income balances. In the spirit of enhancing cooperation, we affirm that carefully calibrated macroeconomic and structural policies tailored to country-specific circumstances are necessary to address excessive imbalances and mitigate the risks to achieving the G20 goal of strong, sustainable, balanced and inclusive growth.

7. Demographic changes, including population aging, pose challenges and opportunities for all G20 members, and these changes will require policy actions that span fiscal, monetary, financial, labour market and other structural policies. To strengthen financial inclusion in the aging society, we endorse the G20 Fukuoka Policy Priorities on Aging and Financial Inclusion.

Fostering Robust Global Economic Growth

Trade and Investment

8. We welcome the G20 Ministerial Statement on Trade and Digital Economy in Tsukuba. We strive to realize a free, fair, non-

discriminatory, transparent, predictable and stable trade and investment environment, and to keep our markets open. International trade and investment are important engines of growth, productivity, innovation, job creation and development. We reaffirm our support for the necessary reform of the World Trade Organization (WTO) to improve its functions. We will work constructively with other WTO members, including in the lead up to the 12th WTO Ministerial Conference. We agree that action is necessary regarding the functioning of the dispute settlement system consistent with the rules as negotiated by WTO members. Furthermore, we recognize the complementary roles of bilateral and regional free trade agreements that are WTO-consistent. We will work to ensure a level playing field to foster an enabling business environment.

Excess Capacity

9. While we note the progress made so far by the Global Forum on Steel Excess Capacity (GFSEC), we ask relevant Ministers of the members of the GFSEC to explore and reach a consensus by fall 2019 on ways to further the work of the Forum.

Innovation: Digitalization, Data Free Flow with Trust

10. Innovation is an important driver for economic growth, which can also contribute to advancing towards the SDGs and enhancing inclusiveness. We will work toward achieving an inclusive, sustainable, safe, trustworthy and innovative society through digitalization and promoting the application of emerging technologies. We share the notion of a human-centered future society, which is being promoted by Japan as Society 5.0. As digitalization is transforming every aspect of our economies and societies, we recognize the critical role played by effective use of data, as an enabler of economic growth, development and social well-being. We aim to promote international policy discussions to harness the full potential of data.

11. Cross-border flow of data, information, ideas and knowledge generates higher productivity, greater innovation, and improved sustainable development, while raising challenges related to privacy, data protection, intellectual property rights, and security. By continuing to address these challenges, we can further facilitate data

free flow and strengthen consumer and business trust. In this respect, it is necessary that legal frameworks, both domestic and international, should be respected. Such data free flow with trust will harness the opportunities of the digital economy. We will cooperate to encourage the interoperability of different frameworks, and we affirm the role of data for development. We also reaffirm the importance of interface between trade and digital economy, and note the ongoing discussion under the Joint Statement Initiative on electronic commerce, and reaffirm the importance of the Work Programme on electronic commerce at the WTO.

12. To further promote innovation in the digital economy, we support the sharing of good practices on effective policy and regulatory approaches and frameworks that are innovative as well as agile, flexible, and adapted to the digital era, including through the use of regulatory sandboxes. The responsible development and use of Artificial Intelligence (AI) can be a driving force to help advance the SDGs and to realize a sustainable and inclusive society. To foster public trust and confidence in AI technologies and fully realize their potential, we commit to a human-centered approach to AI, and welcome the non-binding G20 AI Principles, drawn from the Organization for Economic Cooperation and Development (OECD) Recommendation on AI. Further, we recognize the growing importance of promoting security in the digital economy and of addressing security gaps and vulnerabilities. We affirm the importance of protection of intellectual property. Along with the rapid expansion of emerging technologies including the Internet of Things (IoT), the value of an ongoing discussion on security in the digital economy is growing. We, as G20 members, affirm the need to further work on these urgent challenges. We reaffirm the importance of bridging the digital divide and fostering the adoption of digitalization among micro, small and medium enterprises (MSMEs) and all individuals, particularly vulnerable groups and also encourage networking and experience-sharing among cities for the development of smart cities.

Quality Infrastructure Investment

13. Infrastructure is a driver of economic growth and prosperity. We endorse the G20 Principles for Quality Infrastructure Investment as

our common strategic direction and high aspiration. These emphasize that quality infrastructure is an essential part of the G20's ongoing efforts to close the infrastructure gap, in accordance with the Roadmap to Infrastructure as an Asset Class. We stress the importance of maximizing the positive impact of infrastructure to achieve sustainable growth and development while preserving the sustainability of public finances, raising economic efficiency in view of life-cycle cost, integrating environmental and social considerations, including women's economic empowerment, building resilience against natural disasters and other risks, and strengthening infrastructure governance. We look forward to continuing advancing the elements to develop infrastructure as an asset class, including by exploring possible indicators on quality infrastructure investment.

Global Finance

14. We reaffirm our commitment to further strengthening the global financial safety net with a strong, quota-based, and adequately resourced International Monetary Fund (IMF) at its center. We remain committed to concluding the 15th General Review of Quotas no later than the 2019 Annual Meetings, and call on the IMF to expedite its work on IMF resources and governance reform as a matter of the highest priority. We support the progress made on work to follow up the Eminent Persons Group (EPG) proposals, including on country platforms, and efforts by the World Bank Group (WBG) to enhance risk insurance in development finance. We welcome the work undertaken by the international organizations on capital flows. The OECD has completed a review of its Code of Liberalization of Capital Movements. We will continue our work on the EPG's proposals, recognizing their multi-year nature.

15. We reiterate the importance of joint efforts undertaken by both borrowers and creditors, official and private, to improve debt transparency and secure debt sustainability. We call on the IMF and WBG to continue their efforts to strengthen borrowers' capacity in the areas of debt recording, monitoring, and reporting, debt management, public financial management, and domestic resource mobilization, including under their multi-pronged approach. In the context of the review of the Debt Limits Policy and Non-Concessional Borrowing Policy, we encourage the IMF and WBG to continue their

efforts to deepen their analysis of collateralized financing practices. We welcome the completion of the voluntary self-assessment of the implementation of the G20 Operational Guidelines for Sustainable Financing and the IMF-WBG note on the survey results and policy recommendation. We applaud G20 and non-G20 members who completed the survey and call for continued discussion of the issues highlighted by this note, aiming to improve financing practices. We support the work of the Institute of International Finance on the Voluntary Principles for Debt Transparency to improve debt transparency and sustainability of private financing and look forward to follow up. We support the ongoing work of the Paris Club, as the principal international forum for restructuring official bilateral debt, towards the broader engagement of emerging creditors and welcome India associating voluntarily with the Paris Club to cooperate in its work on a case-by-case basis.

16. We will continue our cooperation for a globally fair, sustainable, and modern international tax system, and welcome international cooperation to advance pro-growth tax policies. We reaffirm the importance of the worldwide implementation of the G20/OECD Base Erosion and Profit Shifting (BEPS) package and enhanced tax certainty. We welcome the recent progress on addressing the tax challenges arising from digitalization and endorse the ambitious work program that consists of a two-pillar approach, developed by the Inclusive Framework on BEPS. We will redouble our efforts for a consensus-based solution with a final report by 2020. We welcome the recent achievements on tax transparency, including the progress on automatic exchange of information for tax purposes. We also welcome an updated list of jurisdictions that have not satisfactorily implemented the internationally agreed tax transparency standards. We look forward to a further update by the OECD of the list that takes into account all of the strengthened criteria. Defensive measures will be considered against listed jurisdictions. The 2015 OECD report inventories available measures in this regard. We call on all jurisdictions to sign and ratify the multilateral Convention on Mutual Administrative Assistance in Tax Matters. We reiterate our support for tax capacity building in developing countries.

17. Technological innovations can deliver significant benefits to the financial system and the broader economy. While crypto-assets do

not pose a threat to global financial stability at this point, we are closely monitoring developments and remain vigilant to existing and emerging risks. We welcome on-going work by the Financial Stability Board (FSB) and other standard setting bodies and ask them to advise on additional multilateral responses as needed. We reaffirm our commitment to applying the recently amended FATF Standards to virtual assets and related providers for anti-money laundering and countering the financing of terrorism. We welcome the adoption of the Financial Action Task Force (FATF) Interpretive Note and Guidance. We also welcome the FSB's work on the possible implications of decentralized financial technologies and how regulators can engage other stakeholders. We also continue to step up efforts to enhance cyber resilience.

18. We welcome the United Nations Security Council Resolution 2462, which stresses the essential role of the FATF in setting global standards for preventing and combatting money laundering, terrorist financing and proliferation financing. We reiterate our strong commitment to step up efforts to fight these threats, including by strengthening the FATF's global network of regional bodies. We call for the full, effective and swift implementation of the FATF Standards.

19. An open and resilient financial system, grounded in agreed international standards, is crucial to support sustainable growth. We remain committed to the full, timely and consistent implementation of the agreed financial reforms. We ask the FSB to continue to evaluate their effects. We will continue to monitor and, as necessary, address vulnerabilities and emerging risks to financial stability, including with macroprudential tools. While non-bank financing provides welcome diversity to the financial system, we will continue to identify, monitor and address related financial stability risks as appropriate. We welcome the work on market fragmentation, and will address its unintended, negative effects, including through regulatory and supervisory cooperation. We continue to monitor and address the causes and consequences of the withdrawal of correspondent banking relationships. Mobilizing sustainable finance and strengthening financial inclusion are important for global growth. We welcome private sector participation and transparency in these areas.

Anti-corruption

20. We remain committed to play a leading role in the global efforts to prevent and fight against corruption, as well as promoting integrity, by implementing the G20 Anti-Corruption Action Plan 2019-2021 while strengthening synergies among related international instruments and mechanisms. Recognizing that countering corruption is an important requisite for ensuring quality and reliability of infrastructure, we welcome the Compendium of Good Practices for Promoting Integrity and Transparency in Infrastructure Development as part of our further work. We endorse the High Level Principles for Effective Protection of Whistleblowers. We renew our commitment to pursuing high level international cooperation between G20 members in the fight against corruption and to lead by example through the effective implementation of the United Nations Convention against Corruption, including its review process. We will intensify our efforts to combat foreign bribery and to ensure that each G20 country has a national law in force for criminalizing foreign bribery as soon as possible. We take note of the efforts towards adherence to the OECD Convention on Combating Bribery of Foreign Public Officials in International Business Transactions. We will continue practical cooperation to fight corruption and reaffirm our commitment to deny safe haven to persons sought for corruption and their proceeds of corruption consistent with our G20 and international commitments and our domestic legal systems and will work more closely on asset recovery cooperation. We look forward to the scoping paper on international cooperation dealing with serious economic offenders and recovery of stolen assets in relation to corruption to be prepared by relevant international organizations. In addition, we also welcome the work on the linkages between corruption and gender being undertaken by relevant international organizations.

Creating a Virtuous Cycle of Growth by Addressing Inequalities

Labour and Employment

21. Population ageing is progressing in G20 members at different rates. Taking into account the commonalities and differences among G20 demographics, we recognize the importance of promoting an healthy

and active ageing society that enables workers to participate in the labour market at older ages, while continuing to increase participation of youth, women and persons with disabilities in economic activities. We will boost job creation and flexible work arrangements, seek to raise quality of employment and enhance employability of workers through lifelong learning as working lives are expected to be longer, and strive towards improving the working conditions for all including, long-term care workers in accordance with national circumstances. We will also continue to promote employment opportunities for and employability of the young population. We ask Ministers of Labour and Employment to identify possible policy priorities for adapting to demographic trends when they meet in Matsuyama in September. We recognize that emerging new forms of work, particularly those driven by technological innovation can be a source of job opportunities but may also pose challenges for decent work and social protection systems. We encourage Labour and Employment Ministers to further exchange experiences and good practices as we endeavor to develop adequate policy responses to these new forms of work, taking into account the view of the private sector. We remain committed to promote decent work and reaffirm our commitment to take actions to eradicate child labour, forced labour, human trafficking and modern slavery in the world of work, including through fostering sustainable global supply chains.

Women's Empowerment

22. Gender equality and women's empowerment are essential for achieving sustainable and inclusive economic growth. We reconfirm their importance in all aspects of our policies and as a cross-cutting issue at upcoming Summits. We note that further progress has been made towards the Brisbane Goal, to reduce the gap in labour force participation between men and women by 25 per cent by 2025. We take note of the progress report Women at Work in G20 Countries prepared by the International Labour Organization (ILO) and OECD, and acknowledge the need to accelerate our efforts. Building on the continued efforts by Labour and Employment Ministers, we will exchange our respective progress and actions taken in the G20 towards the Brisbane Goal, including the quality of women's employment, on the basis of the annual report. We will also address

the gender gap in unpaid care work which remains a major obstacle to women's participation in the labour market. We commit to take further action to improve the quality of women's employment, reduce gender pay gaps, and end all forms of discrimination against women and combat stereotypes and to recognize women as agents of peace, and in the prevention and resolution of conflict.

23. We commit to continue support for girls' and women's education and training, including providing quality primary and secondary education, improved access to STEM (Science, Technology, Engineering and Mathematics) education and raising awareness toward eliminating gender stereotypes. In order to close the digital gender gap, we will continue enhancing girls' and women's access to digital technology with a focus on the needs of those in poverty and rural areas. We reaffirm the importance of taking measures to eradicate all gender-based violence, abuse and harassment, including in the digital context. We welcome efforts, particularly by the private sector, to promote women's access to managerial and decision making positions and foster women business leaders and entrepreneurship. We reaffirm the importance of taking measures to support skills development and provide access to funding to promote women's entrepreneurship and welcome the continued implementation of the Women Entrepreneurs Finance Initiative (We-Fi) in support of women's entrepreneurship in developing countries including in Africa. We recognize the importance of encouraging efforts by the private sector including by acknowledging companies that are taking measures to increase the number of women in management and decision making positions and making gender responsive investments. We welcome the launch of the private sector alliance for the 'Empowerment and Progression of Women's Economic Representation (EMPOWER)' and call upon the alliance to advocate for the advancement of women in the private sector, and we will take stock of their progress and share their concrete efforts at our upcoming Summits.

Tourism

24. Tourism accounts for a significant share of the world's GDP and is expected to continue to be an important driver of global economic growth. We will work to maximize the sector's contribution to the

creation of quality jobs and entrepreneurship, especially for women and youth and in the creative industry; economic resilience and recovery; the preservation of natural resources through sustainable tourism planning and management; and the achievement of inclusive and sustainable development.

Agriculture

25. In order to achieve food security and improve nutrition for the growing world population, agricultural productivity needs to increase and distribution needs to be more efficient, including by reducing food loss and waste, in a way more compatible with the sustainable management of natural resources. To this end, we highlight the importance of access to and utilization of existing, new and advanced technologies, such as Information and Communication Technology (ICT), Artificial Intelligence (AI) and robotics among others, and encourage cross-sectoral collaboration among stakeholders. We also encourage innovation, skills training and lifelong education for all, in attracting new entrants and empowering youth and women in the agro-food sector. We recognize the importance of developing sustainable, science-based and resilient agro-food value chains, in an inclusive and equitable manner, including family farming and small scale farmers, which will also contribute to revitalizing rural areas. We emphasize the need for continued and enhanced information sharing and research collaboration to respond to existing and emerging animal and plant health issues. We will further encourage voluntary exchange of good practices and knowledge towards more sustainable agro-food sector.

Realizing an Inclusive and Sustainable World

Development

26. With a view to the United Nations High Level Political Forum and High-level Dialogue on Financing for Development in September, we remain resolved to playing a leading role in contributing to the timely implementation of the 2030 Agenda for Sustainable Development and the Addis Ababa Action Agenda. We recognize that international public and private finance for development as well as other innovative financing mechanisms, including blended finance,

can play an important role in upscaling our collective efforts. Building on the G20's Action Plan on the 2030 Agenda for Sustainable Development, the Osaka Update underscores the G20's collective and concrete actions contributing to the implementation of the 2030 Agenda and helping to ensure that "no one is left behind". We welcome the Osaka Comprehensive Accountability Report.

27. We support developing countries in their efforts to advance progress towards the timely implementation of the SDGs in such areas as poverty eradication, quality infrastructure investment, gender equality, health, education, agriculture, environment, energy, and industrialization, using all means of implementation, such as the mobilization of private sector resources and capacity building assistance. We reiterate our continued support to the G20 Africa partnership, including the Compact with Africa (CwA), with strengthened bilateral engagement by G20 members and enhanced roles for WBG, African Development Bank, and IMF in implementing the CwA, and G20 initiative on supporting the industrialization of Africa and other relevant initiatives that contribute to the realization of the African vision as set out in the African Union's Agenda 2063. We remain committed to address illicit financial flows and will take stock at future Summits.

28. We reaffirm our commitment to invest in human capital and promote inclusive and equitable quality education for all as emphasized in the G20 Initiative on Human Capital Investment for Sustainable Development. Recognizing the importance of science, technology and innovation (STI) for SDGs, we endorse the Guiding Principles for the Development of STI for SDGs Roadmaps. We recognize the importance of further efforts on North-South, South-South and triangular co-operation as well as disaster risk reduction including disaster risk financing and insurance schemes as a means to promote financial resilience against natural disasters.

29. We will continue our work towards achieving a successful 19th replenishment of the International Development Association, as well as a 15th replenishment of the African Development Fund. We call for full and timely implementation of the capital increase package of the International Bank for Reconstruction and Development and the International Finance Corporation in view of their expanded roles.

Global Health

30. Health is a prerequisite for sustainable and inclusive economic growth. We recall our commitment to moving towards achieving universal health coverage according to national contexts and priorities. We look forward to the United Nations General Assembly High Level Meeting on Universal Health Coverage (UHC). Primary health care including access to medicines, vaccination, nutrition, water and sanitation, health promotion and disease prevention is a cornerstone for advancing health and inclusion. We will strengthen health systems with a focus on quality including through enhancing health workforce and human resources for policy development and promoting public and private sector innovation, such as cost-effective and appropriate digital and other innovative technologies. Recognizing the importance of sustainable financing for health, we will call for greater collaboration between health and finance authorities in accordance with the G20 Shared Understanding on the Importance of UHC Financing in Developing Countries, to which our commitment was affirmed by our Finance and Health Ministers at their Joint Session. We encourage international organizations and all stakeholders to collaborate effectively and we look forward to the upcoming presentation of the global action plan for healthy lives and well-being for all.

31. We will promote healthy and active ageing through policy measures to address health promotion, prevention and control of communicable and non-communicable diseases, and through people-centered, multi-sectoral, community-based integrated health and long-term care over the life course in accordance with national context including demographic trends. We will implement comprehensive set of policies to address dementia, including promoting risk reduction and sustainable provision of long-term care as well as inclusive societies aiming to improve quality of lives of people with dementia and caregivers.

32. We are committed to improving public health preparedness and response including strengthening our own core capacities and supporting capacities of other countries in compliance with the World Health Organization (WHO) International Health Regulations (2005). We will support countries suffering from the current Ebola outbreak in Africa, through both timely financial and technical assistance and

in line with the central coordination responsibility that WHO has for international responses to health emergencies. We will work for the sustainability and efficiency of global health emergency financing mechanisms. We reaffirm our commitment to eradicate polio as well as to end the epidemics of AIDS, tuberculosis and malaria and look forward to the success of the sixth replenishment of the Global Fund to fight AIDS, Tuberculosis, and Malaria.

33. We will accelerate efforts based on the One-Health approach to tackle antimicrobial resistance (AMR). Recognizing the UN Secretary-General's report on AMR, which was informed by the recommendations of the UN Interagency Coordination Group on AMR and other relevant initiatives, we encourage all stakeholders including international organizations to act and coordinate on those items relevant to their missions that contribute to global efforts to combat AMR. We recognize the need for policy measures for infection prevention and reduction of excessive antimicrobial usage. Further action should be taken to promote stewardship of and access to antimicrobials. Noting the ongoing work done by Global AMR R&D Hub, we will promote R&D to tackle AMR. We call on interested G20 members and Global AMR R&D Hub to analyze push and pull mechanisms to identify best models for AMR R&D and to report back to relevant G20 Ministers.

Global Environmental Issues and Challenges

34. Noting the important work of the International Panel on Climate Change (IPCC) and Intergovernmental Science-policy Platform on Biodiversity and Ecosystem Sources (IPBES), and in the light of recent extreme weather events and disasters, we recognize the urgent need for addressing complex and pressing global issues and challenges, including climate change, resource efficiency, air, land, fresh water and marine pollution, including marine plastic litter, biodiversity loss, sustainable consumption and production, urban environmental quality and other environmental issues, and for promoting and leading energy transitions, with the best available science, while promoting sustainable growth. A paradigm shift is needed where the virtuous cycle of environment and growth is accelerated through innovations, and with business communities playing an important role, in synergy with the public sector. To this end we stress the

importance of accelerating the virtuous cycle and leading transformations to a resilient, inclusive, and sustainable future. We emphasize the importance of taking concrete and practical actions and collecting international best practices and wisdom from around the world, mobilizing public and private finance, technology and investment and improving business environments.

Climate Change

35. To this end, we strive to foster inclusive finance for sustainable development, including public and private financing mobilization and alignment between them, as well as innovation in a wide range of areas for low emissions and resilient development. Climate actions at all levels with broad participation, including by non- state actors, will be the key to realizing such a paradigm shift. In further enhancing this effort, as appropriate to each country's circumstances, we will look into a wide range of clean technologies and approaches, including smart cities, ecosystem and community based approaches, nature based solutions and traditional and indigenous knowledge. We need to enhance efforts to support actions and cooperation in adaptation and disaster risk reduction, in particular, for the most vulnerable communities, and to elaborate further and foster coherence between mitigation action, adaptation measures, environmental protection, and resilient infrastructure. We note the successful adoption of the implementation guidelines for the Paris Agreement and the completion of the stocktaking of the Talanoa Dialogue at the United Nations Framework Convention on Climate Change Conference of Parties (UNFCCC COP) 24 and the outcomes of the meeting of G20 energy and environment ministers in Karuizawa, subsequent to the successful G20 Buenos Aires Summit. We are determined to make best use of this momentum, and thus look forward to a successful Climate Action Summit of the UN Secretary-General and concrete outcomes at UNFCCC COP 25 in Santiago, Chile. Signatories to the Paris Agreement who confirmed at Buenos Aires its irreversibility and are determined to implement it, reaffirm their commitment to its full implementation, reflecting common but differentiated responsibilities and respective capabilities, in the light of different national circumstances. By 2020 we aim to communicate, update or maintain our NDCs, taking into account that further global

efforts are needed. We emphasize the importance of providing financial resources to assist developing countries with respect to both mitigation and adaptation in accordance with the Paris Agreement.

36. The United States reiterates its decision to withdraw from the Paris Agreement because it disadvantages American workers and taxpayers. The U.S. reaffirms its strong commitment to promoting economic growth, energy security and access, and environmental protection. The U.S.'s balanced approach to energy and environment allows for the delivery of affordable, reliable, and secure energy to all its citizens while utilizing all energy sources and technologies, including clean and advanced fossil fuels and technologies, renewables, and civil nuclear power, while also reducing emissions and promoting economic growth. The United States is a world leader in reducing emissions. U.S. energy-related CO2 emissions fell by 14% between 2005 and 2017 even as its economy grew by 19.4% largely due to the development and deployment of innovative energy technologies. The United States remains committed to the development and deployment of advanced technologies to continue to reduce emissions and provide for a cleaner environment.

Energy

37. We acknowledge the importance of energy transitions that realize the "3E+S" (Energy Security, Economic Efficiency, and Environment + Safety) in order to transform our energy systems into affordable, reliable, sustainable and low GHG emissions systems as soon as possible, recognizing that there are different possible national paths to achieve this goal. Recalling the G20 Ministerial Meeting on Energy Transitions and Global Environment for Sustainable Growth Communique, we acknowledge the role of all energy sources and technologies in the energy mix and different possible national paths to achieve cleaner energy systems. We also recognize opportunities offered by further development of innovative, clean and efficient technologies for energy transitions, including hydrogen as well as, depending on national circumstances, the Carbon Capture, Utilization and Storage (CCUS) taking note of work on "Carbon Recycling" and "Emissions to Value". We acknowledge the G20 Japanese Presidency's initiative called Research and Development 20 for clean energy technologies ("RD20"). In light of recent events highlighting concern

about safe flow of energy, we acknowledge the importance of global energy security as one of the guiding principles for the transformation of energy systems, including resilience, safety and development of infrastructure and undisrupted flow of energy from various sources, suppliers, and routes. We recognize the value of international cooperation on a wide range of energy-related issues including energy access, affordability and energy efficiency, and energy storage. We reaffirm our joint commitment on medium term rationalization and phasing-out of Inefficient Fossil Fuel Subsidies that encourage wasteful consumption, while providing targeted support for the poorest.

Environment

38. We recognize that improving resource efficiency through policies and approaches, such as circular economy, sustainable materials management, the 3Rs (reduce, reuse, recycle) and waste to value, contributes to the SDGs, as well as to addressing a wide range of environmental challenges, enhancing competitiveness and economic growth, managing resources sustainably, and creating jobs. We encourage work with the private sector towards innovation in the cooling sector. We will also work with stakeholders in order to increase the demand for recycled products. We look forward to the development of a roadmap of the G20 Resource Efficiency Dialogue under the Japanese Presidency.

39. We reiterate that measures to address marine litter, especially marine plastic litter and microplastics, need to be taken nationally and internationally by all countries in partnership with relevant stakeholders. In this regard, we are determined to swiftly take appropriate national actions for the prevention and significant reduction of discharges of plastic litter and microplastics to the oceans. Furthermore, looking ahead beyond those initiatives and existing actions by each member, we share, and call on other members of the international community to also share, as a common global vision, the "Osaka Blue Ocean Vision" that we aim to reduce additional pollution by marine plastic litter to zero by 2050 through a comprehensive life-cycle approach that includes reducing the discharge of mismanaged plastic litter by improved waste management and innovative solutions while recognizing the

important role of plastics for society. We also endorse the G20 Implementation Framework for Actions on Marine Plastic Litter.

40. As illegal, unreported, and unregulated (IUU) fishing remains in many parts of the world a serious threat to the sustainability of the ocean, we recognize the importance of addressing IUU fishing for ensuring the sustainable use of marine resources and conserving the marine environment including biodiversity, and reaffirm our commitment to end IUU fishing.

Displacement and Migration

41. We note the 2019 Annual International Migration and Displacement Trends and Policies Report to the G20 prepared by the OECD in cooperation with ILO, International Organization for Migration (IOM) and United Nations High Commissioner for Refugees (UNHCR). We will continue the dialogue on the various dimensions of these issues in the G20.

42. Large movements of refugees are a global concern with humanitarian, political, social and economic consequences. We emphasize the importance of shared actions to address the root causes of displacement and to respond to growing humanitarian needs.

43. We thank Japan for its Presidency and for hosting a successful Osaka Summit and its contribution to the G20 process, and we look forward to meeting again in Saudi Arabia in 2020, in Italy in 2021 and in India in 2022.

(7) RIYADH 2020

SAUDI ARABIA 2020
RIYADH SUMMIT

LEADERS' DECLARATION

Riyadh Summit, November 21, 2020

1. We, the G20 Leaders, meeting for the second time under the Saudi Presidency, stand united in our conviction that coordinated global action, solidarity, and multilateral cooperation are more necessary today than ever to overcome the current challenges and realize opportunities of the 21st century for all by empowering people, safeguarding the planet, and shaping new frontiers. We are committed to leading the world in shaping a strong, sustainable, balanced and inclusive post- A. Rising to the Challenge Together

2. The COVID-19 pandemic and its unprecedented impact in terms of lives lost, livelihoods and economies affected, is an unparalleled shock that has revealed vulnerabilities in our preparedness and response and underscored our common challenges. We reiterate the commitments of our Extraordinary Summit on March 26, welcome the progress achieved since, and will continue to spare no effort to protect lives, provide support with a special focus on the most vulnerable, and put our economies back on a path to restoring growth, and protecting and creating jobs for all. We express our gratitude to and support for health and other frontline workers as we continue to fight this pandemic. We remain determined to support all developing and least developed countries as they face the intertwined health,

economic, and social effects of COVID-19, recognizing the specific challenges in Africa and small island developing states.

3. We have mobilized resources to address the immediate financing needs in global health to support the research, development, manufacturing, and distribution of safe and effective COVID-19 diagnostics, therapeutics and vaccines. We will spare no effort to ensure their affordable and equitable access for all people, consistent with members' commitments to incentivize innovation. In this regard, we fully support all collaborative efforts, especially the Access to COVID-19 Tools Accelerator (ACT-A) initiative and its COVAX facility, and the voluntary licensing of intellectual property. We commit to addressing the remaining global financing needs, welcome the efforts made by the multilateral development banks to strengthen the financial support for countries' access to COVID-19 tools, in line with existing multilateral efforts, and encourage them to do more. We recognize the role of extensive immunization as a global public good.

4. While the global economy experienced a sharp contraction in 2020 due to the impact of the COVID-19 pandemic, global economic activity has partially picked up as our economies gradually reopened and the positive impact of our significant policy actions started to materialize. However, the recovery is uneven, highly uncertain and subject to elevated downside risks, including those arising from renewed virus outbreaks in some economies, with some countries reintroducing restrictive health measures. We underscore the urgent need to bring the spread of the virus under control, which is key to supporting global economic recovery. We are determined to continue to use all available policy tools as long as required to safeguard people's lives, jobs and incomes, support the global economic recovery, and enhance the resilience of the financial system, while safeguarding against downside risks. We also reaffirm the exchange rate commitments made by our Finance Ministers and Central Bank Governors in March 2018.

5. We are taking immediate and exceptional measures to address the COVID-19 pandemic and its intertwined health, social and economic impacts, including through the implementation of unprecedented fiscal, monetary and financial stability actions, consistent with governments' and central banks' respective mandates, while ensuring

that the international financial institutions and relevant international organizations continue to provide critical support to emerging, developing and low-income countries. Based on the International Labour Organization (ILO) estimates, our efforts to temporarily extend social protection measures have supported the livelihoods of nearly 645 million people.

6. The G20 Action Plan sets out key principles and commitments to drive forward international economic cooperation as we navigate this crisis and take steps to support the recovery and achieve strong, sustainable, balanced and inclusive growth. Recognizing that members are in different stages of responding to the crisis and that the global economic outlook continues to evolve, we endorse the October 2020 updates to the G20 Action Plan, which will ensure that we continue to promptly respond to the evolving health and economic situation and make the most of ongoing economic, social, environmental, technological and demographic changes. We also endorse the second G20 Action Plan Progress Report, which provides up to date information on progress made against Action Plan commitments. The G20 Action Plan is a living document, and we ask our Finance Ministers and Central Bank Governors to continue to regularly review, update, track implementation of, and report on it.

7. We are committed to implementing the Debt Service Suspension Initiative (DSSI) including its extension through June 2021, allowing DSSI-eligible countries to suspend official bilateral debt service payments. We welcome the progress achieved thus far. The preliminary reporting from the International Monetary Fund (IMF) and the World Bank Group (WBG) highlighted that, together with exceptional financing, the DSSI is significantly facilitating higher pandemic-related spending. The IMF and WBG will continue to work on their proposal of a process to strengthen the quality and consistency of debt data and improve debt disclosure. We reiterate the importance of joint efforts by both borrowers and creditors, official and private, to improve debt transparency. Our Finance Ministers and Central Bank Governors will examine by the time of the 2021 IMF/WBG Spring Meetings if the economic and financial situation requires further extension of the DSSI by another 6 months, which is also agreed by the Paris Club. All official bilateral creditors should

implement this initiative fully and in a transparent manner. We will continue to closely coordinate its ongoing implementation to provide maximum support to DSSI-eligible countries. There is a lack of participation from private creditors, and we strongly encourage them to participate on comparable terms when requested by eligible countries. While protecting their current rating and low cost of funding, multilateral development banks (MDBs) are encouraged to go further on their collective efforts in supporting the DSSI, including through providing net-positive flows to DSSI-eligible countries during the suspension period, including the extension period. As of 13 November 2020, 46 countries have requested to benefit from the DSSI, amounting to an estimated USD 5.7 billion of 2020 debt service deferral.

8. Given the scale of the COVID-19 crisis, the significant debt vulnerabilities and deteriorating outlook in many low-income countries, we recognize that debt treatments beyond the DSSI may be required on a case-by-case basis. In this context, we endorse the "Common Framework for Debt Treatments beyond the DSSI", which is also endorsed by the Paris Club.

9. Our ongoing response to the crisis caused by COVID-19 marks a defining moment in our history. Building on the benefits of our interconnectedness, we will address the vulnerabilities revealed by this crisis, take the necessary steps to recover stronger, and work to ensure that future generations are safer than we have been.

B. Building a Resilient and Long-Lasting Recovery

10. **Health:** We commit to advancing global pandemic preparedness, prevention, detection, and response. We reaffirm our commitment to full compliance with the International Health Regulations (IHR 2005), to improving their implementation, including through supporting capacities of countries in need, and to the continued sharing of timely, transparent, and standardized data and information. We emphasize the important mandates of the United Nations' system and agencies, primarily the WHO, while considering the ongoing evaluations, its stated commitment to transparency, and the need to strengthen its overall effectiveness, in coordinating and supporting the global response to the pandemic and the central efforts of Member States. We take note of the assessments of gaps in

pandemic preparedness undertaken by relevant international organizations and we look forward to the work of the Independent Panel for Pandemic Preparedness and Response and the IHR Review Committee on evaluating the global health response to the pandemic as outlined in the World Health Assembly (WHA) Resolution on COVID-19. We commend the Saudi Presidency for initiating discussions on the need for long-term solutions to address gaps in global pandemic preparedness and response, including its proposal towards establishing access to pandemic tools, and we look forward to furthering this discussion during the Italian Presidency.

11. Well-functioning, value-based, inclusive, and resilient health systems are critical to move towards achieving Universal Health Coverage (UHC). We reconfirm the importance of UHC financing in developing countries. We welcome the establishment of the Global Innovation Hub for Improving Value in Health, with which countries can engage on a voluntary basis. We will continue tackling antimicrobial resistance (AMR) and zoonotic diseases based on the One-Health approach; supporting and accelerating research and development (R&D) of new antimicrobials; ensuring access to existing antimicrobials, while enhancing their prudent stewardship; and maintaining our efforts in tackling infectious and non-communicable diseases.

12. **Trade and Investment:** Supporting the multilateral trading system is now as important as ever. We strive to realize the goal of a free, fair, inclusive, non-discriminatory, transparent, predictable, and stable trade and investment environment, and to keep our markets open. We will continue to work to ensure a level playing field to foster an enabling business environment. We endorse the G20 Actions to Support World Trade and Investment in Response to COVID-19. We recognize the contribution that the Riyadh Initiative on the Future of the World Trade Organization (WTO) has made by providing an additional opportunity to discuss and reaffirm the objectives and foundational principles of the multilateral trading system as well as to demonstrate our ongoing political support for the necessary reform of the WTO, including in the lead up to the 12th WTO Ministerial Conference. We recognize the need to increase the sustainability and resilience of national, regional, and global supply chains that foster the sustainable integration of developing and least developed

countries into the trading system, and share the objective of promoting inclusive economic growth including through increased participation of micro-, small-, medium-sized enterprises (MSMEs) in international trade and investment. We note that structural problems in some sectors, such as excess capacities, can cause a negative impact.

13. **International Financial Architecture:** We reiterate our commitment to ensure a stronger global financial safety net with a strong, quota-based, and adequately resourced IMF at its center. We remain committed to revisiting the adequacy of quotas and will continue the process of IMF governance reform under the 16th general review of quotas, including a new quota formula as a guide, by 15 December 2023. We call on the IMF to continue exploring additional tools that could serve its members' needs as the crisis evolves, drawing on relevant experiences from previous crises. We also support the IMF's enhanced assistance to help address particular challenges faced by small developing states. Beyond the crisis response, we call on the IMF to prepare an analysis of the external financing needs in low income developing countries in the coming years and sustainable financing options, and on the WBG, to scale up its work and deploy instruments in new ways to mobilize private financing to these countries. We welcome the G20 Reference Framework for Effective Country Platforms and the country-owned pilot platforms that have been deployed and look forward to further updates by MDBs on progress in this area. We will strengthen long-term financial resilience and support growth, including through promoting sustainable capital flows and developing domestic capital markets.

14. **Transportation and Travel:** We commit to ensuring that global transportation routes and supply chains remain open, safe, and secure, and that any restrictive measures related to COVID-19, including for air and sea crews, are targeted, proportionate, transparent, temporary, and in accordance with obligations under international agreements. We will continue to explore concrete ways to facilitate the movement of people in a way that does not impede our efforts to protect public health.

15. **Infrastructure Investment:** Infrastructure is a driver of growth and prosperity and is critical to promoting economic recovery and resilience. We endorse the G20 Riyadh InfraTech Agenda, which promotes the use of technology in infrastructure, with the aim of

improving investment decisions, enhancing value for money, and promoting quality infrastructure investments for the delivery of better social, economic and environmental outcomes. In line with the G20 Roadmap for Infrastructure as an Asset Class, we welcome the G20/ OECD Report on the Collaboration with Institutional Investors and Asset Managers on Infrastructure Investment, which reflects investors' view on issues and challenges affecting private investment in infrastructure and presents policy options to address them. We look forward to exploring options to continue this work in a flexible manner and without duplications with other initiatives, with the participation of interested MDBs and international organizations. We will advance the work related to the G20 Principles for Quality Infrastructure Investment.

16. **Financial Sector Issues:** We commit to the Financial Stability Board (FSB)'s principles underpinning the national and international responses to COVID-19, including the need to act consistently with international standards, and ask the FSB to continue monitoring financial sector vulnerabilities, working on procyclicality and credit worthiness, and coordinating on regulatory and supervisory measures. We welcome the FSB's holistic review of the March 2020 turmoil, and its forward work plan to improve the resilience of the non-bank financial sector. The pandemic has reaffirmed the need to enhance global cross-border payment arrangements to facilitate cheaper, faster, more inclusive and more transparent payment transactions, including for remittances. We endorse the G20 Roadmap to Enhance Cross-Border Payments. We ask the FSB, in coordination with international organizations and standard-setting bodies, to monitor the progress, review the roadmap and annually report to the G20. We look forward to the FSB completing the evaluation of the effects of the too-big-to-fail reforms in 2021. Moreover, we reaffirm the importance of orderly transition away from LIBOR to alternative reference rates before end-2021. Mobilizing sustainable finance and strengthening financial inclusion are important for global growth and stability. The FSB is continuing to examine the financial stability implications of climate change. We welcome growing private sector participation and transparency in these areas.

17. While responsible technological innovations can deliver significant benefits to the financial system and the broader economy, we are

closely monitoring developments and remain vigilant to existing and emerging risks. No so-called 'global stablecoins' should commence operation until all relevant legal, regulatory and oversight requirements are adequately addressed through appropriate design and by adhering to applicable standards. We welcome the reports on the so-called 'global stablecoins' and other similar arrangements submitted by the FSB, the Financial Action Task Force (FATF) and the IMF. We look forward to the standard setting bodies engaging in the review of existing standards in light of these reports and making adjustments as needed. We look forward to the IMF's further work on macro-financial implications of digital currencies and so-called 'global stablecoins'.

18. We support the Anti-Money Laundering (AML)/Counter-Terrorist Financing (CFT) policy responses detailed in FATF's paper on COVID-19, and reaffirm our support for the FATF, as the global standard-setting body for preventing and combating money laundering, terrorist financing and proliferation financing. We reiterate our strong commitment to tackle all sources, techniques and channels of these threats. We reaffirm our commitment to strengthening the FATF's Global Network of regional bodies, including by supporting their expertise in mutual evaluations, and call for the full, effective and swift implementation of the FATF standards worldwide. We welcome the strengthening of the FATF standards to enhance global efforts to counter proliferation financing.

19. **Digital Economy:** Connectivity, digital technologies, and policies have played a key role in strengthening our response to the pandemic and facilitating the continuation of economic activity. We take note of the Policy Options to Support Digitalization of Business Models during COVID-19. We acknowledge that universal, secure, and affordable connectivity, is a fundamental enabler for the digital economy as well as a catalyst for inclusive growth, innovation and sustainable development. We acknowledge the importance of data free flow with trust and cross-border data flows. We reaffirm the role of data for development. We support fostering an open, fair, and non-discriminatory environment, and protecting and empowering consumers, while addressing the challenges related to privacy, data protection, intellectual property rights, and security. By continuing to address these challenges, in accordance with relevant applicable

legal frameworks, we can further facilitate data free flow and strengthen consumer and business trust. We recognize the importance of working with stakeholders to connect humanity by accelerating global internet penetration and bridging digital divides. We recognize the importance of promoting security in the digital economy and welcome the G20 Examples of Practices Related to Security in the Digital Economy. We will continue to promote multi-stakeholder discussions to advance innovation and a human-centered approach to Artificial Intelligence (AI), taking note of the Examples of National Policies to Advance the G20 AI Principles. We welcome both the G20 Smart Mobility Practices, as a contribution to the well-being and resilience of smart cities and communities, and the G20 Roadmap toward a Common Framework for Measuring the Digital Economy.

20. **International Taxation:** We will continue our cooperation for a globally fair, sustainable, and modern international tax system. We welcome the Reports on the Blueprints for Pillar 1 and Pillar 2 approved for public release by the G20/OECD Inclusive Framework on Base Erosion and Profit Shifting (BEPS). Building on this solid basis, we remain committed to further progress on both pillars and urge the G20/OECD Inclusive Framework on BEPS to address the remaining issues with a view to reaching a global and consensus-based solution by mid-2021. We welcome the report approved by the G20/OECD Inclusive Framework on BEPS on the tax policy implications of virtual currencies. We welcome the progress made on implementing the internationally agreed tax transparency standards and on the established automatic exchange of information. We will continue our support to developing countries in strengthening their tax capacity to build sustainable tax revenue bases.

21. **Anti-corruption:** We will continue to lead by example in the global fight against corruption. In this regard, we welcome the first G20 Anti-Corruption Ministerial Meeting. We will continue to promote global integrity in response to the pandemic, and we endorse the G20 Call to Action on Corruption and COVID-19. We commit to taking and promoting a multi-stakeholder approach, including with international organizations, the civil society, the media, and the private sector, to preventing and combating corruption. We welcome the Riyadh Initiative for Enhancing International Anti-Corruption Law Enforcement Cooperation. We endorse the G20 Action on

International Cooperation on Corruption and Economic Crimes, Offenders and the Recovery of Stolen Assets. We welcome the reformed approach to the G20 Anti-corruption Accountability Report, and endorse G20 High-Level Principles for: the Development and Implementation of National Anti-Corruption Strategies; Promoting Public Sector Integrity Through the Use of Information and Communications Technologies; and Promoting Integrity in Privatization and Public-Private Partnerships. We will demonstrate concrete efforts by 2021 towards criminalizing foreign bribery and enforcing foreign bribery legislation in line with article 16 of UNCAC, and with a view to possible adherence by all G20 countries to the Organisation for Economic Co-operation and Development (OECD) Anti-Bribery Convention. We welcome Saudi Arabia joining the OECD Working Group on Bribery.

C. Ensuring an Inclusive Recovery that Tackles Inequalities

22. **Sustainable Development:** The social and economic impact of the pandemic makes it even more urgent to accelerate efforts to end poverty and tackle inequalities and work to ensure that no-one is left behind. We endorse the G20 Support to COVID-19 Response and Recovery in Developing Countries, the G20 Guidelines on Quality Infrastructure for Regional Connectivity, and the Financing for Sustainable Development Framework. We remain resolved to play a leading role in contributing to the timely implementation of the 2030 Agenda for Sustainable Development and the Addis Ababa Action Agenda. Building on the G20 Action Plan on the 2030 Agenda for Sustainable Development, the Riyadh Update, with its new Accountability Framework, underscores the collective and concrete actions of the G20 contributing to the implementation of the 2030 Agenda and its Sustainable Development Goals. We are determined to support African countries in overcoming the crisis, including by exploring more sustainable financing options for growth in Africa. We reiterate our continued support for the G20 Initiative on Supporting the Industrialization in Africa and LDCs, G20 Africa Partnership and the Compact with Africa, and other relevant initiatives. We remain committed to addressing illicit financial flows.

23. **Access to Opportunities:** This crisis continues to have disproportionate economic and social impact on the most vulnerable

segments of society, reinforcing the need to enhance access to opportunities for all. We will continue our efforts to reduce inequalities, reaffirming our previous commitments to promote inclusive growth. We endorse the G20 Menu of Policy Options to Enhance Access to Opportunities for All that can be leveraged to support the immediate response to the COVID-19 pandemic and move towards a strong, sustainable, balanced and inclusive recovery. We also endorse the G20 High-level Policy Guidelines on Digital Financial Inclusion for Youth, Women, and SMEs prepared by the Global Partnership for Financial Inclusion (GPFI). We welcome the 2020 G20 Financial Inclusion Action Plan, which will guide the work of the GPFI for the next three years.

24. **Employment:** Tackling the devastating impact of the pandemic on labor markets remains our priority as millions of workers continue to face job and income loss. We recognize the importance of protecting and promoting decent jobs for all, especially for women and youth. We support access to comprehensive, robust, and adaptive social protection for all, including those in the informal economy, and endorse the use of the Policy Options for Adapting Social Protection to Reflect the Changing Patterns of Work. We recognize the importance of employment policies and programs in supporting job creation, and promote the use of social dialogue. We will continue to support workers through training and reskilling policies. We acknowledge the report from the ILO and the OECD on the Impact of COVID-19 on Global Labor Markets. We endorse the G20 Youth Roadmap 2025 in support of achieving the G20 Antalya Youth Goal to reduce the share of young people who are at most risk of being permanently left behind in the labor market by 15 percent by 2025. We call upon the ILO and the OECD to continue monitoring these matters. We will continue our efforts to eradicate child labor, forced labor, human trafficking, and modern slavery in the world of work.

25. **Women's Empowerment:** As many women have been disproportionately affected by the crisis, we will work to ensure that the pandemic does not widen gender inequalities and undermine the progress made in recent decades. Recalling relevant UN declarations, processes, and calls to action to empower women and girls, we reaffirm the importance of women's and girls' empowerment as a cross-cutting issue in all aspects of our policies and recognize

that women are a key driver of economic growth. We will continue to promote gender equality, as well as combat stereotypes, reduce pay gaps, and address the unequal distribution of unpaid work and care responsibilities between men and women. We will step up our efforts towards achieving the Brisbane Goal to reduce the gap in labor force participation between men and women by 25 percent by 2025 along with improving the quality of women's employment; we call on ILO and OECD to continue providing input to support our progress; and look forward to a roadmap under the next Presidency. We will take steps to remove the barriers to women's economic participation and entrepreneurship. We welcome the commencement, under the Saudi Presidency, of the Private Sector Alliance for the Empowerment and Progression of Women's Economic Representation (EMPOWER) for women's advancement in leadership positions.

26. **Education:** We have taken actions to mitigate the impact of the COVID-19 pandemic on education. We stress the importance of continuity of education in times of crisis through the implementation of measures to ensure safe in-person learning, effective quality distance and blended teaching and learning, as appropriate. Inclusive, equitable and quality education for all, especially for girls, remains key to unlocking a brighter future and fighting inequalities. It is the foundation of personal development as it provides children, youth, and adults with the knowledge, skills, values, and attitudes necessary to reach their full potential. We affirm the importance of improving the accessibility and affordability of the quality early childhood education, and building and retaining a qualified workforce. We recognize the value of fostering internationalization in education, while respecting national and sub-national laws, rules and policies.

27. **Tourism:** We will continue our efforts in collaboration with stakeholders, including the private sector, to facilitate the travel and tourism sector's recovery from the pandemic. We welcome the Tourism Community Initiative as a catalyst of sector recovery, including the creative economy. We endorse the G20 Guidelines for Inclusive Community Development through Tourism and encourage the use of the AlUla Framework for Inclusive Community Development Through Tourism that aim to create jobs, empower local communities, especially rural, safeguard the planet, and preserve

cultural heritage. We also endorse the G20 Guidelines for Action on Safe and Seamless Travel and welcome the establishment of the G20 Tourism Working Group.

28. **Migration and Forced Displacement:** We emphasize the importance of shared actions to: mitigate the impact of the pandemic on those in vulnerable situations, which may include refugees, migrants and forcibly displaced people; respond to growing humanitarian needs; and address the root causes of displacement. We note the 2020 Annual International Migration and Forced Displacement Trends and Policies Report to the G20 prepared by the OECD in cooperation with ILO, International Organization for Migration (IOM) and United Nations High Commissioner for Refugees (UNHCR). We will continue the dialogue on the various dimensions of these issues in the G20.

D. Ensuring a Sustainable Future

29. **Environment, Energy, Climate:** Preventing environmental degradation, conserving, sustainably using and restoring biodiversity, preserving our oceans, promoting clean air and clean water, responding to natural disasters and extreme weather events, and tackling climate change are among the most pressing challenges of our time. As we recover from the pandemic, we are committed to safeguarding our planet and building a more environmentally sustainable and inclusive future for all people.

30. We strengthen our resolve to conserve our marine and terrestrial environment in advance of the upcoming Conference of the Parties (COP15) to the Convention on Biological Diversity (CBD). We launch the Global Coral Reef R&D Accelerator Platform to conserve coral reefs and the Global Initiative on Reducing Land Degradation and Enhancing Conservation of Terrestrial Habitats to prevent, halt, and reverse land degradation. Building on existing initiatives, we share the ambition to achieve a 50 percent reduction of degraded land by 2040, on a voluntary basis. We reaffirm our commitment to reduce additional pollution by marine plastic litter, as articulated by the Osaka Blue Ocean Vision, and to end illegal, unreported, and unregulated fishing.

31. We stress our continued resolve to ensure a stable and uninterrupted supply of energy to achieve economic growth as we respond to the

challenges brought about by the pandemic. We recognize the importance of expediting universal access, relying on innovation across fuels and technology options, to affordable and reliable energy for all, in accordance with national circumstances, including ensuring access to clean cooking and electricity. In this regard, we recognize the importance of utilizing the widest variety of fuels and technology options, according to national context, and leading energy transitions to realize the "3E+S" (Energy Security, Economic Efficiency, and Environment + Safety). We acknowledge the importance of maintaining undisrupted flows of energy and exploring paths to enhanced energy security and markets stability, while promoting open, competitive, and free international energy markets. We endorse the G20 Initiative on Clean Cooking and Energy Access and G20 Energy Security and Markets Stability Cooperation. We welcome the measures and recommendations of the Energy Focus Group (EFG), as endorsed by the Energy Ministers party to the EFG, to rebalance the energy markets and continue short and long-term investments. We reaffirm our joint commitment on medium term rationalization and phasing-out of inefficient fossil fuel subsidies that encourage wasteful consumption, while providing targeted support for the poorest.

32. We endorse the Circular Carbon Economy (CCE) Platform, with its 4Rs framework (Reduce, Reuse, Recycle and Remove), recognizing the key importance and ambition of reducing emissions, taking into account system efficiency and national circumstances. The CCE is a voluntary, holistic, integrated, inclusive, pragmatic, and complementary approach to promote economic growth while enhancing environmental stewardship through managing emissions in all sectors including, but not limited to, energy, industry, mobility, and food. We acknowledge, in this context, the various voluntary opportunities and their acceleration highlighted by the CCE Guide. We acknowledge the Presidency Reports of the Climate Stewardship Working Group that can be utilized as a toolbox in addressing sustainability including climate change in the context of national circumstances. We also acknowledge the importance of fostering synergies between adaptation and mitigation, including through nature-based solutions and ecosystem-based approaches.

33. In advance of the United Nations Framework Convention on Climate

Change (UNFCCC) COP26 in Glasgow and the UNCBD COP15 in Kunming, we reiterate our support for tackling pressing environmental challenges, such as climate change and biodiversity loss, as we promote economic growth, energy security and access for all, and environmental protection. Signatories to the Paris Agreement who confirmed at Osaka their determination to implement it, once again, reaffirm their commitment to its full implementation, reflecting common but differentiated responsibilities and respective capabilities, in the light of different national circumstances. These signatories recall the request by COP21 to communicate or update their nationally determined contributions reflecting their highest possible ambition, in accordance with their obligations under the Paris Agreement, taking into account means of implementation; and emphasize the importance of providing and mobilizing a wide variety of financial resources, to assist developing countries in their adaptation and mitigation efforts, in accordance with the UNFCCC and the Paris Agreement, reaffirming the importance of international cooperation. In addition, these signatories reiterate the invitation to communicate by 2020 long-term low greenhouse gas emission development strategies. These signatories recall the commitment made by developed countries to a goal of mobilizing jointly USD 100 billion per year by 2020 to address the needs of developing countries. All G20 members also continue to support efforts and utilize all available approaches aimed at advancing environmental stewardship for future generations, and emphasize that further global efforts are needed to address these challenges, while maintaining healthy economies conducive to growth, decent jobs, and innovation.

34. **Agriculture:** We reaffirm our commitment to tackling the challenges in food security and nutrition, as well as reinforcing the efficiency, resilience, and sustainability of food and agriculture supply-chains, especially in light of the effects of the pandemic. A significant increase in responsible investment in agriculture and food systems is needed to meet the challenge of feeding the global population and we endorse the G20 Riyadh Statement to Enhance Implementation of Responsible Investment in Agriculture and Food Systems. We acknowledge the goal of voluntarily establishing intermediate country-specific targets to strengthen efforts towards halving global per capita food loss and waste by 2030.

35. **Water:** We acknowledge that affordable, reliable, and safe water, sanitation, and hygiene services are essential for human life and that access to clean water is critical to overcome the pandemic. We welcome the G20 Dialogue on Water as a basis to share best practices and promote innovation, and new technologies, on a voluntary basis, that will foster sustainable, resilient, and integrated water management.

36. We value the efforts to safeguard people's health through the postponement of major public events. As a symbol of humanity's resilience and global unity in overcoming COVID-19, we commend Japan's determination to host the Olympic and Paralympic Games Tokyo 2020 next year. We further commend the United Arab Emirates' resolve to host World Expo 2020 next year. We look forward to the Beijing Winter Olympics in 2022.

37. We thank Saudi Arabia for hosting a successful Riyadh Summit and its contribution to the G20 process. We look forward to our next meetings in Italy in 2021, Indonesia in 2022, India in 2023 and Brazil in 2024.

38. We thank the international organizations for their valuable input through their reports and technical advice. We commemorate the 75th anniversary of the United Nations. We express our appreciation for the valuable work undertaken by the G20 Engagement Groups.

(8) ROME 2021

G20 ROME LEADERS' DECLARATION

Rome, October 31, 2021

1. We, the Leaders of the G20, met in Rome on October 30th and 31st, to address today's most pressing global challenges and to converge upon common efforts to recover better from the COVID-19 crisis and enable sustainable and inclusive growth in our Countries and across the world. As the premier forum for international economic cooperation, we are committed to overcoming the global health and economic crisis stemming from the pandemic, which has affected billions of lives, dramatically hampered progress towards the achievement of the Sustainable Development Goals and disrupted global supply chains and international mobility. With this in mind, we express our profound gratitude to the health and care professionals, frontline workers, international organizations and scientific community for their relentless efforts to cope with COVID-19.
2. Underlining the crucial role of multilateralism in finding shared, effective solutions, we have agreed to further strengthen our common response to the pandemic, and pave the way for a global recovery, with particular regard to the needs of the most vulnerable. We have taken decisive measures to support Countries most in need to

overcome the pandemic, improve their resilience and address critical challenges such as ensuring food security and environmental sustainability. We have agreed upon a shared vision to combat climate change, and taken important steps towards the achievement of gender equality. We have also further advanced in our common efforts to ensure that the benefits of digitalization are shared broadly, safely and contribute to reducing inequalities.

3. **Global economy.** Over 2021, global economic activity has been recovering at a solid pace, thanks to the roll-out of vaccines and continued policy support. However, the recovery remains highly divergent across and within countries, and exposed to downside risks, in particular the possible spread of new variants of COVID-19 and uneven vaccination paces. We remain determined to use all available tools for as long as required to address the adverse consequences of the pandemic, in particular on those most impacted, such as women, youth, and informal and low-skilled workers, and on inequalities. We will continue to sustain the recovery, avoiding any premature withdrawal of support measures, while preserving financial stability and long-term fiscal sustainability and safeguarding against downside risks and negative spill-overs. Central banks are monitoring current price dynamics closely. They will act as needed to meet their mandates, including price stability, while looking through inflation pressures where they are transitory and remaining committed to clear communication of policy stances. We remain vigilant to the global challenges that are impacting on our economies, such as disruptions in supply chains. We will work together to monitor and address these issues as our economies recover and to support the stability of the global economy. We commit to advancing the forward-looking agenda set in the G20 Action Plan as updated in April 2021 and we welcome the fourth Progress Report. We reaffirm the commitments on exchange rates made by our Finance Ministers and Central Bank Governors in April 2021.

4. **Health.** Recognizing that vaccines are among the most important tools against the pandemic, and reaffirming that extensive COVID-19 immunization is a global public good, we will advance our efforts to ensure timely, equitable and universal access to safe, affordable, quality and effective vaccines, therapeutics and diagnostics, with particular regard to the needs of low- and middle-income countries.

To help advance toward the global goals of vaccinating at least 40 percent of the population in all countries by the end of 2021 and 70 percent by mid-2022, as recommended by the World Health Organization (WHO)'s global vaccination strategy, we will take steps to help boost the supply of vaccines and essential medical products and inputs in developing countries and remove relevant supply and financing constraints. We ask our Health Ministers to monitor progress toward this end and to explore ways to accelerate global vaccination as necessary.

5. We will reinforce global strategies to support research and development as well as to ensure their production and swift and equitable distribution worldwide, also by strengthening supply chains and by expanding and diversifying global vaccine manufacturing capacity at local and regional level, while promoting vaccine acceptance, confidence and fighting disinformation. To this end, we commit to refrain from WTO inconsistent export restrictions and to increase transparency and predictability in the delivery of vaccines. We reiterate our support to all pillars of the ACT-Accelerator, including COVAX, and will continue to improve its effectiveness. We support the extension of ACT-A's mandate throughout 2022 and acknowledge the formation of the Multilateral Leaders Task Force on COVID-19. We welcome the work undertaken by the COVAX ACT-A Facilitation Council Vaccine Manufacturing Working Group and its report aimed at creating a broader base for vaccine manufacturing. In particular, we will support increasing vaccine distribution, administration and local manufacturing capacity in LMICs, including through technology transfer hubs in various regions, such as the newly established mRNA Hubs in South Africa, Brazil and Argentina, and through joint production and processing arrangements. We will work together towards the recognition of COVID-19 vaccines deemed safe and efficacious by the WHO and in accordance with national legislation and circumstances, and to strengthen the organization's ability regarding approval of vaccines, including optimizing procedures and processes, with the aim of broadening the list of vaccines authorized for emergency use (EUL), while continuing to protect public health and ensuring privacy and data protection. As a collective G20 effort, and in light of the enduring vaccination gaps, we commit to substantially increase the provision of and access to

vaccines, as well as to therapeutics and diagnostics. We will enhance our efforts to ensure the transparent, rapid and predictable delivery and uptake of vaccines where they are needed. We call on the private sector and on multilateral financial institutions to contribute to this endeavor. We acknowledge the work of the World Bank Group in this respect and of the IMF and the WHO through the vaccine supply forecast dashboard.

6. We reaffirm our commitment to the Global Health Summit Rome Declaration as a compass for collective action and are committed to strengthening global health governance. We support the ongoing work on strengthening the leading and coordination role of an adequately and sustainably funded WHO. We acknowledge that financing for pandemic prevention, preparedness and response (PPR) has to become more adequate, more sustainable and better coordinated and requires a continuous cooperation between health and finance decision-makers, including to address potential financing gaps, mobilizing an appropriate mix of existing multilateral financing mechanisms and explore setting up new financing mechanisms. We establish a G20 Joint Finance-Health Task Force aimed at enhancing dialogue and global cooperation on issues relating to pandemic PPR, promoting the exchange of experiences and best practices, developing coordination arrangements between Finance and Health Ministries, promoting collective action, assessing and addressing health emergencies with cross-border impact, and encouraging effective stewardship of resources for pandemic PPR, while adopting a One Health approach. Within this context, this Task Force will work, and report back by early 2022, on modalities to establish a financial facility, to be designed inclusively with the central coordination role of the WHO, G20-driven and engaging from the outset Low- and Middle-Income Countries, additional non-G20 partners and Multilateral Development Banks, to ensure adequate and sustained financing for pandemic prevention, preparedness and response.

7. We reaffirm our commitment to achieve the health-related SDGs, in particular Universal Health Coverage. We welcome multilateral efforts aimed at supporting and strengthening pandemic preparedness and response, including consideration of a possible international instrument or agreement in the context of the WHO, and at strengthening implementation of and compliance with the

International Health Regulations 2005. We commit to pursue a One Health approach at global, regional, national and local levels. To this end, we will enhance global surveillance, early detection and early warning systems, under the coordinating role of the WHO, FAO, OIE and UNEP, and address risks emerging from the human-animal-environment interface, particularly the emergence of zoonotic diseases, while pursuing global efforts to fight antimicrobial resistance, while ensuring access to antimicrobials and their prudent stewardship, and continuing to address other critical issues, including non-communicable diseases and mental health. Acknowledging the importance of swiftly reacting to pandemics, we will support science to shorten the cycle for the development of safe and effective vaccines, therapeutics and diagnostics from 300 to 100 days following the identification of such threats and work to make them widely available.

8. We reaffirm the importance of ensuring the continuity of health services beyond COVID-19 and of strengthening national health systems and primary health care services, in light of the repercussions of the pandemic on mental health and well-being, due to isolation, unemployment, food insecurity, increased violence against women and girls and constrained access to education as well as health services, including sexual and reproductive health, paying special attention to women and girls and to the needs of the most vulnerable. We will continue to support initiatives aimed at fighting AIDS, Tuberculosis and Malaria. We will pursue our efforts to enhance innovation in digital and other health-related technologies, taking into account the need to protect personal health data, encourage voluntary technology transfer on mutually agreed terms, and work with the WHO towards updating and reinforcing public health workforce operation standards through enhanced health curricula and training materials. To this end, we will pursue our engagement with the Global Innovation Hub for Improving Value in Health and we welcome the launch of the WHO Academy and initiatives such as the Public Health Workforce *Laboratorium* proposed by the Italian G20 Presidency.

9. **Sustainable Development.** We remain deeply concerned about the impacts of the COVID-19 crisis, especially in developing countries, which has set back progress towards the 2030 Agenda for Sustainable Development and the Addis Ababa Action Agenda. We reaffirm our

commitment to a global response to accelerate progress on the implementation of the SDGs and to support a sustainable, inclusive and resilient recovery across the world, able to promote equity and accelerate progress on all SDGs, recognizing the importance of nationally owned strategies, SDG localization, women and youth empowerment, sustainable production and responsible consumption patterns, and access to affordable, reliable, sustainable and modern energy for all. We will strengthen our actions to implement the G20 Action Plan on the 2030 Agenda and the G20 Support to COVID-19 Response and Recovery in developing countries, building on the 2021 Rome Update, with particular regard to the most vulnerable countries. We welcome the progress made and reiterate our continued support to African Countries, in particular through the G20 Initiative on Supporting the Industrialization in Africa and LDCs, the G20 Africa Partnership, the Compact with Africa and other relevant initiatives. We remain committed to addressing illicit financial flows.

10. **Support to vulnerable countries.** We welcome the new general allocation of Special Drawing Rights (SDR), implemented by the International Monetary Fund (IMF) on 23 August 2021, which has made available the equivalent of USD 650 billion in additional reserves globally. We are working on actionable options for members with strong external positions to significantly magnify its impact through the voluntary channelling of part of the allocated SDRs to help vulnerable countries, according to national laws and regulations We welcome the recent pledges worth around USD [45] billion, as a step towards a total global ambition of USD 100 billion of voluntary contributions for countries most in need. We also welcome the ongoing work to significantly scale up the Poverty Reduction and Growth Trust's lending capacity and call for further voluntary loan and subsidy contributions from countries able to do so. We also call on the IMF to establish a new Resilience and Sustainability Trust (RST) – in line with its mandate – to provide affordable long-term financing to help low-income countries, including in the African continent, small island developing states, and vulnerable middle-income countries to reduce risks to prospective balance of payments stability, including those stemming from pandemics and climate change. The new RST will preserve the reserve asset characteristics of the SDRs channelled through the Trust. Our Finance Ministers look forward to

further discussion of surcharge policy at the IMF Board in the context of the precautionary balances interim review.

11. We welcome the progress achieved under the G20 Debt Service Suspension Initiative (DSSI), which is also agreed to by the Paris Club. Preliminary estimates point to at least USD 12.7 billion of total debt service deferred, under this initiative, between May 2020 and December 2021, benefitting 50 countries. We welcome the recent progress on the Common Framework for debt treatment beyond the DSSI. We commit to step up our efforts to implement it in a timely, orderly and coordinated manner. These enhancements would give more certainty to debtor countries and facilitate the IMF's and MDBs' quick provision of financial support. We look forward to progress in the current negotiations under the Common Framework. We stress the importance for private creditors and other official bilateral creditors to provide debt treatments on terms at least as favourable, in line with the comparability of treatment principle. We recall the forthcoming work of the MDBs, as stated in the Common Framework, in light of debt vulnerabilities. We affirm the importance of joint efforts by all actors, including private creditors, to continue working towards enhancing debt transparency. We look forward to progress by the IMF and World Bank Group on their proposal of a process to strengthen the quality and consistency of debt data and improve debt disclosure.

12. We reaffirm the crucial role of the Multilateral Development Banks' (MDBs) long-term support towards achieving the SDGs. Acknowledging the high financing needs of low income countries, we look forward to an ambitious IDA20 replenishment by December 2021, including through the sustainable use of IDA's balance sheet. We also look forward to the future African Development Fund-16 replenishment. We welcome the launch of the Independent Review of MDBs' Capital Adequacy Frameworks and the G20 Recommendations on the use of Policy-Based lending, which will help maximize the impact of MDB operations.

13. **International Financial Architecture.** We reiterate our commitment to strengthening long-term financial resilience and supporting inclusive growth, including through promoting sustainable capital flows, developing local currency capital markets and maintaining a strong and effective Global Financial Safety Net with a strong, quota-

based, and adequately resourced IMF at its centre. We look forward to the forthcoming review of the IMF's Institutional View on the liberalisation and management of capital flows, informed, among others, by the Integrated Policy Framework. We remain committed to revisiting the adequacy of IMF quotas and will continue the process of IMF governance reform under the 16th General Review of Quotas, including a new quota formula as a guide, by 15 December 2023.

14. Recognizing the importance of strengthening the alignment of all sources of Financing for Sustainable Development with the SDGs and the need to address the related financing gaps, in line with existing commitments, we endorse the G20 Framework for Voluntary Support to Integrated National Financing Frameworks, the G20 High-Level Principles on Sustainability-Related Financial Instruments and the G20 Common Vision on SDG Alignment, noting the importance of transparency and mutual accountability. We also ask our Development and Finance Ministers to further enhance their cooperation.

15. **Food security, nutrition, agriculture and food systems.** We are committed to achieving food security and adequate nutrition for all, leaving no one behind. To this end, we endorse the Matera Declaration and its Call to Action. We encourage partners and stakeholders to collaborate with or join the Food Coalition launched by the FAO as a means to respond to the impacts of COVID-19 on food security and nutrition. We are concerned by famine conditions and acute food insecurity fuelled by armed conflicts in many parts of the world, particularly in the countries listed in the 2021 Global Report on Food Crises. We will foster sustainable and resilient food systems and agriculture innovation, which are vital to end hunger and malnutrition, eradicate poverty and ensure sustainability, also by increasing access to finance through responsible investment, developing and improving early warning programmes, reducing food loss and waste along the food value chain, improving livelihoods for small-holder and marginal farmers and better integrating urban-rural interface. We recognize that promoting sustainable food systems, including by strengthening global, regional and local food value-chains and international food trade, will contribute not only to food security, but also make a major contribution to tackling the interlinked global challenges of climate change and biodiversity loss. We

acknowledge the outcomes of the Food Systems Summit, including initiatives such as the School Meals Coalition, and invite all partners to contribute to its follow-up, highlighting the importance of reinforced co-ordination in food system policy-making and of improved financing tools for sustainable food systems.

16. **Environment.** We commit to strengthen actions to halt and reverse biodiversity loss by 2030 and call on CBD Parties to adopt an ambitious, balanced, practical, effective, robust and transformative post 2020 Global Biodiversity Framework at COP15 in Kunming. We welcome the launch of the UN Decade on Ecosystem Restoration 2021-2030, reaffirm the shared ambition to achieve a 50% reduction of degraded land by 2040 on a voluntary basis, and will strive to achieve Land Degradation Neutrality by 2030. We will build on the G20 Global Initiative on Reducing Land Degradation and Enhancing Conservation of Terrestrial Habitats launched under Saudi Presidency and look forward to its upcoming Implementation Strategy. We recognize the efforts made by a number of countries to adhere to the Leaders' Pledge for Nature and to ensure that at least 30 % of global land and at least 30 % of the global ocean and seas are conserved or protected by 2030, and we will help to make progress towards this objective in accordance with national circumstances. We encourage and support others to make similarly ambitious commitments. We will pursue our efforts to ensure the conservation, protection and sustainable use of natural resources and will take concrete measures to end overfishing, deliver on our commitment to end illegal, unreported and unregulated fishing, and combat crimes that affect the environment such as illegal logging, illegal mining, illegal wildlife trade and illegal movement and disposal of waste and hazardous substances. We underline the many synergies in financial flows for climate, biodiversity and ecosystems, and we will strengthen those synergies to maximize co-benefits. In this context, we recognize the importance of work on nature-related financial disclosure.

17. We will scale up and encourage the implementation of Nature-based Solutions or Ecosystem-based Approaches as valuable tools providing economic, social, climate and environmental benefits including in and around cities, in an inclusive manner and through the participation of local communities and Indigenous Peoples. We will integrate the implementation of a One Health approach in relevant

policies and decision-making processes. We recognize that water resources are globally at risk due to anthropogenic pressure. We will continue to share innovation and best practices, also as a means to support integrated water resources management, including through the G20 Dialogue on Water and the G20 Water Platform adopted under Saudi Presidency.

18. We commit to intensify our actions to conserve, protect, restore and sustainably use marine biodiversity and reiterate our commitment to the Global Coral Reef R&D Accelerator Platform launched under Saudi Presidency. We highlight the importance of parties to UNCLOS making progress as soon as possible in the ongoing negotiations for an ambitious and balanced international legally binding instrument under UNCLOS on the conservation and sustainable use of marine biodiversity of areas beyond national jurisdiction. In the context of the Antarctic Treaty System, we fully support, and encourage further progress to implement the long-standing commitment of the Commission for the Conservation of Antarctic Marine Living Resources (CCAMLR), recognizing Marine Protected Areas (MPAs) can serve as a powerful tool for protecting sensitive ecosystems representative of the Convention Area, in particular in East Antarctica, the Weddell Sea and in the Antarctic Peninsula. We reaffirm our commitment to prohibit fishing subsidies that contribute to overfishing and overcapacity, in line with the SDGs. In line with the Osaka Blue Ocean Vision, we reaffirm our commitment to end Illegal, Unreported and Unregulated fishing and to address marine plastic litter, building on the initiatives conducted, inter alia, by the UNEA, in view of strengthening existing instruments and developing a new global agreement or instrument.

19. Acknowledging the urgency of combating land degradation and creating new carbon sinks, we share the aspirational goal to collectively plant 1 trillion trees, focusing on the most degraded ecosystems in the planet, and urge other countries to join forces with the G20 to reach this global goal by 2030, including through climate projects, with the involvement of the private sector and civil society.

20. **Cities and Circular Economy.** We commit to increase resource efficiency, including through the G20 Resource Efficiency Dialogue and recognize the importance of cities as enablers of sustainable development and the need to improve sustainability, health, resilience

and well-being in urban contexts as underlined by the Habitat III New Urban Agenda. With the involvement of businesses, citizens, academia and civil society organizations, we will enhance our efforts towards achieving sustainable consumption and production patterns and management and reduction of emissions, including by adopting circular economy approaches, and will support local actions for climate mitigation and adaptation. We endorse the G20 Platform on SDG Localization and Intermediary Cities, with the support of the OECD and UN-Habitat. We will support intermediary cities in adopting integrated and inclusive urban planning; accelerating their transitions towards clean and sustainable energy and sustainable mobility for all; improving waste management; fostering empowerment and decent work for women, youth, migrants and refugees; assisting disabled and elderly persons; enhancing food systems sustainability; and enabling more equitable access to digital innovations. Partnerships like the Coalition for Disaster Resilience Infrastructure could act as a vehicle to accelerate this agenda.

21. **Energy and Climate.** Responding to the call of the scientific community, noting with concern the recent reports of the IPCC and mindful of our leadership role, we commit to tackle the critical and urgent threat of climate change and to work collectively to achieve a successful UNFCCC COP26 in Glasgow. To this end, we reaffirm our commitment to the full and effective implementation of the UNFCCC and of the Paris Agreement, taking action across mitigation, adaptation and finance during this critical decade, on the basis of the best available scientific knowledge, reflecting the principle of common but differentiated responsibilities and respective capabilities, in light of different national circumstances. We remain committed to the Paris Agreement goal to hold the global average temperature increase well below 2°C and to pursue efforts to limit it to 1.5°C above pre-industrial levels, also as a means to enable the achievement of the 2030 Agenda.

22. We recognize that the impacts of climate change at 1.5°C are much lower than at 2°C. Keeping 1.5°C within reach will require meaningful and effective actions and commitment by all countries, taking into account different approaches, through the development of clear national pathways that align long-term ambition with short- and medium-term goals, and with international cooperation and support,

including finance and technology, sustainable and responsible consumption and production as critical enablers, in the context of sustainable development. We look forward to a successful COP26.

23. In this endeavour, informed by the IPCC assessments, we will accelerate our actions across mitigation, adaptation and finance, acknowledging the key relevance of achieving global net zero greenhouse gas emissions or carbon neutrality by or around mid-century and the need to strengthen global efforts required to reach the goals of the Paris Agreement. Accordingly, recognizing that G20 members can significantly contribute to the reduction of global greenhouse gas emissions, we commit, in line with the latest scientific developments and with national circumstances, to take further action this decade and to formulate, implement, update and enhance, where necessary, our 2030 NDCs, and to formulate Long-Term Strategies that set out clear and predictable pathways consistent with the achievement of a balance between anthropogenic emissions and removal by sinks by or around mid-century, taking into account different approaches, including the Circular Carbon Economy, socio-economic, economic, technological, and market developments, and promoting the most efficient solutions. We acknowledge the efforts made to date, including net zero and carbon neutrality commitments and new and ambitious NDCs and LTSs by G20 members, and those to come by or at COP26.

24. We will deliver national recovery and resilience plans that allocate, according to national circumstances, an ambitious share of the financial resources to mitigating and adapting to climate change and avoid harm to the climate and environment. We acknowledge the Sustainable Recovery Tracker developed in cooperation with the IEA, encouraging its update. In order to deploy the full potential of zero, low-emission, innovative, modern and clean solutions, we will collaborate to accelerate the development and deployment of the most efficient and effective solutions and help them rapidly achieve cost parity and commercial viability, including to ensure access to clean energy for all, especially in developing countries. We commit to scale up public Research, Development and Deployment. We will increase our cooperation on enhanced country-driven capacity building and technology development and transfer on mutually agreed terms, including through key global initiatives and joint or bilateral projects

on the most efficient solutions in all sectors of economy.

25. Impacts of climate change are being experienced worldwide, particularly by the poorest and most vulnerable. We stress the importance of the effective implementation of the global goal on adaptation and will submit adaptation communications. We also commit to scale up adaptation finance, with a view to achieving a balance with the provision of finance for mitigation to address the needs of developing countries including by facilitating mechanisms, conditions and procedures to access available funds, taking national strategies, priorities and needs into account. We recall and reaffirm the commitment made by developed countries, to the goal of mobilizing jointly USD 100 billion per year by 2020 and annually through 2025 to address the needs of developing countries, in the context of meaningful mitigation actions and transparency on implementation and stress the importance of meeting that goal fully as soon as possible. In this regard, we welcome the new commitments made by some of the members of the G20 to each increase and improve their overall international public climate finance contributions through to 2025 and look forward to new commitments from others. We note the Climate Finance Delivery Plan, which shows, based on OECD estimates, that the goal is expected to be met no later than 2023. We also recall the Paris Agreement aim to strengthen the global response to the threat of climate change, in the context of sustainable development and efforts to eradicate poverty, and that one of its goals is to make finance flows consistent with a pathway towards low GHG emissions and climate-resilient development. We encourage International Financial Institutions, including MDBs, to step up their efforts to pursue alignment with the Paris Agreement within ambitious timeframes, to support sustainable recovery and transition strategies, NDCs and long-term low greenhouse gas emission development strategies in emerging markets and developing economies, and to set out plans to mobilize private finance, in line with their mandates and internal approval procedures, while continuing to support the achievement of the UN 2030 Agenda.

26. We commit to significantly reduce our collective greenhouse gas emissions, taking into account national circumstances and respecting our NDCs. We acknowledge that methane emissions represent a significant contribution to climate change and recognize, according

to national circumstances, that its reduction can be one of the quickest, most feasible and most cost-effective ways to limit climate change and its impacts. We welcome the contribution of various institutions, in this regard, and take note of specific initiatives on methane, including the establishment of the International Methane Emissions Observatory (IMEO). We will further promote cooperation, to improve data collection, verification, and measurement in support of GHG inventories and to provide high quality scientific data.

27. We will increase our efforts to implement the commitment made in 2009 in Pittsburgh to phase out and rationalize, over the medium term, inefficient fossil fuel subsidies that encourage wasteful consumption and commit to achieve this objective, while providing targeted support for the poorest and the most vulnerable.

28. We acknowledge the close link between climate and energy and commit to reduce emission intensity, as part of mitigation efforts, in the energy sector to meet timeframes aligned with the Paris temperature goal. We will cooperate on deployment and dissemination of zero or low carbon emission and renewable technologies, including sustainable bioenergy, to enable a transition towards low-emission power systems. This will also enable those countries that commit to phasing out investment in new unabated coal power generation capacity to do so as soon as possible. We commit to mobilize international public and private finance to support green, inclusive and sustainable energy development and we will put an end to the provision of international public finance for new unabated coal power generation abroad by the end of 2021.

29. As we are recovering from the crisis, we are committed to maintain energy security, while addressing climate change, and guaranteeing just and orderly transitions of our energy systems that ensures affordability, including for the most vulnerable households and businesses. In this endeavour, we will remain vigilant of the evolution of energy markets, taking into account trends over the years, and promote an intensive dialogue. Accordingly, the G20 in collaboration with the International Energy Forum (IEF) will facilitate a dialogue between producers and consumers to bolster the efficiency, transparency and stability of the energy markets. We emphasize the importance of maintaining undisrupted flows of energy from various sources, suppliers and routes, exploring paths to enhanced energy

security and markets stability, while promoting open, competitive and free international energy markets. We recognize the role of digitalization in enhancing energy security and market stability through improved energy planning, while ensuring the security of energy systems against risks of attacks, including through malicious use of ICT. In addition to continuing to address traditional energy security challenges, we are mindful that clean energy transitions require an enhanced understanding of energy security, integrating aspects such as the evolving share of intermittent energy sources; the growing demand for energy storage, system flexibility changing climate patterns; the increase in extreme weather events; responsible development of energy types and sources; reliable, responsible and sustainable supply chains of critical minerals and materials, as well as semiconductors and related technologies.

30. **Policies for the transition and sustainable finance.** We welcome the agreement by Finance Ministers and Central Bank Governors to coordinate their efforts to tackle global challenges such as climate change and environmental protection, and to promote transitions towards green, more prosperous and inclusive economies. We welcome the introduction of a Pillar dedicated to Protecting the Planet in the G20 Action Plan. We agree on the importance of a more systematic analysis of macroeconomic risks stemming from climate change and of the costs and benefits of different transitions, as well as of the macroeconomic and distributional impact of risk prevention strategies and mitigation and adaptation policies, including by drawing on well-established methodologies. We ask the different G20 work streams to act in synergy, within their respective mandates and while avoiding duplication, to inform our discussions on the most appropriate policy mix to move towards low-greenhouse gas emission economies, taking into account national circumstances. Such policy mix should include investment in sustainable infrastructure and innovative technologies that promote decarbonisation and circular economy, and a wide range of fiscal, market and regulatory mechanisms to support clean energy transitions, including, if appropriate, the use of carbon pricing mechanisms and incentives, while providing targeted support for the poorest and the most vulnerable. We welcome the constructive discussions held at the Venice International Conference on Climate and at the G20 High Level

Tax Symposium on Tax Policy and Climate Change and we recognise that the policy dialogue on the macroeconomic and fiscal impact of climate change policies could benefit from further technical work.

31. **Sustainable finance** is crucial for promoting orderly and just transitions towards green and more sustainable economies and inclusive societies, in line with the 2030 Agenda for Sustainable Development and the Paris Agreement. We welcome the establishment of the G20 Sustainable Finance Working Group (SFWG) and we endorse the G20 Sustainable Finance Roadmap and the Synthesis Report. The Roadmap, initially focused on climate, is a multi-year action-oriented document, voluntary and flexible in nature, which will inform the broader G20 agenda on climate and sustainability. We recognise the importance of gradually expanding the Roadmap's coverage to include additional issues, such as biodiversity and nature as well as social matters, based on mutual agreement by G20 members in the coming years. We welcome the Financial Stability Board (FSB) Roadmap for addressing financial risks from climate change, which will complement the work carried out by the SFWG. We welcome the FSB report on the availability of data on climate-related financial stability risks and the FSB report on promoting globally consistent, comparable and reliable climate-related financial disclosures and its recommendations. We also welcome the work programme of the International Financial Reporting Standards Foundation to develop a baseline global reporting standard under robust governance and public oversight, building upon the FSB's Task Force on Climate-Related Financial Disclosures framework and the work of sustainability standard-setters.

32. **International taxation**. The final political agreement as set out in the Statement on a Two-Pillar Solution to Address the Tax Challenges Arising from the Digitalisation of the Economy and in the Detailed Implementation Plan, released by the OECD/G20 Inclusive Framework on Base Erosion and Profit Shifting (BEPS) on 8 October, is a historic achievement through which we will establish a more stable and fairer international tax system. We call on the OECD/G20 Inclusive Framework on BEPS to swiftly develop the model rules and multilateral instruments as agreed in the Detailed Implementation Plan, with a view to ensure that the new rules will

come into effect at global level in 2023. We note the OECD report on Developing Countries and the OECD/G20 Inclusive Framework on BEPS identifying developing countries' progress made through their participation in the OECD/G20 Inclusive Framework on BEPS and possible areas where domestic resource mobilisation efforts could be further supported.

33. **Gender Equality and Women's Empowerment.** We reaffirm our commitment to gender equality and emphasize the pivotal role of women's and girls' empowerment and leadership at all levels for inclusive and sustainable development. We commit to put women and girls, who have been disproportionately affected by the pandemic, at the core of our efforts to build forward better. We will work on key factors such as equal access to education and opportunities, including in STEM sectors, the promotion of women's entrepreneurship and leadership, the elimination of gender-based violence, the enhancement of social, health, care and educational services, the overcoming of gender stereotypes, and the uneven distribution of unpaid care and domestic work. We commit to implement the G20 Roadmap Towards and Beyond the Brisbane Goal and to rapidly enhance the quality and quantity of women's employment, with a particular focus on closing the gender pay gap. We reiterate our commitment to share progress and actions taken towards the Brisbane Goal in the related annual report and ask the ILO and the OECD to continue reporting annually on our progress, taking into account the Roadmaps' Auxiliary Indicators.

34. We welcome the hosting of the first G20 conference on Women's Empowerment and will continue to enhance our concrete measures towards a systemic and cross-cutting approach to gender equality in our national policies, with adequate implementation tools. We will work on women's empowerment in cooperation with academia, civil society and the private sector. To this end, we support the convening of a G20 Conference on Women's Empowerment under the upcoming Presidencies. We welcome the work of the EMPOWER Alliance and its engagement with the G20, to be reviewed in 2025. We acknowledge the Women Entrepreneurs Finance Initiative as an important partnership to support women-led SMEs.

35. **Employment and social protection.** The Covid-19 pandemic has exacerbated inequalities in our labour markets, disproportionately

affecting vulnerable workers. In cooperation with social partners, we will adopt human-centered policy approaches to promote social dialogue and to ensure greater social justice; safe and healthy working conditions; and decent work for all, including within global supply chains. To reduce inequalities, eradicate poverty, support worker transitions and reintegration in labour markets and promote inclusive and sustainable growth, we will strengthen our social protection systems, as outlined in the G20 Policy Principles to Ensure Access to Adequate Social Protection for All in a Changing World of Work. We welcome the G20 Policy Options to Enhance Regulatory Frameworks for Remote Working Arrangements and Work through Digital Platforms. We will work to ensure decent working conditions for remote and platform workers and strive to adapt our regulatory frameworks to new forms of work, ensuring that these are fair and inclusive, leaving no one behind, while paying special attention to addressing the digital gender divide and intergenerational inequalities. We also ask the ILO and the OECD to continue monitoring progress towards the Antalya Youth Goal. We underscore our commitment to further international cooperation to strengthen safe and healthy working conditions for all workers and welcome the G20 Approaches on Safety and Health at Work.

36. **Education.** Access to education is a human right and a pivotal tool for inclusive and sustainable economic recovery. We commit to ensure access to quality education for all, with particular attention to women and girls and vulnerable students. We will increase our efforts to make education systems inclusive, adaptable and resilient, and will enhance the coordination between education, employment and social policies to improve the transition from education to quality employment, also through lifelong learning.

37. We recognize the critical role of education for sustainable development, including environmental stewardship, in empowering younger generations with the necessary skills and mindset to address global challenges. We commit to enhance cooperation and to foster stronger, effective measures to this end.

38. **Migration and forced displacement.** The impact of the pandemic has confronted us with new challenges with regard to migration in our globalized economies. We commit to take steps to support the full inclusion of migrants, including migrant workers, and refugees

in our pandemic response and recovery efforts, in the spirit of international cooperation and in line with national policies, legislation and circumstances, ensuring full respect for their human rights and fundamental freedoms regardless of their migration status. We also recognize the importance of preventing irregular migration flows and the smuggling of migrants, as part of a comprehensive approach for safe, orderly and regular migration, while responding to humanitarian needs and the root causes of displacement. We note the 2021 Annual International Migration and Forced Displacement Trends and Policies Report to the G20 prepared by the OECD in cooperation with ILO, International Organization for Migration (IOM) and United Nations High Commissioner for Refugees (UNHCR). We will continue the dialogue on migration and forced displacement in future Presidencies.

39. **Transportation and Travel.** We will endeavor to restart international travel in a safe and orderly manner, consistent with the work of relevant international organizations such as the WHO, the International Civil Aviation Organization, the International Maritime Organization and the OECD. To this end, taking into consideration national public health policies, we acknowledge the relevance of shared standards to ensure seamless travel, including testing requirements and results, vaccination certificates and interoperability and mutual recognition of digital applications, while continuing to protect public health and ensuring privacy and data protection. We reiterate the essential role of transport personnel and the need for a coordinated approach to the treatment of air, maritime and land crews, consistent with public health standards and with the principle of non-discrimination.

40. **Financial regulation.** We welcome the FSB final report on the lessons learnt from the COVID-19 pandemic from a financial stability perspective and the proposed next steps. While the global financial system has been largely resilient, gaps in the regulatory framework remain which we are committed to addressing, including by completing the remaining elements of the G20 regulatory reforms agreed after the 2008 financial crisis. We are also committed to strengthening the resilience of the non-bank financial intermediation (NBFI) sector with a systemic perspective, and reducing the need for extraordinary central bank interventions, by implementing the FSB

NBFI work programme. We endorse the FSB final report on policy proposals to enhance money market fund (MMF) resilience and we will assess and address MMF vulnerabilities in our jurisdictions, using the framework and policy toolkit in the report, recognizing the need to tailor measures to jurisdictions' specific circumstances, as well as taking account of cross-border considerations.

41. We welcome the progress reported against milestones set for 2021 by the G20 Roadmap to enhance cross-border payments, and we endorse the ambitious but achievable quantitative global targets for addressing the challenges of cost, speed, transparency and access by 2027 set out in the FSB report. We call on public authorities and the private sector to work together to make the practical improvements to achieve these goals. We reiterate that no so-called "global stablecoins" should commence operation until all relevant legal, regulatory and oversight requirements are adequately addressed through appropriate design and by adhering to applicable standards. We encourage jurisdictions to progress in the implementation of the FSB High-Level Recommendations, and standard setting bodies to complete their assessment of whether to make any adjustments to standards or guidance in light of the FSB Recommendations. We encourage the Committee on Payments and Market Infrastructures, Bank for International Settlements Innovation Hub, IMF and World Bank to continue deepening the analysis on the potential role of central bank digital currencies in enhancing cross-border payments and their wider implications for the international monetary system. We thank Mr. Randal K. Quarles for his service as FSB Chair and we welcome the appointment of Mr. Klaas Knot as his successor.

42. **Trade and Investment.** We affirm the important role of open, fair, equitable, sustainable, non-discriminatory and inclusive rules-based multilateral trade system in restoring growth, job creation and industrial productivity and promoting sustainable development, as well as our commitment to strengthen it with the WTO at its core. Recalling the Riyadh Initiative on the future of the WTO, we remain committed to working actively and constructively with all WTO Members to undertake the necessary reform of the WTO, improving all its functions, and we highlight the need to implement this commitment in practice through an inclusive and transparent approach including tackling the development issues. We commit to

a successful and productive WTO 12th Ministerial Conference (MC12) as an important opportunity to advance that reform and revitalize the organization. We will work with all WTO members in the lead-up to the MC12 and beyond to enhance the capacity of the multilateral trading system to increase our pandemic and disaster preparedness and resilience through a multifaceted response, with a view to deliver an outcome on trade and health by MC12, including to work towards enhancing timely, equitable and global access to vaccines. We support reaching a meaningful WTO agreement on harmful fisheries subsidies by the MC12, in line with the SDG 14.6, and we welcome the ongoing work on agriculture.

43. We recognize the importance of sound, predictable and transparent domestic regulatory frameworks for trade in services and investment. We underscore the importance of fair competition and we will continue to work to ensure a level playing field to foster a favourable trade and investment environment. Reducing trade tensions, tackling distortions in all sectors of trade and investment, addressing supply chain disruptions and fostering mutually beneficial trade and investment relations will be critical as economies respond to and recover from the COVID-19 pandemic. We believe that trade and environmental policies should be mutually supportive and WTO consistent and contribute to the optimal use of the world's resources in accordance with the objectives of sustainable development. We highlight the importance of strengthening MSMEs' capacity to become more integrated into the global economy.

44. **Infrastructure investment**. We recognize the critical role of quality infrastructure investments in the recovery phase. We acknowledge that resilient, properly funded, well maintained and optimally managed systems are essential to preserve infrastructure assets over their life-cycles, minimising loss and disruption, and securing the provision of safe, reliable and high-quality infrastructure services. To this end, we endorse the G20 Policy Agenda on Infrastructure Maintenance. In line with the G20 Roadmap for Infrastructure as an Asset Class, and building on the G20 Infrastructure Investors Dialogue, we will continue, in a flexible manner, to develop further the collaboration between the public and private investors to mobilise private capital. We underline the importance of promoting knowledge sharing between local authorities and national governments to foster

more inclusive infrastructure. We will continue to advance the work related to the G20 Principles for Quality Infrastructure Investment. We agree to extend the Global Infrastructure Hub mandate until the end of 2024.

45. **Productivity**. Digital transformation has the potential of boosting productivity, strengthening the recovery and contributing to broad-based and shared prosperity. We endorse the G20 Menu of Policy Options – Digital Transformation and Productivity Recovery, which provides policy options, shares good practices, promotes inclusion and sheds light on the key role of international cooperation to make use of the growth opportunities of digitalization. Drawing on the Menu we will continue discussing policies to sustain productivity growth, and to help ensure that the benefits are evenly shared within and across countries and sectors. We recognise the importance of good corporate governance frameworks and well-functioning capital markets to support the recovery, and look forward to the review of the G20/OECD Principles of Corporate Governance.

46. **Digital economy, higher education and research**. We recognize the role of technology and innovation as key enablers for the global recovery and sustainable development. We recognize the importance of policies to create an enabling, inclusive, open, fair and non-discriminatory digital economy that fosters the application of new technologies, allows businesses and entrepreneurs to thrive, and protects and empowers consumers, while addressing the challenges related to privacy, data protection, intellectual property rights, and security. Mindful of the need to support a better inclusion of MSMEs in the digital economy, we commit to reinforce our actions and international cooperation towards the digital transformation of production, processes, services and business models, also through the use of consensus-based international standards and the improvement of consumer protection, digital skills and literacy. We welcome the results of the G20 Innovation League, as a platform through which multilateral endeavors can boost partnerships, collaboration, co-creation, and private investments in technologies and applications benefitting humankind, highlighting how trade and digital policies can help strengthen the competitiveness of MSMEs in global markets and address the particular challenges they face. We have also begun to address the application of distributed ledger

technologies such as blockchain networks to protect consumers through increased traceability. We recognize the growing role that Information and Communication Technologies play in our societies. In this context, we emphasize the need to address the increased security challenges in the digital environment, including from ransomware and other forms of cyber crime. With this in mind, we will work to strengthen bilateral and multilateral cooperation to secure our ICT, address shared vulnerabilities and threats, and combat cyber crime.

47. Well aware of the benefits stemming from the responsible use and development of trustworthy human-centered Artificial Intelligence (AI), we will advance the implementation of the G20 AI Principles, while considering the specific needs of MSMEs and start-ups to encourage competition and innovation, as well as diversity and inclusion, and the importance of international cooperation to promote research, development and application of AI. We welcome the G20 Policy Examples on How to Enhance the Adoption of AI by MSMEs and Start-ups.

48. We acknowledge the importance of data free flow with trust and cross-border data flows. We reaffirm the role of data for development. We will continue to work on addressing challenges such as those related to privacy, data protection, security and intellectual property rights, in accordance with the relevant applicable legal frameworks. We will also continue to further common understanding and to work towards identifying commonalities, complementarities and elements of convergence between existing regulatory approaches and instruments enabling data to flow with trust, in order to foster future interoperability. Recognizing the responsibility of digital service providers, we will work in 2022 towards enhancing confidence in the digital environment by improving internet safety and countering online abuse, hate speech, online violence and terrorism while protecting human rights and fundamental freedoms. We remain committed to protecting the most vulnerable, and acknowledge the G20 High Level Principles for Children Protection and Empowerment in the Digital Environment, drawn from the OECD Recommendation on Children in the Digital Environment and other relevant tools, such as the ITU 2020 Guidelines on Child Online Protection.

49. **Financial inclusion**. We reaffirm our commitment to enhancing digital financial inclusion of vulnerable and underserved segments of society, including micro, small and medium-sized enterprises (MSMEs), carrying forward the work of the Global Partnership for Financial Inclusion (GPFI) and implementing the G20 2020 Financial Inclusion Action Plan. We endorse the G20 Menu of Policy Options for digital financial literacy and financial consumer and MSME protection "Enhancing digital financial inclusion beyond the COVID-19 crisis", with the aim to provide a guide for policymakers in their efforts to lay the ground for new financial inclusion strategies in the post-pandemic world. We welcome the 2021 GPFI Progress Report to G20 Leaders and the 2021 Update to Leaders on Progress Towards the G20 Remittance Target. We support the GPFI in bringing forward the monitoring of National Remittances Plans, also gathering more granular data, and strongly encourage the continued facilitation of the flow of remittances and the reduction of average remittance transfer costs.

50. **Data gaps**. Improving data availability and provision, including on environmental issues, and harnessing the wealth of data produced by digitalization is critical to better inform our decisions. We take note of the work done so far by the IMF, in close cooperation with the FSB and the Inter-Agency Group on Economic and Financial Statistics (IAG) towards a possible new G20 Data Gaps Initiative and we look forward to its further development.

51. Recognizing the importance of an efficient use of digital tools within public administrations, we will continue to promote agile regulatory frameworks and will provide digital public services that are human-centric, proactive, easy to use and accessible to all. We welcome the novel emphasis on secure, interoperable and trusted digital identity solutions that can provide better access to public and private sector services while promoting privacy and personal data protection. We will pursue further work on designing digital identity tools, deployable also in emergency scenarios.

52. Recognizing that sustainable investment in quality digital infrastructure can greatly contribute to reducing the digital divide, we will promote universal, and affordable access to connectivity for all by 2025. Recognizing universal, secure, affordable, advanced and well-functioning digital infrastructure as an important driver for the

economic recovery, we endorse the G20 Guidelines for Financing and Fostering High-Quality Broadband Connectivity for a Digital World, developed with the support of the OECD.

53. We will enhance our efforts to ensure that our research and work forces are able to adapt their skills to the rapidly evolving digital environment and harness the potential of innovation and digital tools whilst upholding shared ethical principles and values. We will also leverage common digital infrastructures to promote research collaboration, open science and higher education. Firmly convinced about the crucial relevance of scientific progress in improving the lives of billions around the world and effectively addressing global challenges, we will also continue to ensure that scientific research, including on digital technology, is carried out in a responsible, safe, transparent, equitable, inclusive and secure manner, taking into account the risks stemming from cutting-edge technologies.

54. We welcome the transformation of the Digital Economy Task Force into a Working Group and invite our Digital Ministers to further their discussions on the digital economy as appropriate.

55. **Tourism.** Building on the work made in 2020, we will continue to support a rapid, resilient, inclusive and sustainable recovery of the tourism sector, which is among those hardest hit by the pandemic, with a particular focus on developing countries and MSMEs. We endorse the G20 Rome Guidelines for the Future of Tourism, and commit to take action to fulfill its objectives, in particular with regard to safe mobility and seamless travel and sustainability and digitalization. We will explore collaboration in the fields of creative economy and innovation in support of tourism. To this end, we ask our Ministers of Tourism to pursue their collaboration with the OECD, the UNWTO and other relevant international organizations.

56. **Culture.** Recalling that culture has intrinsic value, we underline the role of culture and of cultural and creative professionals and businesses as drivers for sustainable development and in fostering the resilience and the regeneration of our economies and societies, stressing the importance of international efforts to safeguard and promote culture, with a key role to be played by UNESCO, and the need to support workers, including in the cultural field, also by facilitating access to employment, social protection, digitalization and business support measures. We emphasize the importance of

addressing threats to irreplaceable cultural resources and protecting and preserving cultural heritage damaged, trafficked or endangered by conflicts and disasters, recalling the objectives of UNSC Resolution 2347. We ask our relevant institutions to further pursue the G20 cooperation on culture.

57. **Anti-corruption.** Renewing our commitment to zero tolerance for corruption in the public and private sectors and to achieving common goals in the global fight against corruption, we adopt our 2022-2024 Anti-Corruption Action Plan. We will further strengthen our engagement with other stakeholders such as academia, civil society, media and the private sector, and will continue to promote their important role and active participation in this field. We are committed to fight any new and sophisticated forms of corruption. We endorse the G20 High-Level Principles on Corruption related to Organized Crime, on Tackling Corruption in Sport, and on Preventing and Combating Corruption in Emergencies, and adopt the G20 Anti-corruption Accountability Report. We reaffirm our commitment to deny safe haven to corruption offenders and their assets, in accordance to domestic laws and to combat transnational corruption. We will also provide competent authorities with adequate, accurate and up-to-date information by adopting legally appropriate measures to improve international and domestic beneficial ownership transparency of legal persons and arrangements and real estate, especially trans-national flows, in line with the Financial Action Task Force recommendations.

58. We remain committed to promoting a culture of integrity in the private sector, particularly in their relations with the public sector. In our collective efforts to better measure corruption, we welcome the Compendium of Good Practices on Measurement of Corruption. We will ensure that G20 Countries adapt their regulation and legislation to comply with the relevant obligation to criminalize bribery, including bribery of foreign public officials, and bolster efforts to effectively prevent, detect, investigate, prosecute and sanction domestic and foreign bribery. We will demonstrate concrete efforts for the duration of the Action Plan and share information on our actions towards criminalizing foreign bribery and enforcing foreign bribery legislation in line with article 16 of UNCAC, with a view to the possible adherence of all G20 countries to the OECD Anti-Bribery

Convention. As a means to further improve international cooperation on anti-corruption, we welcome the progress made by the GlobE Network.

59. We reaffirm our full support for the Financial Action Task Force (FATF) and the Global Network and recognize that effective implementation of Anti-Money Laundering/Countering the Financing of Terrorism and Proliferation (AML/CFT/CPF) measures is essential for building confidence in financial markets, ensuring a sustainable recovery and protecting the integrity of the international financial system. We stress the relevance of the risk-based approach of the FATF recommendations with the aim to ensure legitimate cross-border payments and to promote financial inclusion. We confirm our support for strengthening the FATF recommendations to improve beneficial ownership transparency and call on countries to fight money laundering from environmental crime, particularly by acting on the findings of the FATF report. We reaffirm the commitments made by Finance Ministers and Central Bank Governors aimed at sustaining and strengthening the work of the FATF-Style Regional Bodies.

60. We look ahead to Beijing Winter Olympics and Paralympics 2022, as opportunities for competition for athletes from around the world, which serves as a symbol of humanity's resilience.

61. We thank the international organizations and the G20 Engagement Groups for their valuable inputs and policy recommendations. We thank Italy for its Presidency, for successfully hosting the Global Health Summit, co-Chaired with the European Commission, and the Rome Leaders' Summit, and for its contribution to the G20 process, and we look forward to meeting again in Indonesia in 2022, in India in 2023 and in Brazil in 2024.

(9) BALI 2022

G20
INDONESIA
2022 RECOVER TOGETHER RECOVER STRONGER

G20 BALI LEADERS' DECLARATION

Bali, 15-16 November 2022

1. Fourteen years ago, the Leaders of the G20 met for the first time, facing the most severe financial crisis in our generation. We recognized, as large global economies, that collectively we carry responsibilities and that our cooperation was necessary to global economic recovery, to tackle global challenges, and lay a foundation for strong, sustainable, balanced, and inclusive growth. We designated the G20 the premier forum for global economic cooperation, and today we reaffirm our commitment to cooperate as we, once again, address serious global economic challenges.
2. We met in Bali on 15-16 November 2022, at a time of unparalleled multidimensional crises. We have experienced the devastation brought by the Covid-19 pandemic, and other challenges including climate change, which has caused economic downturn, increased poverty, slowed global recovery, and hindered the achievement of the Sustainable Development Goals.
3. This year, we have also witnessed the war in Ukraine further adversely impact the global economy. There was a discussion on the issue. We reiterated our national positions as expressed in other fora, including the UN Security Council and the UN General Assembly,

which, in Resolution No. ES-11/1 dated 2 March 2022, as adopted by majority vote (141 votes for, 5 against, 35 abstentions, 12 absent) deplores in the strongest terms the aggression by the Russian Federation against Ukraine and demands its complete and unconditional withdrawal from the territory of Ukraine. Most members strongly condemned the war in Ukraine and stressed it is causing immense human suffering and exacerbating existing fragilities in the global economy - constraining growth, increasing inflation, disrupting supply chains, heightening energy and food insecurity, and elevating financial stability risks. There were other views and different assessments of the situation and sanctions. Recognizing that the G20 is not the forum to resolve security issues, we acknowledge that security issues can have significant consequences for the global economy.

4. It is essential to uphold international law and the multilateral system that safeguards peace and stability. This includes defending all the Purposes and Principles enshrined in the Charter of the United Nations and adhering to international humanitarian law, including the protection of civilians and infrastructure in armed conflicts. The use or threat of use of nuclear weapons is inadmissible. The peaceful resolution of conflicts, efforts to address crises, as well as diplomacy and dialogue, are vital. Today's era must not be of war.

5. At today's critical moment for the global economy, it is essential that the G20 undertakes tangible, precise, swift and necessary actions, using all available policy tools, to address common challenges, including through international macro policy cooperation and concrete collaborations. In doing so, we remain committed to support developing countries, particularly the least developed and small island developing states, in responding to these global challenges and achieving the SDGs. In line with the Indonesian G20 Presidency theme

   - **Recover Together, Recover Stronger**—we will take coordinated actions to advance an agenda for a strong, inclusive and resilient global recovery and sustainable development that delivers jobs and growth. With the above in mind, we will: Stay agile and flexible in our macro-economic policy responses and cooperation. We will make public investments and structural reforms, promote private investments, and strengthen multilateral trade and resilience of global supply chains, to support long-term growth, sustainable and inclusive, green and just transitions. We will ensure long-term fiscal sustainability, with our central banks committed to achieving price stability.

- Protect macroeconomic and financial stability and remain committed to using all available tools to mitigate downside risks, noting the steps taken since the Global Financial Crisis to strengthen financial resilience and promote sustainable finance and capital flows.
- Take action to promote food and energy security and support stability of markets, providing temporary and targeted support to cushion the impact of price increases, strengthening dialogue between producers and consumers, and increasing trade and investments for long-term food and energy security needs, resilient and sustainable food, fertilizer and energy systems.
- Unlock further investments for low- and middle-income and other developing countries, through a greater variety of innovative financing sources and instruments, including to catalyze private investment, to support the achievement of the SDGs. We ask the Multilateral Development Banks to bring forward actions to mobilize and provide additional financing within their mandates, to support achievement of the SDGs including through sustainable development and infrastructure investments, and responding to global challenges.
- Recommit to accelerate achievement of the SDGs, achieving prosperity for all through sustainable development.

6. We are deeply concerned by the challenges to global food security exacerbated by current conflicts and tensions. We therefore commit to taking urgent actions to save lives, prevent hunger and malnutrition, particularly to address the vulnerabilities of developing countries, and call for an accelerated transformation towards sustainable and resilient agriculture and food systems and supply chains. We commit to protect the most vulnerable from hunger by using all available tools to address the global food crisis. We will take further coordinated actions to address food security challenges including price surges and shortage of food commodities and fertilizers globally. Recalling the G20 efforts such as the Global

Agriculture and Food Security Program, we welcome global, regional, and national initiatives in support of food security, and in particular note the progress made by the UN Secretary General's Global Crisis Response Group on Food, Energy and Finance, as well as the World Bank Group's and IMF's food security responses. We emphasize the importance of building on the G20 Matera Declaration, working together to sustainably produce and distribute food, ensure that food systems better contribute to adaptation and mitigation to climate change, and halting and reversing biodiversity loss, diversify food sources, promote nutritious food for all, strengthen global, regional, and local food value chains, and accelerate efforts to reduce food loss and waste. We will also implement the One Health approach, intensify research on food science and technology, and improve stakeholders' capacity along the food supply chains, particularly women, youth, smallholder, and marginal farmers as well as fishers.

7. We support the international efforts to keep food supply chains functioning under challenging circumstances. We are committed to addressing food insecurity by ensuring accessibility, affordability, and sustainability of food and food products for those in needs, particularly in developing countries and least developed countries. We reiterate our support for open, transparent, inclusive, predictable, and non-discriminatory, rules-based agricultural trade based on WTO rules. We highlight the importance of enhancing market predictability, minimizing distortions, increasing business confidence, and allowing agriculture and food trade to flow smoothly. We reaffirm the need to update global agricultural food trade rules and to facilitate trade in agricultural and food products, as well as the importance of not imposing export prohibitions or restrictions on food and fertilizers in a manner inconsistent with relevant WTO provisions. We are committed to sustained supply, in part based on local food sources, as well as diversified production of food and fertilizers to support the most vulnerable from the disruptions in food trade supply chain. We will avoid adversely impacting food security deliberately. We commit to facilitate humanitarian supplies for ensuring access to food in emergency situations and call on UN Member States and all relevant stakeholders with available resources to provide in-kind donations and resources to support countries most affected by the food crisis, as required and based on assessed needs by governments

of affected countries. We continue to support the carve out of humanitarian activities from sanctions and call on all nations to support this aim, including through current efforts at the UN. We will continue to closely monitor the state of global food security and nutrition.

8. We welcome the Türkiye and UN-brokered two Istanbul Agreements signed on 22 July 2022 and consisting of the Initiative on the Safe Transportation of Grain and Foodstuffs from Ukrainian Ports (Black Sea Grain Initiative) and the Memorandum of Understanding between the Russian Federation and the Secretariat of the United Nations on Promoting Russian Food Products and Fertilizers to the World Markets, on the unimpeded deliveries of grain, foodstuffs, and fertilizers/inputs from Ukraine and the Russian Federation, to ease tension and prevent global food insecurity and hunger in developing countries. We emphasize the importance of their full, timely and continued implementation by all relevant stakeholders, as well as the UN Secretary-General's calls for continuation of these efforts by the Parties. In this context we highlight other efforts that ensure the flow of agri-food goods such as the EU Solidarity Lanes and the Russian donations of fertilizers facilitated by the World Food Programme. Moreover, we take note of various initiatives addressing food insecurity such as the Arab Coordination Group initiative.

9. We are committed to supporting the adoption of innovative practices and technologies, including digital innovation in agriculture and food systems to enhance productivity and sustainability in harmony with nature and promote farmers and fishers' livelihoods and increase income, in particular smallholders by increasing efficiency, and equal access to food supply chains. We will promote responsible investments in agricultural research and science and evidence-based approaches. We will continue to strengthen the Agricultural Market Information System (AMIS) as an early warning tool, to enhance food and fertilizer/inputs market transparency, reduce market uncertainties, and support coordinated policy responses for food security and nutrition, through the sharing of reliable and timely data and information.

10. We ask the Food and Agriculture Organization (FAO) and the World Bank Group (WBG) to share with us the results of their mapping exercises on food insecurity, which will be consolidated in the future

with inputs from technical experts and other relevant international organizations, and will provide a systemic analysis of responses to address food security. This will identify any major gaps in global responses; examine food and nutrition variables and funding; examine the supply and demand of fertilizers; build on the G20 Agricultural Market Information System (AMIS); and identify any medium-term issues that require further technical and systemic analysis. The FAO and WBG will report back by the 2023 Spring Meetings.

11. We meet at a time of climate and energy crises, compounded by geopolitical challenges. We are experiencing volatility in energy prices and markets and shortage/disruptions to energy supply. We underline the urgency to rapidly transform and diversify energy systems, advance energy security and resilience and markets stability, by accelerating and ensuring clean, sustainable, just, affordable, and inclusive energy transitions and flow of sustainable investments. We stress the importance of ensuring that global energy demand is matched by affordable energy supplies. We reiterate our commitment to achieve global net zero greenhouse gas emissions/carbon neutrality by or around mid-century, while taking into account the latest scientific developments and different national circumstances. We call for continued support for developing countries, especially in the most vulnerable countries, in terms of providing access to affordable, reliable, sustainable, and modern energy, capacity building, affordable latest technology within the public domain, mutually beneficial technology cooperation and financing mitigation actions in the energy sector.

12. We reaffirm our commitment to achieve SDG 7 targets and strive to close the gaps in energy access and to eradicate energy poverty. Recognising our leadership role, and guided by the Bali Compact and the Bali Energy Transition Roadmap, we are committed to finding solutions to achieve energy markets stability, transparency, and affordability. We will accelerate transitions and achieve our climate objectives by strengthening energy supply chain and energy security, and diversifying energy mixes and systems. We will rapidly scale up the deployment of zero and low emission power generation, including renewable energy resources, and measures to enhance energy efficiency, abatement technologies as well as removal

technologies, taking into account national circumstances. We recognise the importance to accelerate the development, deployment and dissemination of technologies, and the adoption of policies, to transition towards low-emission energy systems, including by rapidly scaling up the deployment of clean power generation, including renewable energy, as well as energy efficiency measures, including accelerating efforts towards the phasedown of unabated coal power, in line with national circumstances and recognising the need for support towards just transitions. We will increase our efforts to implement the commitment made in 2009 in Pittsburgh to phase-out and rationalize, over the medium term, inefficient fossil fuel subsidies that encourage wasteful consumption and commit to achieve this objective, while providing targeted support for the poorest and the most vulnerable. We will strengthen international cooperation as well as relevant producer-consumer dialogues on securing energy affordability and accessibility by limiting volatility in energy prices and scaling up clean, safe, inclusive, and sustainable technologies, including developing regional energy interconnectivity. We are committed to promote investment in sustainable infrastructure and industry, as well as innovative technologies and a wide range of fiscal, market and regulatory mechanisms to support clean energy transitions, including, as appropriate, the use of carbon pricing and non-pricing mechanisms and incentives, while providing targeted support for the poorest and the most vulnerable.

13. Mindful of our leadership role, we reaffirm our steadfast commitments, in pursuit of the objective of UNFCCC, to tackle climate change by strengthening the full and effective implementation of the Paris Agreement and its temperature goal, reflecting equity and the principle of common but differentiated responsibilities and respective capabilities in light of different national circumstances. We will play our part fully in implementing the Glasgow Climate Pact and the relevant outcomes of previous COPs and CMAs, in particular COP 26, including the call to revisit and strengthen the 2030 targets in our NDCs, as necessary to align with the Paris Agreement. In this regard, we welcome enhanced climate actions resulting from the new or updated NDCs and invite parties to urgently scale up mitigation and adaptation ambition and means of implementation as well as make progress on loss and damage at COP 27 which is being held in Africa.

Noting the IPCC assessments that the impact of climate change will be much lower at a temperature increase of 1.5°C compared with 2°C, we resolve to pursue efforts to limit the temperature increase to 1.5°C. This will require meaningful and effective actions and commitment by all countries, taking into account different approaches, through the development of clear national pathways that align long- term ambition with short and medium-term goals, and with international cooperation and support, including finance and technology, and sustainable and responsible consumption and production as critical enablers, in the context of sustainable development.

14. We welcome the progress to date towards achieving a Post 2020 Global Biodiversity Framework (GBF). We urge all parties and countries to finalize and adopt the GBF with the view of realizing of 2050 Vision of "Living in harmony with Nature" at the second part of COP15 CBD as a strong framework of action and accountability for halting and reversing biodiversity loss by 2030 and, as appropriate, to update National Biodiversity Strategies and Action Plans accordingly. We emphasize the importance of achieving and synergizing the objectives of the three Rio Conventions. We stress the need for clear and measurable goals and targets for biodiversity and means of implementation and accountability. We commit to strengthen actions to halt and reverse biodiversity loss by 2030 and call on CBD Parties to adopt an ambitious, balanced, practical, effective, robust and transformative post-2020 Global Biodiversity Framework at COP-15 in Montreal. We urge for increased resource mobilization from all sources, including from countries and entities, to provide new and additional financial resources for the implementation of the GBF, once it is negotiated, including to help enable and support developing country parties, and for aligning private and public financial flows with biodiversity objectives. We will scale up efforts to combat biodiversity loss, deforestation, desertification, land degradation and drought, as well as restoring degraded land to achieve land degradation neutrality by 2030, and in support of the G20's ambition to reduce land degradation by 50% by 2040 on a voluntary basis. We recognize the effort made by a number of countries to ensure that at least 30% of global land and at least 30% of the global ocean and seas are conserved or protected by

2030 and we will help to make progress towards this objective in accordance with national circumstances. We commit to reduce environmental impacts by changing unsustainable consumption and production patterns as well as to enhance environmentally sound waste management including by preventing illegal cross-border traffic of waste.

15. We will step up efforts to halt and reverse biodiversity loss, including through Nature-based Solutions and Ecosystem-based Approaches, support climate mitigation and adaptation, enhance environmental conservation and protection, sustainable use and restoration, responding to natural disasters, reduce ecosystem degradation, enhance ecosystem services and to address issues affecting the marine and coastal environment. We will further promote sustainable development and lifestyles, resource efficiency and circular economy to increase sustainability and work together on scientific knowledge-sharing, raising awareness, and capacity building, particularly to advance on the ocean-based climate action. We are committed to ending illegal, unreported and unregulated fishing. We welcome the WTO multilateral Agreement on Fisheries Subsidies and encourage its rapid entry into force. In line with the UNEA Resolution 5/14, we are committed to develop an international legally binding instrument on plastic pollution, including in the marine environment, with the ambition of completing the work by the end of 2024. We highlight the progress made and call on participating delegations to achieve an ambitious and balanced agreement without delay on an international legally binding instrument under UNCLOS on the conservation and sustainable use of marine biological diversity of areas beyond national jurisdiction, as called for in the UNGA Resolution 69/292. We also acknowledge that ecosystems, including forests, seagrasses, coral reefs, wetland ecosystems in all their diversity, including peatlands and mangrove, support climate change mitigation and adaptation efforts.

16. We acknowledge the urgent need to strengthen policies and mobilize financing, from all sources in a predictable, adequate and timely manner to address climate change, biodiversity loss, and environmental degradation including significantly increasing support for developing countries. We recall and further urge developed countries to fulfil their commitments to deliver on the goal of jointly

mobilizing USD 100 billion per year urgently by 2020 and through to 2025 in the context of meaningful mitigation action and transparency on implementation. We also support continued deliberations on an ambitious new collective quantified goal of climate finance from a floor of USD 100 billion per year to support developing countries, that helps in fulfilling the objective of the UNFCCC and implementation of the Paris Agreement. We emphasize the importance of transparency in the implementation of the pledges. We also recall the Glasgow Climate Pact urging developed countries to at least double their collective provision of climate finance for adaptation to developing countries, from 2019 levels, by 2025, in the context of achieving a balance between mitigation and adaptation in the provision of scaled up financial resource, recalling Article 9 of the Paris Agreement.

17. In the context of strengthening global efforts to reach the objective of the United Nations Framework Convention on Climate Change (UNFCCC) and the goals of the Paris Agreement, as well as implementing the COP26 commitments, we reiterate that our policy mix toward carbon neutrality and net zero should include a full range of fiscal, market and regulatory mechanisms including, as appropriate, the use of carbon pricing and non-pricing mechanisms and incentives, and phase out and rationalize, over the medium term, inefficient fossil fuel subsidies that encourage wasteful consumption and commit to achieve this objective, while providing targeted support to the poorest and most vulnerable, and in line with national circumstances. We acknowledge the macro-economic risks stemming from climate change and will continue discussions on the costs and benefits of different transitions.

18. We are committed to take actions in support of orderly, just and affordable transitions to achieve the objectives of the 2030 Agenda for Sustainable Development in line with the UNFCCC and the Paris Agreement as well as with the convention on Biological Diversity. We welcome the progress made across the G20, international organizations, other international networks and initiatives, and the private sector in addressing the priorities of the G20 Sustainable Finance Roadmap, which is voluntary and flexible in nature, and call for further efforts to advance the Roadmap's recommended actions that will scale up sustainability financing. We welcome the

establishment of the Sustainable Finance Working Group's online dashboard and repository of relevant work, to illustrate ongoing and future progress made on the Roadmap, and encourage members to contribute on a voluntary basis, taking country circumstances into consideration. We endorse the 2022 G20 Sustainable Finance Report which articulates practical and voluntary recommendations for jurisdictions and relevant stakeholders in developing transition finance frameworks, improving the credibility of financial institutions' net zero commitments and scaling up sustainable finance instruments, with a focus on improving accessibility and affordability. We also welcome the valuable discussion during the Presidency's Forum on policy levers that incentivize financing and investment to support the transition.

19. We remain committed to promoting a healthy and sustainable recovery which builds towards achieving and sustaining Universal Health Coverage under the SDGs. While the COVID-19 pandemic is not over, the World Health Organization (WHO) has recently declared monkeypox as another Public Health Emergency International Concern (PHEIC), reinforcing that international health threats are ever present and that the G20 and broader global community must come together to improve our collective prevention, preparedness and response capabilities. We reaffirm the importance of strengthening of national health systems by putting people at the center of preparedness and equip them to respond effectively. We emphasize the need for equitable access to pandemic medical countermeasures, and welcome the efforts of ACT-A, and note that the results of the ACT-A external evaluations can be useful lessons for future discussions. We reaffirm our commitment to strengthen global health governance, with the leading and coordination role of WHO and support from other international organizations. We support the work of the Intergovernmental Negotiating Body (INB) that will draft and negotiate a legally binding instrument that should contain both legally binding and non-legally binding elements to strengthen pandemic PPR and the working group on the International Health Regulations that will consider amendments to the International Health Regulations (IHR) (2005) mindful that the decision will be made by World Health Assembly.

20. The G20 High Level Independent Panel, as well as the WHO and

World Bank have estimated there is an annual pandemic PPR financing gap of approximately USD 10 billion. As initiated by the Saudi Arabian G20 Presidency, the Italian G20 Presidency and continued by the Indonesian G20 Presidency, we welcome the provision of additional financial resources, to assist in financing critical gaps in implementing IHR (2005) and increase PPR capacities. In this regard, we welcome the establishment of a new Financial Intermediary Fund for Pandemic PPR (the 'Pandemic Fund') hosted by the World Bank. It aims to address critical pandemic PPR gaps and build capacity at national, regional and global levels, bring additionality in financial resources for pandemic PPR, catalyze complementary investments, and facilitate a coordinated and coherent approach to pandemic PPR strengthening. We welcome the Pandemic Fund's inclusive membership and representation from low- and middle-income countries, civil society organizations and donors, and acknowledge the WHO's technical expertise and central coordination role in this endeavor, which reflects its leadership role in the global health architecture. We appreciate the work of the Secretariat hosted by the World Bank, with the WHO as technical lead and as chair of the Technical Advisory Panel. We look forward to the launch of the Pandemic Fund's first call for proposals as soon as possible. We commit to increase the capacity of developing countries for pandemic PPR through the Pandemic Fund, and look forward to the stocktaking review of the Pandemic Fund at the end of its first year to draw on lessons learned and incorporate any changes needed to ensure it is operating in accordance with its governing documents and effective at filling critical PPR gaps, and that it continues to have a central coordination role for the WHO, maintains a strong connection to the G20, and is inclusive of the perspectives of low- and middle-income countries and additional non-G20 partners in its decision making. We commend the pledges by current donors, amounting to over USD 1.4 billion, and encourage additional voluntary pledges. We call on new donors to join the Pandemic Fund, as they are able to.

21. It is essential to continue collaboration between Finance and Health Ministries for pandemic PPR. We extend the mandate of the Task Force, and ask the Secretariat of the Task Force to work with the Task Force co-chairs, the incoming Indian G20 Presidency, the G20 Troika,

and G20 members to agree on a Task Force workplan for 2023, taking into account a multi-year planning horizon. We thank the WHO for continuing to host the Secretariat, with support from the World Bank. In 2023 the Task Force will continue to be co-chaired by Indonesia and Italy, representing advanced and emerging economy perspectives, and will continue to draw on expertise of the WHO, International Financial Institutions and other relevant organizations, with the support of the 2023 Indian G20 Presidency. To expand the voice of lower income countries we invite key regional organizations to join the Task Force meetings, as appropriate. We will work closely with the WHO to ensure the Task Force continues to complement the global pandemic PPR architecture and there is no further duplication and fragmentation of the global health governance system. Delivering on the mandate from the G20 Rome Leaders' Declaration, in 2023 the Task Force will continue developing coordination arrangements between Finance and Health Ministries, and share best practices and experiences from past finance-health coordination in order to develop joint responses to pandemics, as appropriate. The Task Force will undertake work to better understand economic risks and vulnerabilities from pandemics, and how to mitigate them, with a focus on finance and health coordination in response to new pandemics, considering country-specific circumstances and recognizing the importance of further work on resource mobilization. We ask the Task Force to report back to Finance and Health Ministers in 2023 on its progress.

22. We recognize that the extensive COVID-19 immunization is a global public good and we will advance our effort to ensure timely, equitable and universal access to safe, affordable, quality and effective vaccines, therapeutics and diagnostics (VTDs). Acknowledging the adoption of the Ministerial Declaration on the WTO Response to the COVID-19 Pandemic and Preparedness for Future Pandemics and the Ministerial Decision on the TRIPS Agreement at the WTO's 12th Ministerial Conference (MC12), we note that, no later than six months from the date of the Ministerial Decision on the TRIPS Agreement, WTO members will decide on its extension to cover the production and supply of COVID-19 diagnostics and therapeutics. We remain committed to embedding a multisectoral One Health approach and enhancing global surveillance, including genomic surveillance, in

order to detect pathogens and antimicrobial resistance (AMR) that may threaten human health. To enable global pathogen surveillance as part of our commitment to implement the IHR (2005), we encourage sharing of pathogen data in a timely manner on shared and trusted platforms in collaboration with WHO. We encourage sharing of benefits arising from the utilization of pathogens consistent with applicable national laws.

23. We recognize the need for strengthening local and regional health product manufacturing capacities and cooperation as well as sustainable global and regional research and development networks to facilitate better access to VTDs globally, especially in developing countries, and underscore the importance of public-private partnership, and technology transfer and knowledge sharing on voluntary and mutually agreed terms. We support the WHO mRNA Vaccine Technology Transfer hub as well as all as the spokes in all regions of the world with the objective of sharing technology and technical know-how on voluntary and mutually agreed terms. We welcome joint research and joint production of vaccines, including enhanced cooperation among developing countries. We acknowledge the importance of shared technical standards and verification methods, under the framework of the IHR (2005), to facilitate seamless international travel, interoperability, and recognizing digital solutions and non-digital solutions, including proof of vaccinations. We support continued international dialogue and collaboration on the establishment of trusted global digital health networks as part of the efforts to strengthen prevention and response to future pandemics, that should capitalize and build on the success of the existing standards and digital COVID-19 certificates.

24. The COVID-19 pandemic has accelerated the transformation of the digital ecosystem and digital economy. We recognize the importance of digital transformation in reaching the SDGs. We acknowledge that affordable and high-quality digital connectivity is essential for digital inclusion and digital transformation, while a resilient, safe and secure online environment is necessary to enhance confidence and trust in the digital economy. We recognize the importance of policies to create an enabling, inclusive, open, fair and non-discriminatory digital economy that fosters the application of new technologies, allows businesses and entrepreneurs to thrive, and protects and empowers

consumers, while addressing the challenges, related to digital divides, privacy, data protection, intellectual property rights, and online safety. We acknowledge the importance to counter disinformation campaigns, cyber threats, online abuse, and ensuring security in connectivity infrastructure. We remain committed to further enable data free flow with trust and promote cross-border data flows. We will advance a more inclusive, human-centric, empowering, and sustainable digital transformation. We also reaffirm the role of data for development, economic growth and social well-being.

25. We encourage international collaboration to further develop digital skills and digital literacy to harness the positive impacts of digital transformation, especially for women, girls, and people in vulnerable situations, and further support efforts to develop reliable skills and literacy. We note the increasing demands for a workforce adept at utilizing emerging technologies, education and training, reskilling and upskilling to meet such demands. We also seek to increase connectivity by accelerating high capacity and secure infrastructure and provide more accessible and affordable resources and tools, while also improve the digital literacy skills of learners, teachers, school leaders, and other educational professional to ensure universal access to education, accelerate learning recovery and promote lifelong learning.

26. We found digital technology becomes the key for recovery and empowerment across various sectors, including in building a resilient and sustainable food system and agriculture, creating sustainable and decent jobs and human capacity development, supporting inclusive trade, industrialization and investment, increasing productivity, as well as opening up the potential of the future economy, especially for Micro, Small and Medium Enterprises (MSMEs) and start-ups. It is essential to ensure that no one is left behind in our effort to digitally transform our society, by involving all stakeholders, including the youth, women, business sector, audit institution, parliaments, scientists, and labours.

27. We support continued implementation of the G20 Roadmap for Enhancing Cross-Border Payments, including the future delivery of the initial estimates for key performance indicators and 2022 Progress Report that sets out priorities for the next stage of work. We encourage central banks, other public authorities and the payments industry to

continue to work collaboratively on these important initiatives to enhance cross-border payments. We welcome the report by the Bank for International Settlements (BIS) Committee on Payments and Market Infrastructures (CPMI) on interlinking payment systems and the role of Application Programming Interfaces (APIs) that was presented in a joint workshop by the Indonesian G20 Presidency in coordination with the BIS CPMI and the BIS Innovation Hub (BISIH) on cross-border payments and interoperability at the Festival Ekonomi Keuangan Digital Indonesia (FEKDI) 2022. We also welcome the joint report by the BIS CPMI, BISIH, IMF, and World Bank on options for access to and interoperability of Central Bank Digital Currencies (CBDCs) for cross-border payments.

28. We endorse the G20 Financial Inclusion Framework on Harnessing Digitalization to Increase Productivity and Foster a Sustainable and Inclusive Economy for Women, Youth and MSMEs or Yogyakarta Financial Inclusion Framework guided by the G20 2020 Financial Inclusion Action Plan. To address digitalization and sustainable finance developments, and support financial inclusion and well-being, we endorse the updated G20/OECD High-Level Principles on Financial Consumer Protection and welcome the updated G20/OECD High-Level Principles on SME Financing.

29. To support our collective ambition to recover together, recover stronger, we commit to well- calibrated, well-planned, and well-communicated policies to support sustainable recovery, with due consideration to country-specific circumstances. We commit to mitigate scarring effects to support strong, sustainable, balanced and inclusive growth. We will stay agile and flexible in our fiscal policy response, standing ready to adjust to the changing circumstances as needed. Temporary and targeted measures to help sustain the purchasing power of the most vulnerable and cushion the impact of commodity price increases, including energy and food prices, should be well designed to avoid adding to high inflationary pressures. We will continue to enhance macro policy cooperation, preserve financial stability and long-term fiscal sustainability, and safeguard against downside risks and negative spillovers. Macroprudential policies need to remain vigilant to guard against rising systemic risks as financial conditions tighten. Recognizing that many currencies have moved significantly this year with increased volatility, we reaffirm

the commitments made on exchange rates by our Finance Ministers and Central Bank Governors in April 2021. We also reiterate the importance of global cooperation and express our appreciation to the Indonesian G20 Presidency for its efforts to maintain an effective system of multilateralism through the G20.

30. G20 central banks are strongly committed to achieving price stability, in line with their respective mandates. To that end, they are closely monitoring the impact of price pressures on inflation expectations and will continue to appropriately calibrate the pace of monetary policy tightening in a data-dependent and clearly communicated manner, ensuring that inflation expectations remain well anchored, while being mindful to safeguard the recovery and limit cross-country spillovers. Central bank independence is crucial to achieving these goals and buttressing monetary policy credibility.

31. We are committed to the swift implementation of the OECD/G20 two-pillar international tax package. We welcome the progress on Pillar One. We also welcome progress on Pillar Two Global Anti-Base Erosion (GloBE) Model Rules, which pave the way for consistent implementation at a global level as a common approach, and we look forward to the completion of the GloBE Implementation Framework. We call on the OECD/G20 Inclusive Framework on Base Erosion and Profit Shifting (BEPS) to finalize Pillar One, including remaining issues and by signing the Multilateral Convention in the first half of 2023, and to complete the negotiations of the Subject to Tax Rule (STTR) under Pillar Two that would allow the development of a Multilateral Instrument for its implementation. We will work to strengthen the tax and development agenda in light of the July 2022 G20 Ministerial Symposium on Tax and Development, and we note the G20/OECD Roadmap on Developing Countries and International Tax. We support the progress made on implementing internationally agreed tax transparency standards, including regional efforts and welcome the signing of the Asia Initiative Bali Declaration in July 2022. We also welcome the Crypto-Asset Reporting Framework and the amendments to the Common Reporting Standard, both of which we consider to be integral additions to the global standards for automatic exchange of information. We call on the OECD to conclude the work on implementation packages, including possible timelines, and invite the Global Forum on Transparency and Exchange of

Information for Tax Purposes to build on its commitment and monitoring processes to ensure widespread implementation of both packages by relevant jurisdictions.

32. We reaffirm our commitment to strengthening the long-term financial resilience of the international financial architecture, including by promoting sustainable capital flows, and developing local currency capital markets. We welcome the IMF's revised Institutional View on Liberalization and Management of Capital Flows and look forward to continued discussions with international organizations on the coherent implementation of international frameworks for the use of capital flow management measures, while being mindful of their original purpose. We look forward to further progress by the IMF in operationalizing the Integrated Policy Framework and welcome the report by the Bank for International Settlements (BIS) on Macro-financial stability frameworks. We welcome continued exploration of how CBDCs could potentially be designed to facilitate cross-border payments, while preserving the stability and integrity of the international monetary and financial system. We welcome the successful completion of the G20 TechSprint 2022, a joint initiative with the BISIH, which has contributed to the debate on the most practical and feasible solutions to implement CBDCs. We reiterate our commitment to maintaining a strong and effective Global Financial Safety Net with a strong, quota-based and adequately resourced IMF at its center. We remain committed to revisiting the adequacy of quotas and will continue the process of IMF governance reform under the 16th General Review of Quotas, including a new quota formula as a guide, by 15 December 2023. We take note on the continuation of discussion of the IMF surcharge policy.

33. We are committed to support all vulnerable countries to recover together, recover stronger. We welcome pledges amounting to USD 81.6 billion through the voluntary channelling of Special Drawing Rights (SDRs) or equivalent contributions, and call for further pledges from all willing and able countries to meet the total global ambition of USD 100 billion of voluntary contributions for countries most in need. We welcome the operationalization of the Resilience and Sustainability Trust (RST) to help eligible low-income countries, small states and vulnerable middle-income countries address longer-term structural challenges that pose macroeconomic risks, including those

stemming from pandemics and climate change. We welcome the voluntary contributions to the RST and call for additional pledges and timely contributions to it and to the Poverty Reduction and Growth Trust (PRGT), especially for subsidy resources, to ensure a broad pool of contributors to meet funding needs. We are open to explore viable options for countries to voluntarily channel SDRs through Multilateral Development Banks (MDBs), while respecting national legal frameworks and the need to preserve the reserve assets status of SDRs. We will explore ways, including through balance sheet optimization measures, and other potential avenues, to maximize MDBs' development impact. We welcome early deliberations and urge MDBs to continue to discuss options for implementing the recommendations of the G20 Independent Review of MDBs' Capital Adequacy Frameworks within their own governance frameworks, and to deliver an update in Spring 2023. This will inform the ongoing development of a roadmap for the implementation of the recommendations, while safeguarding MDBs' long-term financial sustainability, robust credit ratings and preferred creditor status. We acknowledge the concluding report on the 2020 Shareholding Review of the International Bank for Reconstruction and Development (IBRD) and look forward to the 2025 Shareholding Review. At this challenging juncture, we reiterate our commitment to step up our efforts to implement the Common Framework for Debt Treatment beyond the Debt Service Suspension Initiative (DSSI) in a predictable, timely, orderly and coordinated manner. We welcome progress in this regard, including the provision of financing assurances for Zambia. We welcome the conclusion of the debt treatment to Chad and encourage the timely conclusion of the debt treatment for Zambia by early 2023.

We also encourage the conclusion of the debt treatment for Ethiopia under an IMF-supported program. We are concerned about the deteriorating debt situation in some vulnerable middle- income countries. This could be addressed by multilateral coordination that involves all official and private bilateral creditors to take swift action to respond to their requests for debt treatments. We stress the importance for private creditors and other official bilateral creditors to commit to providing debt treatments on terms at least as favourable to ensure fair burden sharing in line with the comparability of treatment principle. We reaffirm the importance of joint efforts by all actors, including private creditors, to continue working toward enhancing debt transparency. We welcome the efforts of private sector lenders who have already contributed data to the joint Institute of International Finance (IIF)/OECD Data Repository Portal, and continue to encourage others to also contribute on a voluntary basis.

34. In the face of a more challenging global economic and financial outlook, we underline the need to reinforce global financial system resilience and ask the Financial Stability Board (FSB) and IMF to continue their monitoring efforts. We commit to sustaining global financial stability, including through continued coordination of policy measures and implementation of international standards. We welcome the FSB's final report on financial sector exit strategies and scarring effects of COVID-19 and its conclusions regarding financial stability issues by the end of 2022. We strongly support global policy actions to increase resilience, in particular against cross-border spillovers, including by addressing the identified structural vulnerabilities in non-bank financial intermediation (NBFI) from a systemic perspective. To this end, we welcome the FSB's NBFI progress report with policy proposals to address systemic risk in NBFI, including in open-ended funds. We welcome the report by the Basel Committee on Banking Supervision (BCBS), the BIS Committee on Payments and Market Infrastructures (CPMI), and the International Organization of Securities Commissions (IOSCO) on the review of margining practices. We support taking forward the implementation of the FSB updated Roadmap for addressing climate-related financial risks which complements the G20 Sustainable Finance Roadmap. Globally consistent data are needed in order to effectively address climate-related financial risks. We look forward to the finalization of standards by the International Sustainability Standards Board (ISSB) in support of globally consistent, comparable and reliable climate-related financial disclosures, and its work beyond climate, and we welcome the efforts to achieve interoperability across disclosure frameworks. We welcome the FSB progress report on achieving consistent and comparable climate-related financial disclosures and the final report on supervisory and regulatory approaches to climate-related risks. We welcome the report by the FSB and the Network for Greening the Financial System (NGFS) on climate-scenario analysis by jurisdictions.

35. We welcome ongoing work by the FSB and international standard setters to ensure that the crypto-assets ecosystem, including so-called stablecoins, is closely monitored and subject to robust regulation, supervision, and oversight to mitigate potential risks to financial stability. We welcome the FSB's proposed approach for establishing a comprehensive international framework for the regulation of crypto-asset activities based on the principle of 'same activity, same risk, same regulation'. We welcome the FSB consultative report on the review of its high- level recommendations for the regulation, supervision and oversight of "global stablecoin" arrangements. We also welcome the FSB consultation report on promoting international consistency of regulatory and supervisory approaches to crypto-assets activities and markets. It is critical to build public awareness of risks, to strengthen regulatory outcomes and to support a level playing field, while harnessing the benefits of innovation. We welcome the final guidance by the BIS CPMI and IOSCO which confirms that the Principles for Financial Market Infrastructures apply to systematically important stablecoin arrangements. We welcome the FSB consultative report on achieving greater convergence in cyber incidents reporting, and look forward to the final report. We welcome the results of the second phase of the Data Gaps Initiative (DGI-2) and will continue to work with partners in addressing the identified remaining challenges. We welcome the workplan on the new Data Gaps Initiative (DGI) prepared by the IMF, FSB and the Inter-Agency Group on Economic and Financial Statistics (IAG) in collaboration with participating members. We ask the IMF, the FSB and the IAG to begin work on filling these data gaps and report back on progress in the second half of 2023, noting that the targets are ambitious and delivery will need to take into account national statistical capacities, priorities, and country circumstances as well as avoiding overlap and duplication at international level. We welcome the progress of work on the review of the G20/OECD Principles of Corporate Governance, including the second report and the ongoing public consultation, and look forward to further updates on the review.

36. We reaffirm that the rules-based, non-discriminatory, free, fair, open, inclusive, equitable, sustainable and transparent multilateral trading system (MTS), with the WTO at its core, is indispensable to advancing our shared objectives of inclusive growth, innovation, job creation

and sustainable development in an open and interconnected world as well as to supporting the resilience and recovery of a global economy under strain due to COVID-19 and global supply chain disruption. We agree that reforming the WTO is key in strengthening trust in the MTS. We will continue to ensure a level playing field and fair competition to foster a favourable trade and investment environment for all. We note the importance of the contribution of the MTS to promote the UN 2030 Agenda and its SDGs. Commending the successful conclusion of the 12th WTO Ministerial Conference (MC12), we commit to seize and advance the positive momentum by engaging in active, constructive, pragmatic, and focused discussions on WTO reform to improve all its functions, including reform of the dispute settlement mechanism, on the path leading to the MC13.

37. We are committed to reinforce international trade and investment cooperation to address supply chain issues and avoid trade disruptions. We believe that trade and climate/environmental policies should be mutually supportive and WTO consistent and contribute to the objectives of sustainable development. We also recognise the importance of inclusive international cooperation on digital trade. We recognize the need to promote value addition through sustainable and inclusive investment in highly productive sectors such as downstream manufacturing, digital trade, and services, and to foster linkages between foreign investors and local enterprises particularly MSMEs. We note the initiative from the Indonesian Presidency to hold discussions on policy coherence between trade, investment and industry, and to continue addressing industry-related issues in the broader G20 process, as appropriate.

38. We recognize the importance of revitalizing infrastructure investment in a sustainable, inclusive, accessible, and affordable way. We endorse the voluntary and non-binding G20/GI Hub Framework on How to Best Leverage Private Sector Participation to Scale Up Sustainable Infrastructure Investment which will consider country circumstances, and which will complement investment from other sources, including public investment and finance provided by MDBs. We note the Outcome Document from the 2022 G20 Infrastructure Investors Dialogue. To enhance social inclusion and address subnational disparities, we endorse the G20-OECD Policy Toolkit on Mobilizing

Funding and Financing for Inclusive and Quality Infrastructure Investment in Regions and Cities, prepared with the support of the Asian Development Bank (ADB). We note the Preliminary Findings Report on Gender Inclusive Approaches in Private Participation in Infrastructure in promoting gender considerations during the infrastructure lifecycle and look forward to the final report. We endorse the InfraTracker 2.0 which will enable both the public and private sectors towards transformative infrastructure investment post-COVID-19, by providing insights into long-term infrastructure strategies and plans. To narrow the digital divide, we endorse the G20 Compendium of Case Studies on Digital Infrastructure Finance: Issues, Practices and Innovations. We endorse the Quality Infrastructure Investment (QII) Indicators and associated guidance note, developed for the G20, which are voluntary and non-binding and consider country circumstances, and we look forward to further discussions on how the QII indicators can be applied. We welcome progress made towards developing a possible new governance model for the Global Infrastructure Hub (GI Hub) and ask that principles to guide the process be finalized as soon as possible.

39. The rise of automation and digital technologies are reshaping the world of work, presenting both opportunities and challenges. Adding to the situation, the COVID-19 pandemic has exacerbated pre-existing inequalities in many countries and continues to disproportionately affect women, youth, older workers, persons with disabilities and migrant workers. We underline that it remains our utmost priority to mitigate the adverse impact of the current trends on the labour market, reduce inequalities while responding effectively to the opportunities that automation and digital technologies present and promote gender equality. We remain committed to the promotion of decent work and the elimination of child and forced labour.

40. We reaffirm our commitment to support the full inclusion of migrants, including migrant workers, refugees, in our recovery efforts, in the spirit of international cooperation and in line with national policies, legislation, and circumstances, ensuring full respect for their human rights and fundamental freedoms regardless of their migration status. We also recognize the importance of preventing irregular migration flows and the smuggling of migrants, as part of a comprehensive approach for safe, orderly and regular migration, while responding

to humanitarian needs and the root causes of displacement. We support strengthening cooperation between countries of origin, transit, and destination. We will continue the dialogue on migration and forced displacement in future Presidencies.

41. We remain committed to a human-centred, inclusive, fair, sustainable approach that leads to greater social justice, decent work, and social protection for all. We will continue our work to integrate persons with disabilities, women, and youth across sectors and levels in pursuit of an inclusive labour market. We are resolved to promote sustainable development of human capacity, labour markets, and productivity, including through community-based vocational education and training, to advance job creation through entrepreneurship, to empower MSMEs, and to accelerate our efforts to foster and adapt labour protection for all workers, including those in the informal sector. We will maximize our approach to skills development to respond effectively to the needs of the labour market, with the involvement of social partners. We will accelerate progress towards the Antalya Youth Goal, as well as universal social protection for all by 2030.

42. We are deeply concerned that multidimensional crises, including the COVID-19 pandemic, as well as lack of fiscal space and unequal access to finance and technology, are posing significant challenges towards realizing the 2030 Agenda for Sustainable Development and the Addis Ababa Action Agenda in a timely manner. We will demonstrate leadership and take collective actions to implement the 2030 Agenda for Sustainable Development and accelerate the achievement of the SDGs by 2030 and address developmental challenges by reinvigorating a more inclusive multilateralism and reform aimed at implementing the 2030 Agenda.

43. In this regard, we will strengthen inclusive and sustainable recovery and build resilience in all developing countries, including SIDS in the Pacific and Caribbean and LDCs, through ambitious and concrete actions. We also reiterate our continued support to Africa, including through the G20 Compact with Africa and the G20 Initiative on Supporting Industrialization in Africa and LDCs. We will focus on MSMEs, adaptive social protection, green economy and blue economy. We recognise the need for partnership to promote mutually beneficial technology cooperation and share good practice, as well

as the need for inclusive and quality infrastructure investment for stronger recovery and resilience. We underscore the need to address the financing gap towards implementation of the 2030 Agenda, through enhancing innovative financing mechanisms, including blended finance, while noting the importance of transparency and mutual accountability. We take note of initiatives such as the Coalition for Disaster Resilience Infrastructure and the Global Blended Finance Alliance, and welcome the Global Platform for Disaster Risk Reduction. We look forward to the success of the SDGs Summit in 2023.

44. Access to education is a human right and a pivotal tool for inclusive and sustainable economic recovery. We welcome the outcome of the Transforming Education Summit. We will act in solidarity in particular with developing countries to rebuild more resilient, tech- enabled, accessible, and effective education systems. We will empower relevant actors within and beyond G20 to remove barriers to education, improve teaching and learning environments, and support transitions within and across all stages of education, with emphasis on women and girls. We also underscore the importance of learners' well-being in their preparation for work and meaningful participation and contribution to more equitable, inclusive and sustainable society. We reaffirm the importance of Education for Sustainable Development (ESD) and our commitment to SDG4 to ensure inclusive and equitable quality education and training. We are committed to promoting lifelong learning at all levels amidst the changing nature of work and encourage partnership in this regard.

45. We acknowledge the importance of research and innovation in sustainable resource utilization in various sectors, especially in the midst of health, climate, food and energy crises. We welcome research and innovation collaboration for the conservation of biodiversity and its use to support the sustainable development including green and blue economy. We also promote inclusive collaborations to further research and innovation, as well as promoting researchers' international mobility.

46. As women and girls continue to be disproportionately affected by the COVID-19 pandemic and other crises, we reaffirm our commitment to put gender equality and women's empowerment at the core of our efforts for an inclusive recovery and sustainable

development. We commit to implement the G20 Roadmap Towards and Beyond the Brisbane Goal foster financial inclusion and access to digital technologies, including to address the unequal distribution in paid and unpaid care and domestic work, with a focus on closing the gender pay gap. We commit to the elimination of gender-based violence, the enhancement of social, health, care and educational services, and the overcoming of gender stereotypes. We will continue to advance women's and girls' equal access to inclusive and quality education, including participations in STEM education, women entrepreneurship through MSMEs, and women's and girls' access in leadership positions. We will promote quality of life for women in rural areas and women with disabilities. We welcome the work that has been done by the EMPOWER Alliance and its engagement with the G20, and support the future convening of G20 Ministerial Conference on Women's Empowerment.

47. We reaffirm the important role of tourism for global recovery, and the community-based approach for rebuilding a more human-centred, inclusive, sustainable, and resilient tourism sector. We acknowledge the vital importance of strengthening safe international mobility and connectivity and seamless post-Covid travel to enable tourism recovery. We further recognize that creative economy, which involve knowledge-based economy, human creativity, and intellectual property rights, contributes to improving the resiliency of tourism local communities and MSMEs through human capital development, digital transformation, innovation, public-private partnerships, sustainable preservation of natural and cultural heritage, and innovative financing while retaining their significant commercial and cultural values.

48. We reaffirm the role of culture as an enabler and driver for sustainable development with intrinsic value beyond its social and economic benefits. We are committed to develop policies that draw on cultural diversity as a resource for sustainable living and promote an inclusive and equitable ecosystem at all levels that values the contribution of those working in the culture, arts and heritage sectors. We will respect, protect and preserve the cultural heritage of our peoples, including local communities and indigenous peoples, as applicable. We support public incentives and sustainable investments from the private sector to strengthen the cultural economy. We will safeguard cultural

heritage as well as fighting illicit trafficking of cultural property and promoting restitution to its rightful owner/countries of origin, in accordance with the relevant UNESCO Conventions and national laws.

49. We will continue to lead by example through strengthening and implementing our obligations and commitments to anti-corruption efforts including through legally binding instruments, while renewing our commitment to zero tolerance for corruption. We emphasize the importance of transparency and accountability for both public and private sector as a crucial part of a collective recovery effort. We underscore the important role of auditing as well as public participation and anti-corruption education in preventing and tackling any form of corruption. We recall our commitments and call on all countries to criminalise bribery, including bribery of foreign public officials, and effectively prevent, combat, detect, investigate, prosecute and sanction bribery. We will further work to strengthen international cooperation and legal frameworks to combat economic crimes including corruption related to organized crime and money laundering, including, on a voluntary basis, through existing networks and initiatives such as GlobE and the G20 Denial of Entry Experts Network. We will share information on our actions towards criminalising foreign bribery and enforcing foreign bribery legislation in line with Article 16 of UNCAC, and look forward to enlarging participation to the OECD Anti-Bribery Convention, as appropriate. We reaffirm our commitment to deny safe haven to corruption offenders and their assets, in accordance to domestic laws. We also recognize the importance of mitigating corruption risk in all sectors. We will further strengthen our engagement with and promote active participation by stakeholders such as academia, civil society, media and the private sector, including to advance a culture of integrity.

50. We recognize the need for the international community to step up their efforts to effectively combat money laundering, terrorism financing, and proliferation financing. We reaffirm our commitment to delivering the strategic priorities of the Financial Action Task Force (FATF) and its FATF Style Regional Bodies (FSRBs) to lead global action to respond to these threats. We welcome the initiative by the FATF to promote implementation of international standards on virtual assets, in particular the "travel rule", and transparency of beneficial

ownership, and acknowledge their role in the fight against systemic corruption and environmental crimes, which gravely impact economies and societies. We support the ongoing work of the FATF to enhance global efforts to seize criminal proceeds and return funds to victims and states in line with domestic frameworks. We encourage all G20 members to strengthen collaboration to adopt and effectively implement the FATF standards.

51. We welcome the Indonesian Presidency's efforts to compile a wide array of national submissions and international coordinated collaborations from G20 members, invited countries, and regional and international organizations. These have been presented in the "G20 Action for Strong and Inclusive Recovery", as annexed. We call for further concrete actions to impart greater momentum and impact to the efforts of international community to recover together and recover stronger.

52. We welcome the outcomes of various G20 working groups and Ministerial meetings. We appreciate and thank Indonesia for its Presidency and for successfully hosting the Bali G20 Leaders' Summit and for its contribution to the G20 process. We look forward to meeting again in India in 2023, in Brazil in 2024 and in South Africa in 2025.

We thank international organizations, including the UN and its Specialised Agencies, World Bank Group, IMF, OECD, Asian Development Bank, ERIA, CEPI, European Investment Bank, GGGI, ICAO, IEA, IEF, IFAD, ILO, IRENA, FAO, FSB, Gavi, Global Fund, IAEA, Islamic Development Bank, ITU, Medicine Patent Pool, Sustainable Energy for All (SEforAll), OPEC, WEF, WFP, WHO, WTO, UNCCD, UNCTAD, UNDESA, UNDP, UNECE, UNESCAP, UNESCO, UNFCCC, UN Global Pulse, UN Habitat,

UNICEF, UNIDO, UNOPS, UN Women, UNWTO and the G20 Engagement Groups (W20, L20, T20, S20, Y20, SAI20, P20, C20, B20, U20) for their valuable inputs and policy recommendations.

Ceremonial Pictures & Logos of G20 Summits 2014-2021

(1) Brisbane 2014

(2) Antalya 2015

(3) Hangzhou 2016

(4) Hamburg 2017

(5) Buenos Aires 2018

(6) Osaka 2019

(7) Riyadh 2020 (Virtual Summit)

(8) Rome 2021

(9) Bali 2022

Bibliography

Aashriti Gautam. India and G20: Strengthening and Shaping Global Governance. *EPRA International Journal of Multidisciplinary Research,* Vol. 8, Issue 10, October 2022. Journal DOI: 10.36713/epra2013

Abbott, Tony. G20 2014: Overview Of Australia's Presidency. www.unescap.org/sites/default/d8files/knowledge-products/G20-Presentation-6Aug2014.pdf Accessed on 10/08/2022.

About C20 Indonesia. www.civil-20.org/about/ Accessed on 14/08/2022.

Aldrich, Daniel. Japan's opportunity to lead. www.nature.com/articles/s41558-019-0510-0 Accessed on 11/08/2022.

Alvin Cheng-Hin Lim. The BRICS at the Hangzhou G20 Summit. www.brics-info.org/adopted-g20-leaders-communique-hangzhou-summit/ Accessed on 02/09/2022.

Amon, Ada and, Ingrid Holmes. What is holding back energy efficiency financing in G20 countries? November 2015, https://www.jstor.org/stable/resrep17783

B20 Argentina Buenos Aires Summit Communiqué. https://www.b20argentina.info/Document/documentb20 Accessed on 12/08/2022.

B20 Bali; advancing innovative, inclusive and collaborative growth. www.b20indonesia2022.org Accessed on 14/08/2022.

B20 Italy final communiqué. Policy recommendations to the G20. www.b20italy2021.org. Accessed on 12/08/2022.

B20 policy recommendations to the G20; realizing opportunities of the 21st century for all. www.groupofnations.com/summits/b20-saudi-arabia/ Accessed on 14/08/2022.

Ban Ki-moon. Letters from Ban Ki-moon to the G20 Leaders, 11 April 2015, https://www.jstor.org/stable/community.30377175

Banu, Saira. India at G20 Osaka Summit. Centre for Public Policy Research. www.cppr.in/articles/india-at-g20-osaka-summit Accessed on 10/08/2022.

Bery, Suman. The G20 turns ten: what's past is prologue, 01 November 2018, https://www.jstor.org/stable/resrep28507

Bhatia, Rajiv. "The G20's Virtual year" in India in the G20: Rule-taker to Rule-maker (Manjeet Kripalani, ed.), Routledge.

Biba, Sebastian and Holbig, Heike. China in the G20: A Narrow Corridor for Sino–European Cooperation. China in the G20: A Narrow Corridor for Sino–European Cooperation on JSTOR. Accessed on 01/09/2022.

Brunner, Christoph. Activist Sense: Affective Media Practices during the G20 Summit in Hamburg, March 2018. https://transversal.at/transversal/0318/brunner/en

C20 Argentina: policy pack. www.civil-20.org/category/papers-statements/ Accessed on 14/08/2022.

C20 Communiqué 2020. https://civil-20.org/2020/ Accessed on 14/08/2022.

C20 Final Communiqué. https://civil-20.org/2020/ Accessed on 14/08/2022.

C20 Principles. https://civil-20.org/2020/wp-content/uploads/2019/12/C20-Principles_final1.pdf Accessed on 14/08/2022.

Callaghan, Mike. The G20 needs a growth strategy, 01 February 2014, https://www.jstor.org/stable/resrep10230

Chin, G. T. and Dobson, H. J. (2016), China's Presidency of the G20 Hangzhou: On Global Leadership and Strategy, Global Summitry, ISSN 2058-7430. https://doi.org/10.1093/global/guw002. Accessed on 2/09/2022.

Communiqué from the Urban 20 (U20), 02 October 2020, Riyadh-U20 Riyadh 2020 Urban, www.urban20.org/u2summit/2020-riyadh/ Accessed on 18/08/2022.

Communiqué of the Forty-Fourth Meeting of the IMFC - International Monetary Fund. https://www.imf.org/en/News/Articles/2021/10/14/communique-of-the-forty-fourth-meeting-of-the-imfc Accessed on 24/04/2022.

Communiqué T20 summit season 17 September –01 November 2020, virtual summit from Riyadh, Saudi Arabia-T20 Saudi Arabia. www.g20.utoronto.ca/t20/2020-T20%20Communique-EN.pdf Accessed on 14/08/2022.

Communiqué, 4th G20 Finance Ministers and Central Bank Governors, Washington DC., 13 October 2021, www.g20.org

Communiqué, Joint G20 Finance and Health Ministers Meeting, 29 October 2021, www.g20.org

Crises: economy, society, law, and culture towards a less vulnerable humankind, SSH20 academies joint statement. https://www.lincei.it/en/news/academies-g20-countries-signed-two-joint-statements Accessed on 14/08/2022.

Cyber Incident Response and Recovery: Progress Report to the G20 Finance Ministers and Central Bank Governors. https://www.fsb.org/2019/05/cyber-incident-response-and-recovery-progress-report-to-the-g20-finance-ministers-and-central-bank-governors/ Accessed on 28/08/2022.

Daniel Neff and Joachim Betz. Gender Justice as an International Objective: India in the G20. 01 June 2017. Stable URL, https://www.jstor.org/stable/resrep24793

Daniel Neff and Joachim Betz. Gender Justice as an International Objective: India in the G20. German Institute of Global and Area Studies (GIGA). https://www.jstor.org/stable/resrep24793 Accessed on 05/09/2022.

Declaration on Delivering Resources through the International Financial Institutions, 24 April 2009, London, United Kingdom, www.g20.org

Declaration on Strengthening the Financial System, 2 April 2009, London United Kingdom, www.g20.org

Declaration—Summit on Financial Markets and the World Economy, 15 November 2008, Washington United States, www.g20.org

Dharmaputra, Radityo. Understanding Indonesia's Response to Russia's war in Ukraine: A Preliminary Analysis of the Discursive Landscape published in *Journal of Global Strategic Studies*, Vol. II, No. 1, June 2022, DOI: 10.36859/jgss.v2i1.1057

Dhruv C. Katoch, Ed. *India Foundation Journal*, Vol. III, November-December 2022. Journal@indiafoundation.in

Engagement Communiqués Osaka Summit. https://www.mofa.go.jp/policy/economy/g20_summit/osaka19/en/engagementgroups/ Accessed on 14/08/2022.

Eran, Oded. The G20 Hamburg Summit. The G20 Hamburg Summit on JSTOR. Accessed on 01/09/2022.

Final Declaration, 2-4 November 2011, Cannes, France, www.g20.org

Finalising post-crisis reforms: an update - A report to G20 Leaders. https://www.bis.org/bcbs/publ/d344.htm Accessed on 01/09/2022.

Framework for Post-Implementation Evaluation of the Effects of the G20 Financial Regulatory Reforms. https://www.fsb.org/2017/07/framework-for-post-implementation-evaluation-of-the-effects-of-the-g20-financial-regulatory-reforms/ Accessed on 28/08/2022.

FSB action plan to assess and address the decline in correspondent banking: Progress report to G20 Summit of July 2017, https://www.fsb.org/2017/07/fsb-action-plan-to-assess-and-address-the-decline-in-correspondent-banking-progress-report-to-g20-summit-of-july-2017/. Accessed on 28/08/2022.

FSB Chair's letter to G20 Leaders: November 2022. https://www.fsb.org/wp-content/uploads/P111122.pdf Accessed on 02/09/2022.

G20 5th Anniversary Vision Statement, 5-6 September 2013, Saint Petersburg, Russia, www.g20.org

G20 Buenos Aires Action Plan, 30 November-01 December 2018, Argentina, www.g20.org

G20 commitment to social justice and decent work welcomed by ILO. https://www.ilo.org/global/about-the-ilo/newsroom/news/WCMS_861583/lang—en/index.htm Accessed on 05/09/2022.

G20 Data Gaps Initiative (DGI-2): The Sixth Progress Report — Countdown to December 2021. https://www.fsb.org/2021/10/g20-data-gaps-initiative-dgi-2-the-sixth-progress-report-countdown-to-december-2021/ Accessed on 25/08/2022.

G20 Germany 2017 Science 20 Dialogue. https://scholar.archive.org/work/445a67ddfrc4bno4x37tg5ncui Accessed on 14/08/2022.

G20 Hamburg Action Plan, 7-8 July 2017, Hamburg, Germany, www.g20.org

G20 Leaders´ Declaration. Shaping an interconnected world. https://www.fsb.org/wp-content/uploads/G20-Leaders-Hamburg-Communique.pdf Accessed on 02/09/2022.

G20 Leaders' Communiqué Antalya Summit, 15-16 November 2015. https://www.fsb.org/wp-content/uploads/G20-Antalya-Leaders-Summit-Communique.pdf Accessed on 02/09/2022.

G20 Leaders' Communiqué Hangzhou Summit, 4-5 September 2016. https://www.fsb.org/wp-content/uploads/G20-Hangzhou-Leaders-Summit-Communique.pdf Accessed on 02/09/2022.

G20 Leaders' Communiqué, 15-16 November 2014, Brisbane, Australia, www.g20.org

G20 Leaders' Communiqué, 15-16 November 2015, Antalya, Turkey, www.g20.org

G20 Leaders' Communiqué, 18-19 June 2012, Los Cabos, Mexico, www.g20.org

G20 Leaders' Communiqué, 2-4 November 2011, Cannes, France, www.g20.org

G20 Leaders' Communiqué, 4-5 September 2016, Hangzhou, China. www.g20.org

G20 Leaders' Communiqué, Brisbane Summit, 15-16 November 2014. https://www.fsb.org/wp-content/uploads/brisbane_g20_leaders_summit_communique.pdf Accessed on 02/09/2022.

G20 Leaders' Declaration, 18-19, 2012, Los Cabos, Mexico, www.g20.org

G20 Leaders' Declaration, 5-6 September 2013, Saint Petersburg, Russia, www.g20.org

G20 Leaders' Declaration, 7-8 July 2017, Hamburg, Germany, www.g20.org

G20 Leaders' Declaration. Building consensus for fair and sustainable development. https://www.fsb.org/wp-content/uploads/buenos_aires_leaders_declaration.pdf Accessed on 02/09/2022.

G20 Osaka Action Plan, 28–29 June 2019, Japan, www.g20.org

G20 Osaka Leaders' Declaration. https://www.fsb.org/wp-content/uploads/G20-Osaka-Leaders-Declaration.pdf Accessed on 02/09/2022.

G20 presidency by Antalya, Turkiye. 15-16 November 2015. https://www.oecd.org/g20/summits/antalya/

G20 presidency by Bali, Indonesia. 15-16 November 2022. https://www.oecd.org/g20/summits/bali/publicationsdocuments/

G20 presidency by Brisbane, Australia, 15-16 November 2014. https://www.oecd.org/g20/summits/brisbane/

G20 presidency by Buenos Aires, Argentina. 30 November 30-01 December 2018. https://www.oecd.org/g20/summits/buenos-aires/publications documents/

G20 presidency by Hamburg, Germany, 7-8 July 2017. https://www.oecd.org/g20/summits/hamburg/publicationsdocuments/#d.en.431545

G20 presidency by Hangjhou, China, September 4-5, 2016, https://www.oecd.org/g20/summits/hangzhou/publicationsdocuments/#d.en.389512

G20 presidency by Osaka, Japan,28-29 June 2019. https://www.oecd.org/g20/summits/osaka/publicationsdocuments/

G20 presidency by Riyadh, Saudi Arabia, 21-22 November 2020, https://www.oecd.org/g20/summits/riyadh/publicationsdocuments/

G20 presidency by Rome, Italy. 30-31 October 2021. https://www.oecd.org/g20/summits/rome/

G20 Presidency of Indonesia, G20 Indonesia 2022, www.g20.org

G20 Riyadh summit Leader's Declaration. https://www.fsb.org/wp-content/uploads/G20_Riyadh_Summit_Leaders_Declaration_EN.pdf Accessed on 02/09/2022.

G20 Roadmap Towards Strengthened Oversight and Regulation of Shadow Banking, 5-6 September 2013, Saint Petersburg, Russia, www.g20.org

G20 Rome Leaders' Declaration, 31 October 2021, www.g20.org

G20 Rome Leaders' Declaration. https://www.fsb.org/wp-content/uploads/G20_Rome_Summit_Leaders_Declaration.pdf.pdf Accessed on 02/09/2022.

G20 starts in Bali as Ukraine war, raging inflation top agenda. Reuters, 15 November 2022.

G20 talks enter final day as emergency meeting held over Poland blasts, https://www.thejakartapost.com/world/2022/11/16/g20-talks-enter-final-day-as-emergency-meeting-held-over-poland blasts.html?Utm_campaign=os&utm_source=mobile&utm_medium=android, 15 November 2022, Jakarta.

G20 Today: India's Opportunity to Lead–Analysis. Gateway House – Eurasia Review, 16 November 2022.

G20: IsDB and ILO pledge to pool resources to support mutual Member states. https://www.ilo.org/beirut/media-centre/news/WCMS_861491/lang—en/index.htm Accessed on 05/09/2022.

Georgieva, Kristalina. 'Facing a Darkening Economic Outlook: How the G20 can Respond' IMF Blog, 13 July 2022. https://www.imf.org/en/Blogs/Articles/2022/07/13/blog-how-g20-can-respond

Hangzhou Action Plan, 4-5 September 2016, Hangzhou, China, www.g20.org

Hotez, Peter J. COVID-19 vaccines: the imperfect instruments of vaccine diplomacy. *Journal of Travel Medicine*, 2022, 1–3, https://doi.org/10.1093/jtm/taac063.

ILO welcomes G20 endorsement of human-centred approach to COVID-19 recovery, https://www.ilo.org/global/about-the-ilo/newsroom/news/WCMS_826032/lang—en/index.html Accessed on 05/09/2022.

IMF Report on G20 Mutual Assessment Process (MAP), 11-12 November 2010, Seoul Summit, Korea, www.imf.org

IMF Staff note to G20, 26-27 June 2010, Toronto Summit, Canada, www.imf.org

IMF Staff Reports for the G-20 Mutual Assessment Process, 3-4 November 2011, Cannes Summit, France, www.imf.org

Implementation and Effects of the G20 Financial Regulatory Reforms: 2020 Annual Report. https://www.fsb.org/2020/11/implementation-and-effects-of-the-g20-financial-regulatory-reforms-2020-annual-report/ Accessed on 28/08/2022.

Implementation and Effects of the G20 Financial Regulatory Reforms. https://www.fsb.org/2016/08/implementation-and-effects-of-the-g20-financial-regulatory-reforms-2/ Accessed on 28/08/2022.

Implementation and effects of the G20 financial regulatory reforms. https://www.fsb.org/2015/11/implementation-and-effects-of-the-g20-financial-regulatory-reforms/ Accessed on 01/09/2022.

Implementation of Basel standards - A report to G20 Leaders on implementation of the Basel III regulatory Reforms. https://www.bis.org/bcbs/publ/d377.htm Accessed on 28/08/2022.

Incentives to centrally clear over-the-counter (OTC) derivatives. https://

www.fsb.org/2018/11/incentives-to-centrally-clear-over-the-counter-otc-derivatives-2/ Accessed on 28/08/2022.

'India@2023, G20 Presidency', Power point presentation by Harsh Vardhan Shringla, India's Chief Coordinator for G20 at a business conference in Mumbai, 5 September 2022.

Institute for Global Dialogue. Argentina's G20 presidency: implications for the G20-Africa partnership. https://www.jstor.org/stable/resrep30613 Accessed on 05/09/2022.

Institute for Global Dialogue. The G20 Osaka Summit: Japan's delicate balancing of diplomacy-led and development-led engagements, 01 September 2019, https://www.jstor.org/stable/resrep19356

Institute for Global Dialogue. The G20 Osaka Summit: Japan's delicate balancing of diplomacy-led and development-led engagements. https://www.jstor.org/stable/resrep19356 Accessed on 05/09/2022.

International Financial Architecture Working Group (IFAWG)–Recent Developments on Local Currency Bond Markets in Emerging Economies, IMF and World Bank Group, 28 January 2020, www.imf.org

International Institute for Sustainable Development. G20 Scorecard: OECD members, 01 January 2020, https://www.jstor.org/stable/resrep29255

International Monetary Fund, Blog by Kristalina Georgieva, Finding a Solid Footing for the Global Economy, 19 February 19 2020, www.imf.org

International Monetary Fund, Blog by Kristalina Georgieva, The Global Economic Reset—Promoting a More Inclusive Recovery, 11 June 2020, www.imf.org

International Monetary Fund, G-20 Background Note, Implementation of the G-20 Action Plan, 16 July 2020, www.imf.org

International Monetary Fund, G-20 Surveillance Note, G-20 Leaders' Summit, 21 November 2020, Riyadh Summit, Virtual Meeting, November 2020, www.imf.org

International Monetary Fund, G-20 Surveillance Note, Group of Twenty Finance Ministers and Central Bank Governors Meetings, 22-23 February 2020, Riyadh, Saudi Arabia, 19 February 2020, www.imf.org

International Monetary Fund, G-20 Surveillance Note, Group of Twenty Finance Ministers and Central Bank Governors Meetings, 15 April 2020, Virtual Meeting, 15 April 2020, www.imf.org

International Monetary Fund, Blog by Kristalina Georgieva, The Next Phase of the Crisis: Further Action Needed for a Resilient Recovery, 16 July 2020, www.imf.org

International Monetary Fund, G-20 Background Note, Enhancing Access to

Opportunities, Prepared by Staff of the IMF and the World Bank, 11 June 2020, www.imf.org

International Monetary Fund, G-20 Report on Strong, Sustainable, Balanced and Inclusive Growth, 02 November 2020, www.imf.org

International Monetary Fund, G-20 Surveillance Note, Group of Twenty Finance Ministers and Central Bank Governors Meetings, 18 July 2020, virtual meeting, www.imf.org

International Monetary Fund, Staff Note for the G20 International Financial Architecture Working Group (IFAWG)–Recent Developments on Local Currency Bond Markets in Emerging Economies, IMF and World Bank Group, 28 January 2020, www.imf.org

Intervention by Prime Minister at G20 Session I on Inclusive Growth and Global Economy, Growth Strategies, Employment and Investment Strategies. 15 November 2021, www.mea.gov.in

Intervention by Prime Minister at G20 Session-II on Enhancing Resilience in Antalya, 16 November 2021, www.mea.gov.in

Intervention by Prime Minister at G20 Working Dinner on Global Challenges–Terrorism and Refugee Crisis, Antalya, 15 November 2021, www.mea.gov.in

Intervention by Prime Minister at G20 Working Lunch on Trade and Energy., Antalya, 16 November 2015, www.mea.gov.in

Issue Priorities (2022). G20 Indonesia 2022. URL https://g20.org/g20-presidency-of-indonesia/#priorities.

J. Kirton and B. Warren. Governing Climate Change at the G20 Rome and UN Glasgow Summits and Beyond. *International Organisations Research Journal.*,2022, Vol. 17, No. 2, pp. 110–134.

Jain, Shruti. India's G20 Presidency 2023: Exploring Areas of Cooperation with Australia, Observer Research Foundation, https://www.orfonline.org/research/indias-g20-presidency-2023/ Accessed on 11/10/2022

James Mcbride and Anshu Siripurapu, 'The Group of Twenty', Council on Foreign Relations, 15 November 2021. https://www.cfr.org/backgrounder/group-twenty

Kevin P. Gallagher. Ruling Capital: Emerging Markets and the Reregulation of Cross-Border Finance, 2015, https://www.jstor.org/stable/10.7591/j.ctt1287ds5.11

Kirton, John and Marina Larionova. Contagious convergent cumulative cooperation: the dynamic development of the G20, BRICS and SCO. *International Politics*. https://doi.org/10.1057/s41311-022-00407-7. Accessed on 05/10/2022.

Kirton, John. 'The G20's Growing Governance, 2008-2022'. 16 June 2022. http:/

/www.g20.utoronto.ca/biblio/Kirton_G20_Governance_UPH_220224.pdf

Kraemer, R. and Andreas. A Sustainable Ocean Economy, Innovation and Growth: a G20 Initiative, 01 July 2017, https://www.jstor.org/stable/resrep16150

Kraemer, R. Andreas. The G20 and Building Global Governance for "Climate Refugees", 01 March 2017, https://www.jstor.org/stable/resrep05208

L20 statement to the Buenos Aires G20 Summit Buenos Aires, Argentina. https://www.ituc-csi.org/l20. Accessed on 14/08/2022.

L20 statement to the G20 leaders´ Summit 30-31 October 2021, Rome, Italy. www.ituc-csi.org/l20 Accessed on 14/08/2022.

L20 statement to the G20 leaders' Summit, 21-22 November 2020, Riyadh, Saudi Arabia. https://www.ituc-csi.org/l20 Accessed on 14/08/2022.

Lay, Jann. The G20 under Argentina's Presidency: Time to Deliver on the Hamburg Promises, 01 December 2017, https://www.jstor.org/stable/resrep21172

Lead Intervention by Prime Minister at G20 Working Lunch on Development and Climate Change, Antalya, 15 November 2021, www.mea.gov.in

Lesage, Dries. From Washington to Hangzhou: Does the G20 Live up to its Potential? www.jstor.org/stable/26531657#metadata_info_tab_contents Accessed on 02/09/2022.

Lombardi, Domenico. How the G20 Can Stimulate Innovation, 01 January 2017, https://www.jstor.org/stable/resrep17312.22

Mabera, Faith. Argentina's G20 presidency: implications for the G20-Africa partnership, 01 September 2018, https://www.jstor.org/stable/resrep30613

Mabera, Faith. Japan's G20 presidency: affirming the Asian century's positive role for global economic governance, 01 September 2019. https://www.jstor.org/stable/resrep30629#metadata_info_tab_contents Accessed on 10/08/2022.

Manish Chand, India at G20: A Fine Balance, dated 13 November 2021, www.mea.gov.in

Marianne Dutkiewicz and Amanda Ellis. Women's Economic Empowerment and the G20 Agenda, 01 February 2018, https://www.jstor.org/stable/resrep21067

Maupin, Julie. Blockchains and the G20: Building an Inclusive, Transparent and Accountable Digital Economy, 01 March 2017, https://www.jstor.org/stable/resrep05191

Meeting between Prime Minister and President of the Republic of Korea,

Prime Minister of Italy and Prime Minister of Norway in G20 Summit, 2017 in Hamburg, 8 July 2018., www.mea.gov.in

Narlikar, Amrita. Can the G20 Save Globalisation? 01 March 2017, https://www.jstor.org/stable/resrep21167

Ncuma Grobbelaar and Iwazi Ngubevana. Ensuring a Just Energy Transition through Hydrogen: How the G20 can Support Africa, 01 January 2022, https://www.jstor.org/stable/resrep40064

New York Times, Biden Praises G20 Discussion as Summit ends, 31 October 2021, www.nytimes.com

Ntandoyenkosi Sibindi. G20 Compact with Africa: Consolidating and Accelerating Rwanda's Transformation Agenda. www.jstor.org/stable/resrep25955#metadata_info_tab_contents Accessed on 10/08/2022.

Nuclear wars cannot be fought in Ukraine, https://www.thejakartapost.com/world/2022/11/15/nuclear-wars-cannot-be-fought-in-ukraine-china-.html?Utm_campaign=os&utm_source=mobile&utm_medium=android 14 November 2022.

Nugraha, Ogi Nanda and Raka Ade Candra. Diplomatic Bluff against Indonesia's G20 Presidency amid the Ukraine-Russia Conflict: A View from Political Psychology. https://nbn-resolving.org/urn:nbn:de:0168-ssoar-80700-8. Accessed on 01/10/2022.

Obstfeld, Maurice and Posen, Adam S. Introduction: The G20 not only should but can be meaningfully useful to recovery from the COVID-19 pandemic, April, 2020, https://www.jstor.org/stable/resrep43897.3

Ole Jacob Sending and Joachim Nahem. Wielding influence in a new governance architecture: Norway, the G20 and the 2030 Agenda, 01 January 2017, https://www.jstor.org/stable/resrep07992

Opening Remarks by Prime Minister at BRICS Leaders' Meeting, 15 November 2021, www.mea.gov.in

Opening Statement by Prime Minister at BRICS Leaders' Meeting in Brisbane, Australia, 15 November 2021, www.mea.gov.in

Overview of Progress in the Implementation of the G20 Recommendations for Strengthening Financial stability. https://www.fsb.org/2013/09/r_130905c/ Accessed on 01/09/2022.

Pandemic preparedness and the role of science,S20 academies joint statement. https://www.lincei.it/en/news/academies-g20-countries-signed-two-joint-statements Accessed on 14/08/2022.

PIB Delhi, Prime Minister meets Italian Prime Minister Mario Draghi on the margins of G20 Summit in Rome, 29 October 2021, www.pib.gov.in

Pigman, Geoffrey Allen. 5 Conclusions: The G20 an Economic 'Security

Council' in the Making? 01 January 2012, https://www.jstor.org/stable/resrep07757.8

PM's address at the G-20 Summit in Bali, Session III: Digital Transformation. https://www.pmindia.gov.in/en/ 16 November 2022.

PM's meeting with Chancellor of the Federal Republic of Germany on the sidelines of G-20 Summit in Bali. https://www.pmindia.gov.in/en/ 16 November 2022.

PM's meeting with the PM of Australia on the sidelines of G-20 Summit in Bali. htps://www.pmindia.gov.in/en/ 16 November 2022.

PM's meeting with the PM of the United Kingdom on the sidelines of G-20 Summit in Bali. https://www.pmindia.gov.in/en/ 16 November 2022.

PM's meeting with the President of France on the sidelines of G-20 Summit in Bali. https://www.pmindia.gov.in/en/ 16 November 2022.

PM's meeting with the Prime Minister of Italy on the sidelines of G-20 Summit in Bali. https://www.pmindia.gov.in/en/ 16 November 2022.

PM's remarks at the Closing Session of G-20 Summit in Bali. https://www.pmindia.gov.in/en/ 16 November 2022.

PM's remarks at the unveiling of logo, theme and website of India's G20 Presidency via video conferencing. https://www.pmindia.gov.in/en/ 08 November 2022.

Prabhakar, S.V.R.K. and others. Ecosystem-based Approaches in G20 Countries: Current Status and Priority Actions for Scaling Up, 01 January 2019, https://www.jstor.org/stable/resrep21870.9

Prime Minister Draghi's Opening Address, Rome, 30 October 2021, www.g20.org

Progress report to G20 on the FSB action plan to assess and address the decline in correspondent banking. https://www.fsb.org/2016/08/progress-report-to-g20-on-the-fsb-action-plan-to-assess-and-address-the-decline-in-correspondent-banking/ Accessed on 28/08/2022.

Rana, Pradumna B. and J, Xianbai. Osaka G20 Summit: Mixed Outcome. www.eurasiareview.com/12072019-osaka-g20-summit-mixed-outcome-analysis/ Accessed on 10/08/2022.

Reducing misconduct risks in the financial sector: Progress report to G20 Leaders. https://www.fsb.org/2017/07/reducing-misconduct-risks-in-the-financial-sector-progress-report-to-g20-leaders/ Accessed on 28/08/2022.

Report to the G20 on actions taken to assess and address the decline in correspondent banking. https://www.fsb.org/2015/11/report-to-the-g20-on-actions-taken-to-assess-and-address-the-decline-in-correspondent-banking/ Accessed on 01/09/2022.

Reports to the G20 summit - November 2022-Financial Services Board. https://www.fsb.org/work-of-the-fsb/implementation-monitoring/reports-to-the-g20/reports-to-the-g20-summit-november-2022/ Accessed on 25/08/2022.

Ridpath, Barbara. G20 Working Group Issues: Reform and Rules, 01 March 2009, https://www.jstor.org/stable/resrep03547.7

Rieck, Christian E., Moncayo, Gunter Rieck and Meyer, Lilian. From Hangzhou to Hamburg: Outlines of a Multiyear Agenda for the G20. www.jstor.org/stable/resrep10088#metadata_info_tab_contents Accessed on 02/09/2022.

Rizqi, Miftakhul. A deixis analysis in Joko Widodo's statement on Indonesia's G20 presidency. http://journal.ubm.ac.id/. Accessed on 01/10/2022.

Road to the Bali Summit. www.g20.utoronto.ca/2022/2022-road.html Accessed on 10/08/2022.

Roadmap for Enhancing Cross-border Payments - First consolidated progress report. https://www.fsb.org/wp-content/uploads/P131021-1.pdf Accessed on 02/09/2022.

Rumble, Olivia. A New South African Climate Diplomacy: G7, G20 and Beyond, 01 October 2021, https://www.jstor.org/stable/resrep37455

S20 Argentina 2018, Food and nutrition security: improving soils and increasing productivity. https://t20argentina.org/joint-statement-by-the-c20-l20-s20-t20-w20-and-y20-on-addressing-gender-labour-gaps/ Accessed on 14/08/2022.

S20 Japan 2019 Science 20. G20 Osaka. www.g20.utoronto.ca/s20/2019-revised_S20Japan2019Statement.pdf Accessed on 14/08/2022.

S20 Saudi Arabia 2020 Science Communiqué. https://s20saudiarabia.org.sa Accessed on 14/08/2022.

Schadler, Susan. Trump and the IMF, 01 October 2017, https://www.jstor.org/stable/resrep05225

Schirm, Stefan A. The G20, Emerging Powers, and Transatlantic Relations, 01 May 2011, https://www.jstor.org/stable/resrep19025.5

Science 20 joint statement G20 Indonesia—recover together recover stronger-S20 Indonesia. https://s20indonesia.org Accessed on 14/08/2022.

Second Phase of the G20 Data Gaps Initiative (DGI-2): First Progress Report. https://www.fsb.org/2016/09/second-phase-of-the-g20-data-gaps-initiative-dgi-2-first-progress-report/ Accessed on 28/08/2022.

See, Multiple authors (2012). Think-20 Meeting: report to Sherpas. www.g20.utoronto.ca/t20/2012-FINAL_Think-20_Report_to_Sherpas.pdf

Seidu, Dode. G20 Compact with Africa: The Case of Ghana. South African

Institute of International Affairs (2020). www.jstor.org/stable/resrep25951 Accessed on 10/08/2022.

Shafiah F. Muhiba. Domestic constraints on Indonesia's global leadership aspirations. *East Asia Forum Quarterly,* April–June 2022, https://search.informit.org/doi/pdf/10.3316/informit.639738767615357

Shah, Bipin. Resurrection of Mao at G20 meeting, held at Hangzhou, China. Resurrection of Mao at G20 meeting, held at Hangzhou, China | Bipin Shah - Academia.edu Accessed on 02/02/2022.

Srinivas, V. Talk on G20@2023: The Road Map to Indian Presidency, New Delhi. ICWA, 2 August 2022. p.10.

Stewart M. Patrick. 'The G20 was made for moments like this', Council on Foreign Relations, 25 October 2021. https://www.cfr.org/blog/g20-wasmade-moments

T20 Italy - 2021 final communiqué. T20-Italy-Final-Communique.pdf (t20italy.org) Accessed on 18/08/2022.

T20 Summit 2018 Cumbre T20 2018. https://sai20.org/wp-content/uploads/2022/01/2018-Communique-T20-Argentina-18-September-2018.pdf Accessed on 14/08/2022.

Tanaka, Kenta. G20 Summit and emergency medical services in Osaka, Japan. Doi: 10.1002/ams2.661. Accessed on 02/09/2022.

The Cannes Action Plan for Growth and Jobs, 2-4 November 2011, Cannes France, www.g20.org

The G20 Osaka Summit: Japan's delicate balancing of diplomacy-led and development-led engagements, Institute for Global Dialogue (2019). www.jstor.org/stable/resrep19356#metadata_info_tab_contents. Accessed on 10/08/2022.

The G20 Seoul Summit Leaders' Declaration, 11-12 November, 2010, Seoul, Korea, www.g20.org

The G20 Toronto Summit Declaration, 26-27 June 2010, Toronto, Canada, www.g20.org

The Global Plan for Recovery and Reform, 2 April 2009, London, United Kingdom, www.g20.org

The Hindu, "A Welcome Decision–Vaccine Production must be ramped up to sustain exports and meet domestic demand"., Editorial dated 22 September 2021, www.thehindu.com

The Leaders' Statement—The Pittsburgh Summit, 24-25 September 2009, Pittsburgh, USA, www.g20.org

The Seoul Development Consensus for Shared Consensus for Shared Growth, 11-12 November, 2010, Seoul, Korea, www.g20.org

The Seoul Summit Document, 11-12 November, 2010, Seoul, Korea, www.g20.org

Thornton, Phil. United G20 Must Pave the Way for Robust Post-COVID-19 Recovery, 01 July 2020, https://www.jstor.org/stable/resrep26010

Timmer, C. Peter. Top priority for Indonesian leadership of G20 cooperation. *East Asia Forum Quarterly*. April–June 2022, https://search.informit.org/doi/pdf/10.3316/informit.522295149774922

Tomita, Koji. On the upcoming Osaka G20 Summit. Www.jiia.or.jp/en/ajiss_commentary/column-317.html Accessed on 02/09/2022.

Transcript of Media Briefing by official spokesperson in Hangzhou on Prime Minister's visit to China, 4 September 2016, www.mea.gov.in

Transcript of Media Briefing by Shri Suresh Prabhu, Prime Minister's Sherpa for G-20 and Official Spokesperson on G20 Summit in Brisbane, 16 November 2014., www.mea.gov.in

U20 cities call on the G20 to prioritize an urban perspective in tackling global issues: an official communiqué from Urban 20 (U20)-U20 Buenos Aires 2018. www.urban20.org/wp-content/uploads/2020/09/U20-2018-Communique.pdf Accessed on 18/08/2022.

Urban 20 calls on G20 to empower cities to ensure a green and just recovery-U20 Rome-Milan 2021. www.urban20.org/u20summit/2021-rome-milan/ Accessed on 20/08/2022.

Ussal Sahbaz and FerideInan. Turkey and the G-20 Presidency: Implications for LIDCs and Africa, 01 June 2015, https://www.jstor.org/stable/resrep25965

Viswanathan, Balasubramanian. G20 Scorecard of Fossil Fuel Funding: India, 01 January 2020, https://www.jstor.org/stable/resrep29249

W20 Communiqué 2022 - Women20 Communiqué edition 2022. W20 (w20indonesia.org) Accessed on 20/08/2022.

W20 Japan 2019 Communiqué - W20 Japan 2019. https://w20japan.org/en/index.html Accessed on 20/08/2022.

Welcoming Speech of the President of the Republic of Indonesia at the Opening of the 1st FMCBG Indonesia G20 Presidency 2022, 17 February 2022, Jakarta, Indonesia. https://www.g20.org/g20-presidency-of-indonesia/

Which leaders will attend G20 summit? https://www.thejakartapost.com/world/2022/11/13/which-leaders-will-attend-g20-summit.html, 13 November 2022, Jakarta.

Women 20 Communiqué - W20 Saudi Arabia 2020. www.w20saudiarabia.org.sa Accessed on 20/08/2022.

Women at Work in G20 countries: Progress and policy action in 2021 – presentation. https://www.ilo.org/global/about-the-ilo/how-the-ilo-works/multilateral-system/g20/WCMS_849141/lang—en/index.htm Accessed on 05/09/2022.

Women20 Communiqué Edition 2021-W20 Italia 2021. W20-Italy-Communiqueì.pdf (dlii.org) Accessed on 20/08/2022.

World Health Organization, COVAX, www.who.int/initiatives/act-accelerator/covax

Wrenn Yennie Lindgren. The G20 Comes to Japan: Making Sense of the Osaka Agenda. How do the outcomes of the G-20's eight engagement groups factor into this year's Osaka Summit? *The Diplomat*. 25 June 2019.

Xinhua, G20 Rome Summit ends with commitment to address multiple global challenges, 01 November 2021, www.xinhua.net.com

Y20 2021 Communiqué-Y20 Italia - Digitalization, Innovation, Future of Work. https://www.y20italy.it Accessed on 24/08/2022.

Y20 Argentina 2018 youth 20. Shaking the present, building the future- Y20 Summit, Cordoba Policy Recommendations. https://www.youth20.org/pdfs/PolicyRP.pdf Accessed on 20/08/2022.

Y20 Indonesia 2022 Communiqué- Sustainable and Liveable Planet. https://y20-indonesia.org/y20-communique-indonesia/ Accessed on 20/08/2022.

Yellinek, Roie. G20 2017: China and Germany Step Up. G20 2017: China and Germany Step Up (besacenter.org). Accessed on 01/09/2022.

Youth at Work in G20 countries: Progress and policy action in 2021 towards the Antalya goal – presentation. https://www.ilo.org/global/about-the-ilo/how-the-ilo-works/multilateral-system/g20/WCMS_849142/lang—en/index.htm Accessed on 05/09/2022.

Zvi Magen and Udi Deke. The Trump-Putin Meeting: From Hamburg to Southern Syria. https://www.jstor.org/stable/resrep08833 Accessed on 01/09/2022.

Index